AN ILLUSTRATED HISTORY OF
ISLAMIC ARCHITECTURE

AN ILLUSTRATED HISTORY OF ISLAMIC ARCHITECTURE

An introduction to the architectural wonders of Islam, from mosques, tombs and mausolea to gateways, palaces and citadels

Consultant: Moya Carey

CAROLINE CHAPMAN • MELANIE GIBSON •
GEORGE MANGINIS • ANNA McSWEENEY •
CHARLES PHILLIPS • IAIN ZACZEK

southwater

This edition is published by Southwater
an imprint of Anness Publishing Ltd
Blaby Road, Wigston, Leicestershire LE18 4SE; info@anness.com
www.southwaterbooks.com; www.annesspublishing.com

Anness Publishing has a new picture agency outlet for images
for publishing, promotions or advertising. Please visit our website
www.practicalpictures.com for more information.

Publisher: Joanna Lorenz
Editorial Director: Helen Sudell
Cover Design: Nigel Partridge
Production Controller: Christine Ni

Produced for Anness Publishing by Toucan Books
Managing Editor: Ellen Dupont
Editor: Theresa Bebbington
Designer: Ralph Pitchford
Picture Researcher: Marian Pullen
Cartography: Cosmographics, UK
Proofreader: Marion Dent
Indexer: Michael Dent

© Anness Publishing Ltd 2012

All rights reserved. No part of this publication may be reproduced, stored in a retrieval system, or transmitted in any way or by any means, electronic, mechanical, photocopying, recording or otherwise, without the prior written permission of the copyright holder.

A CIP catalogue record for this book
is available from the British Library.

Previously published as part of a larger volume,
The Illustrated Encyclopedia of Islamic Art and Architecture

ETHICAL TRADING POLICY
At Anness Publishing we believe that business should be conducted in an ethical and ecologically sustainable way, with respect for the environment and a proper regard to the replacement of the natural resources we employ.

As a publisher, we use a lot of wood pulp in high-quality paper for printing, and that wood commonly comes from spruce trees. We are therefore currently growing more than 750,000 trees in three Scottish forest plantations: Berrymoss (130 hectares/320 acres), West Touxhill (125 hectares/305 acres) and Deveron Forest (75 hectares/ 185 acres). The forests we manage contain more than 3.5 times the number of trees employed each year in making paper for the books we manufacture.

Because of this ongoing ecological investment programme, you, as our customer, can have the pleasure and reassurance of knowing that a tree is being cultivated on your behalf to naturally replace the materials used to make the book you are holding.

Our forestry programme is run in accordance with the UK Woodland Assurance Scheme (UKWAS) and will be certified by the internationally recognized Forest Stewardship Council (FSC). The FSC is a non-government organization dedicated to promoting responsible management of the world's forests. Certification ensures forests are managed in an environmentally sustainable and socially responsible way. For further information about this scheme, go to www.annesspublishing.com/trees.

PUBLISHER'S NOTE
Although the information in this book is believed to be accurate and true at the time of going to press, neither the authors nor the publisher can accept any legal responsibility or liability for any errors or omissions that may have been made.

Page 1 The Taj Mahal.
Page 2 Azem Palace.
Page 3 Dome of the Rock.

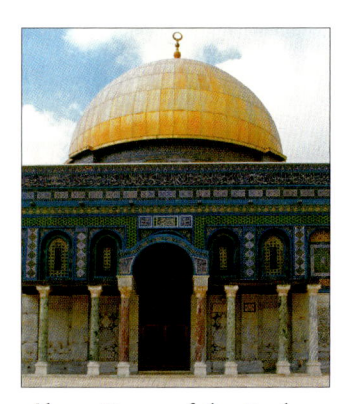

Above Dome of the Rock, a Muslim shrine built in Jerusalem 691.

Above Brickwork from the 9th-century Mausoleum of Ismail Samani in Bukhara.

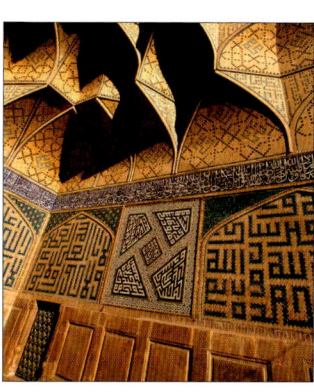

Above Muqarnas *and tiles in the Seljuks' 11th-century Friday Mosque in Isfahan.*

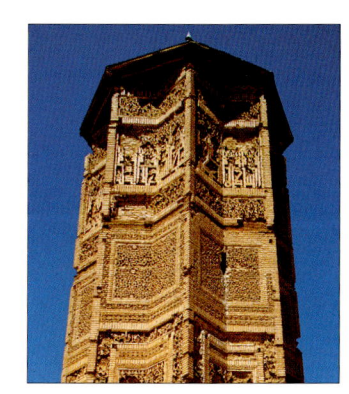

Above *The early 12th-century Bahram Shah minaret, in Ghazni.*

CONTENTS

Introduction	6
Timeline	10
THE ARCHITECTURE OF THE ISLAMIC WORLD	**16**
The Mosque	18
The *Qibla*	20
The Mosque Interior	22
The *Madrasa*	24
Memorials for the Dead	26
The City	28
Trade and Travel	30
Hajj: Pilgrimage to Makkah	32
ISLAMIC ARCHITECTURE THROUGH THE CENTURIES	**34**
The Umayyad Period	36
Dome of the Rock	38
The Great Mosque of Damascus	40
Desert Palaces	42
Baghdad	44
Samarra	46
The Fatimid Caliphate	48
Sicily	50
The Samanid Dynasty	52
The Ghaznavid and Ghurid Dynasties	54
The Great Seljuks	56
Monuments and *Madrasas*	58
Caravanserais	60
The Anatolian Seljuks	62
The Zangids of Mosul	64
The Ayyubid Dynasty	66
Aleppo and Damascus	68
The Mamluks	70
Mamluk Mausoleum Complexes	72
The Umayyads of Spain	74
Córdoba	76
Early Islamic Rule in North Africa	78
The Almoravids and Almohads	80
Rabat and Marrakech	82
The Nasrids	84
The Garden in Islamic Architecture	86
Islamic Architecture in Africa	88
The Ilkhanids and Their Architecture	90
Takht-i Sulayman	92
The Timurid Dynasty	94
Samarkand Tombs	96
Timurid Herat	98
Safavid Isfahan	100
Mughal Tombs	102
The Taj Mahal	104
Red Fort	106
Lahore	108
Early Ottoman Architecture	110
Constantinople (Istanbul)	112
Topkapi Palace	114
Damascus, Aleppo and Iznik	116
Revivalist Trends	118
The Modern Age	120
Modern Architecture	122
Glossary	124
Index	126
Acknowledgements	128

Above Detail of tiles from the Gur-e Amir Mausoleum, in Samarkand.

Above Alhambra, residence of Muslim rulers in Granada, built in the 14th century.

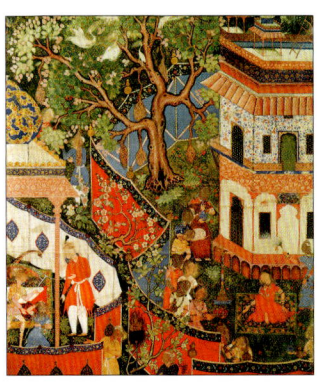

Above Detail from a mid-16th-century illustration, produced in Mughal India.

Above Sultan Qaboos Mosque, built in Oman between 1995 and 2001.

INTRODUCTION

THE RELIGION OF ISLAM WAS FOUNDED BY THE PROPHET MUHAMMAD (DIED 632) IN THE ARABIAN CITIES OF MAKKAH AND MADINAH. THE ARABIC WORD 'ISLAM' LITERALLY MEANS 'SUBMISSION'.

The Prophet Muhammad was born in Makkah, around 570. Orphaned at a young age, he was raised by his extended family, a minor clan of the powerful Quraysh tribe. Makkah was a merchant city with an important pilgrimage sanctuary at its heart. Known as the *Kaabah*, the sanctuary was dedicated to a pantheon of pagan deities. As a young man, Muhammad travelled widely beyond his hometown. He married Khadijah (died 619), a wealthy merchant widow, and they ran her business together. In 610, during a period of solitary reflection on Mount Hira outside Makkah, Muhammad, now about 40, began to receive divine revelations instructing him to preach a new, monotheistic faith, that would challenge and eventually overturn the pagan beliefs of his own community.

THE EMERGENCE OF ISLAM

Revelations came to the Prophet periodically over the rest of his life, for the next 22 years. They were carefully remembered and retained

Above During the annual Hajj to Makkah, pilgrims also visit the Mosque of the Prophet in Madinah.

Below It is estimated that one million or so pilgrims visit the Kaabah in Makkah every year for the annual Hajj *rituals*.

by the Prophet and his growing community of Muslim converts, and together these revealed passages constitute the Quran, the Holy

6

Book of Islam. As such, Muslims consider the Quran to be of divine authorship, a perfect text. The essential message of this new religion was monotheism: Muslims believe in only one God, and avoid idolatry. Islam also holds sacred a long lineage of ancient prophets including Adam, Noah, Abraham and Jesus. In these aspects, Islam shares a great deal with both Judaism and Christianity, and these fellow monotheistic faiths are described in the Quran as the 'People of the Book' because Jews and Christians also possess sacred texts (the Torah and the Bible).

THE PROPHET'S MISSION IN ARABIA

Following his first revelation, Muhammad obeyed the divine command to 'Recite!' and started to preach. He began seeking converts, first among his family and friends, and then gradually from the wider Makkah community. This soon met with hostility from the dominant Quraysh tribe, whose power in Makkah rested with their responsibility for the pagan sanctuary of the *Kaabah*. The new religion also undermined the tribal system of family loyalty, as it created a new community bound by religious commitment rather than blood relationships. After many years under threat, the Prophet and his followers were finally forced to leave Makkah in the year 622, and they fled to the security of a small Muslim community recently established in nearby Yathrib. There they built a house for the Prophet and his family, which became the first mosque. This migration, or *hijrah*, was an important moment for the first Muslims, and marks the beginning of Islamic history: 622 is the first year in the Muslim calendar, 1AH ('Anno Hegirae') – the year of the *hijrah*. In honour of this reception, Yathrib was renamed Madinat al-Nabi ('The City of the Prophet'), and is now known as Madinah.

Muslims prospered in Madinah and surrounding tribal areas, extending their political and religious influence, but hostility with Makkah remained unresolved. Eventually, in 630, the Muslim forces conquered Makkah, defeating the Quraysh, and reclaimed the *Kaabah* pilgrimage sanctuary for Islam. This had long been the Prophet's intention: he had already designated the holy *Kaabah* as the direction for Muslim prayer; now he cleared the site of its pagan idols, and it became part of Muslim tradition – and the destination for the annual *Hajj* pilgrimage, one of the five basic requirements of Islam. Following this victory, the Prophet continued to live in his house in Madinah, where he passed away in 632.

Above The text of this 16th-century Quran is beautifully framed within panels of illumination.

THE FIVE PILLARS OF ISLAM

Islam requires that all Muslims perform five basic duties, as follows:

1. *Shahadah*, or profession of faith, reciting the creed statement 'There is no god but God, and Muhammad is his messenger'.
2. *Salat*, or daily prayers, to be performed every day at five determined times between early dawn and evening.
3. *Zakat*, or charitable donation of alms to the poor.
4. *Sawm*, or annual fasting during the daylight hours of the month of Ramadhan every year.
5. *Hajj*, the pilgrimage to the *Kaabah* in Makkah, which must be undertaken at least once in every Muslim's lifetime.

INTRODUCTION

Following the death of the Prophet Muhammad in 632, the Muslim community, or *ummah*, sought a means of agreement on his successor, or caliph.

THE RIGHTEOUS CALIPHS

Until the emergence of the Umayyad dynasty in 661, leadership of the new Islamic state was determined by consensus rather than family inheritance. The initial principle was based on the Prophet's own views about his succession, which were unclear and hotly debated. When weak and close to death, the Prophet Muhammad had asked his companion and father-in-law, Abu Bakr, to lead the community's prayers on his behalf. This was considered significant, and the community chose Abu Bakr (died 634) as the first of the four Righteous Caliphs, or al-Rashidun.

The following three caliphs were also close friends or family of the Prophet: Umar (died 644), Uthman Ibn-Affan (died 656) and Ali (died 661), and all were elected with the consensus of the community. The years of the Rashidun Caliphs saw the Islamic state expand with great military energy from its Arabian heartland, conquering first Syria, then Palestine, North Africa and Iraq, and then Iran. The Byzantine emperor was beaten into retreat in Anatolia, and the last Sasanian Shah Yazdagird III (died 651) was completely defeated. Both great empires were severely damaged by Muslim conquest, but both also contributed a considerable cultural heritage to the new Islamic state – in terms of government infrastructure and court ceremony, as well as art and architecture. This was particularly felt after the capital moved to Damascus in 661, and eventually to Baghdad in 750.

THE EMERGENCE OF SHIAH ISLAM

The fourth caliph was Ali ibn Abu Talib (d.661), who ruled from Kufa in Iraq. He was a close companion of the Prophet Muhammad, as the first three caliphs had also been. Ali was the Prophet's younger cousin. He had been fostered by him as a child, and later married the Prophet's daughter Fatima.

Left A manuscript illustration that depicts the first three Shiah Imams: Ali with his sons Hasan and Husayn.

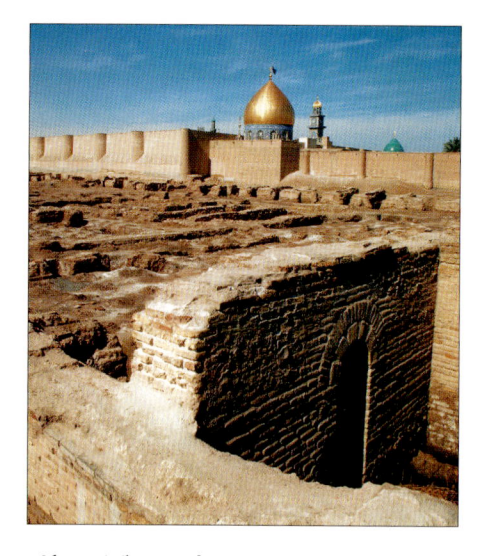

Above The Kufa Mosque in Iraq was the headquarters of Ali ibn Abu Talib (died 661).

Ali and Fatima had two sons, Hasan and Husayn, who were therefore part of a bloodline descending directly from the Prophet – who had had no surviving sons.

This lineage became ever more significant with regard to the Muslim leadership: while Ali was caliph, he was challenged by Muawiyah, the governor of Syria and eventual founder of the Umayyad dynasty (661–750). Importantly, Ali was from the same clan as the Prophet, while Muawiyah and the third caliph, Uthman, were from the Umayyad clan (another branch of the Quraysh tribe of Makkah). When Ali was murdered in 661 by members of the radical Khariji sect, Muawiyah was quick to seize the Caliphate – establishing his own dynasty, which ruled from Damascus. Ali's son Hasan (died 669) did not pursue the Caliphate, but on Muawiyah's death in 680, his brother Husayn claimed the leadership as a direct descendant of the Prophet. Husayn led his forces to Karbala in Iraq, and was greatly outnumbered by the Umayyad forces of Muawiyah's son, Yazid. Besieged, Husayn and his supporters were eventually massacred

INTRODUCTION

Above A painting of the Battle of Karbala, showing Husayn's half-brother, Abbas, heroically defeating an Umayyad soldier.

by the Umayyads (10 October 680). Ashura, the anniversary of Husayn's martyrdom, is mourned every year by Muslims, but has an especially strong significance for the sect that emerged from orthodox or Sunni Islam. Known as Shiat-Ali, or the partisans of Ali, Shiah Muslims hold that the leadership of the Islamic state should fall only to those descended directly from the Prophet: Ali is therefore regarded by them as the first such leader, or Imam, with Hasan and Husayn the second and third, and a succession of further Imams thereafter. The first three caliphs are therefore regarded by Shiah Muslims as invalid, while the Umayyad dynasty and its successor, the Abbasid, are considered usurpers. There are different important branches within Shiism, according to views about the

Right Shiah pilgrims visit the holy shrine of Imam Ali in the Iraqi city of Najaf.

succession of later Imams: these include Twelver Shiism, the state religion of Iran since the 16th century, and Ismaili Shiism – of which the Aga Khan is the current leader. Shiah reverence for the tombs of Imams and their families is very strong, particularly for the shrine of Imam Ali in Najaf, of Imam Husayn at Karbala (both in Iraq), and of Imam Reza in Mashhad in Iran. These and other Shiah shrines remain important pilgrimage destinations to this day.

IN THIS BOOK

The culture of Islam has had far-reaching influences around the world, and the pages that follow explore its beautiful architecture. A timeline puts the main events into context, and then the main types of structure are described, including mosques, *qiblas*, *madrasas* and tombs. The chapter that follows consists of a chronological survey of Islamic architecture through the centuries, and the book concludes with a useful glossary of Arabic terms.

9

Timeline

The following timeline lists some of the major works in the long history of Islamic art and architecture.

- 610–32 The Prophet receives the revelations of the Quran.
- c.654 A standardized version of the Quran is issued by Rashidun Caliph Uthman ibn-Affan (reigned 644–56) and sent to the four cities of Madinah, Damascus, Kufa and Basra.
- 691 Umayyad Caliph Abd al-Malik (reigned 685–705) oversees the building of the Dome of the Rock in Jerusalem.
- 696–98 A major reform of coinage in the Umayyad Caliphate replaces figurative images with Islamic epigraphy.
- 705–15 The Great Mosque in Damascus is built under Umayyad Caliph al-Walid I (reigned 705–15). It is one of the first mosques to have minarets.
- c.712–715 The Qusayr Amra 'desert palace', or hunting lodge, is built by Caliph al-Walid I in Jordan.
- c.715 The rebuilding of the Al-Aqsa Mosque in Jerusalem is completed by al-Walid I. According to tradition the original Al-Aqsa Mosque was built in c.644.
- 724–27 Umayyad Caliph al-Hisham (reigned 724–43) builds the desert palace of Qasr al-Hayr al-Gharbi in the Syrian desert.
- 743–44 Umayyad Caliph al-Walid II (reigned 743–44) builds the palace of Mshatta in Jordan.
- 762 Madinat al-Salam (the 'City of Peace'), later called Baghdad, is founded by Abbasid Caliph al-Mansur (reigned 754–75) beside the river Tigris in Iraq.

Above Ruins of the Qusayr Azraq fortress in Jordan, which was expanded by the Mamluks in the 13th century.

- c.775 The fortified palace of Ukhaydir is built near Kufa, 200km (125 miles) from Baghdad.
- 775–85 Abbasid Caliph al-Mahdi (reigned 775–85) is the first Islamic ruler to put his name on official coinage.
- 784–86 Umayyad ruler Abd al-Rahman I (reigned 756–88) begins construction of the Mezquita in Córdoba, Spain.
- 805 Abbasid Caliph Harun al-Rashid (reigned 786–809) founds a public hospital in Baghdad. It is the first such institution in the Islamic world: within a few years many major cities in the Abbasid Empire have a public hospital named *bimaristan* (a Pahlavi word meaning 'place of the sick').
- 817–63 The Great Mosque at Kairouan, Tunisia, is built.
- 830 The Bayt al-Hikma ('House of Wisdom') – a library and centre for the translation of classical texts – is established in Baghdad by Abbasid Caliph al-Mamun (reigned 813–33).
- 836 Abbasid Caliph al-Mutasim (reigned 833–42) establishes a new royal capital at Samarra, on the river Tigris.
- 848–52 Abbasid Caliph al-Mutawakkil (reigned 847–61) builds the Great

Above Seljuk stonework adorns the portal of the Ince Minareli Madrasa in Konya, Turkey, built in the 1260s.

Mosque of Samarra, with its spiral minaret.
- c.850–70 Muhammad al-Bukhari (810–70), a scholar resident in Samanid Bukhara (now in Uzbekistan), compiles the Sahih Bukhari, a collection of *hadith*, or sayings, of the Prophet Muhammad, that is considered the most authentic of all extant books of *hadith*.
- 859 The Qarawiyyin *madrasa* is established in Fez in Morocco. This is the oldest known *madrasa*.
- 886–940 Abbasid vizier Ibn Muqla (886–940) identifies the 'Six Pens' or classic scripts of calligraphy: *naskhi, muhaqqaq, thuluth, rayhani, riqa* and *tawqi*.
- 892 Abbasid Caliph al-Mutamid (reigned 870–92) returns the capital to Baghdad from Samarra.
- 892–943 A brick tomb is built in Bukhara (now Uzbekistan) to honour Samanid ruler Ismail Samani (reigned 892–907).
- 921 Fatimid leader Ubayd Allah al-Mahdi Billah builds the palace city of Mahdia on the coast of Tunisia.
- c.935 Iranian poet Rudaki (859–c.941) is active at the court of Samanid ruler Nasr II (reigned 914–43).
- 936–940 Umayyad Caliph Abd al-Rahman III (reigned 912–61)

TIMELINE

- builds the city of Madinat al-Zahra near Córdoba in Islamic Spain.
- c.955 A woven silk textile now known as the Shroud of Saint Josse is made for Samanid official Abu Mansur Bukhtegin (d.960).
- 959 A *madrasa* is set up alongside the al-Azhar Mosque in Cairo, Egypt. This eventually develops into the prestigious al-Azhar University.
- 969 The Fatimids found the city of Cairo as a royal capital in Egypt.
- 1006–7 The Gunbad-i-Qabus tomb tower is built in Gurgan, Iran, for Ziyarid ruler Qabus ibn Wushnigr (reigned 978–1012).
- 1009–10 Iranian poet Firdawsi compiles his 60,000-couplet epic, *Shahnama* (Book of Kings).
- 1012 The Mosque of al-Hakim is completed in Cairo.
- 1033 Fatimids under Caliph Ali al-Zahir (reigned 1021–36) rebuild the Al-Aqsa Mosque in Jerusalem in the form it retains today. The mosque had been damaged by an earthquake.
- 1065 The al-Nizamiyya *madrasa* is set up in Baghdad by Seljuk vizier Nizam al-Mulk (1018–92). It is the first of a series of *madrasas* he establishes in Iran.
- 1078–79 The Ribat-i Malik *caravanserai* is built on the road between Bukhara and Samarkand (now in Uzbekistan) by the Qarakhanid Sultan Nasr (reigned 1068–80).
- 1082 The Great Mosque of Tlemcen (in Algeria) is built by Almoravid leader Yusuf ibn Tashfin (reigned 1060–1106).
- 1086–87 Nizam al-Mulk, vizier for Seljuk Sultan Malik Shah (reigned 1072–92), builds the south *iwan* (hall) at the Friday Mosque of Isfahan, Iran.
- 1088–89 Taj al-Mulk, Malik Shah's imperial chamberlain, adds the north *iwan* to Isfahan's Friday Mosque.
- c.1096 Fatimid vizier Badr al-Jamali rebuilds Cairo's city walls; he constructs the fortified gates of Bab al-Nasr and Bab al-Futuh.
- 1096 The Almoravid Great Mosque of Algiers is completed.
- 1125 Fatimid vizier Mamum al-Bataihi founds the Aqmar Mosque in Cairo.
- 1132–40 Norman King Roger II of Sicily (reigned 1130–54) builds the Palatine Chapel in his royal palace in Palermo.
- 1135-46 The Grand Mosque in Zavareh, central Iran, is built. It is one the earliest surviving mosques built with four *iwans*, or vaulted halls, opening on to the courtyard.
- 1142 The Mosque of Taza in Algeria is founded by Almohad leader Abd al-Mumin (reigned 1130–63).
- 1147-48 The Gunbad-i-Surkh tomb tower is built in Maragha, Iran, by architect Bakr Muhammad.
- 1154 Moroccan geographer Muhammad al-Idrisi (1100–66) completes his celebrated world map, probably the most accurate made during the medieval period. It is called the 'Tabula Rogeriana' because it is made for King Roger II of Sicily at his court in Palermo.
- 1157 The Mausoleum of Sultan Sanjar, is built at Merv (now in Turkmenistan).
- 1158–60 Another Seljuk four-*iwan* mosque is built at Ardestan, Iran.
- 1169 Zangid ruler of Syria Nur al-Din (reigned 1146–74) commissions four Aleppo craftsmen to make a beautiful new *minbar* for the Al-Aqsa Mosque, Jerusalem. It is installed in 1187 after Ayyubid general Salah al-Din takes the city.
- 1172–98 In Seville, Spain, the Almohads build the Great Mosque, which later becomes the city's Christian cathedral.

Above 14th-century tilework on the walls of one of the tombs in the Shah-i Zinda Mausoleum in Samarkand, Uzbekistan.

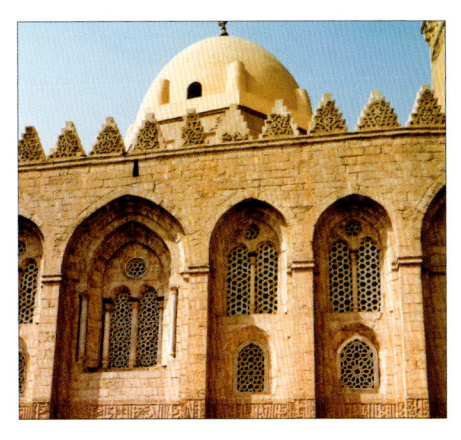

Above The Mamluk Sultan Qalawun built this mausoleum in 1285 as part of his much larger complex in Cairo, Egypt.

Above Inscriptions from the Quran were carved into the red sandstone of the Qutub Minar, a tall minaret in Delhi, India.

TIMELINE

Above A scene from the 1514 Battle of Chaldiran, when the Ottoman Empire defeated the Safavids.

Above Detail of one of the exquisite 16th-century Iznik tiles in the Rüstem Pasha Mosque in Istanbul, Turkey.

Above The dome inside the Selimiye Mosque in Edirne, Turkey, built by the architect Mimar Sinan, 1568–74.

- 1176–83 Ayyubid ruler Salah al-Din builds the Citadel on Muqattam Hill, Cairo.
- 1190 Ghurid Sultan Ghiyath al-Din Muhammad builds the Minaret of Jam in Afghanistan. It is 60m (197ft) in height.
- 1193 Qutb-al-din Aybak – Turkic Muslim general and self-styled Sultan of Delhi – begins construction of the Qutb Minar in Delhi to mark the triumph of Islam in India.
- 1199 The *Kitab al-Diryaq* (Book of Antidotes) is one of many exquisite books made for the Zangid rulers of Mosul (Iraq). Zangid Mosul is also celebrated for its metalworking at this time.
- 1227–34 Abbasid Caliph al-Mustansir (reigned 1226–42) is responsible for the building of the Mustansiriya *madrasa* in Baghdad. It is designed with three *iwans* that lead on to a central courtyard.
- 1229 Anatolian Seljuk Sultan Ala al-Din Kaykubad I (reigned 1220–37) builds a *caravanserai* on the road from Konya to Aksaray, Turkey. He builds a second *caravanserai* on the road between Kayseri and Sivas (also in Turkey) in 1232–36.

- *c.*1240 The Mosque of Djénné is built in Mali, western Africa.
- 1242–44 The *madrasa* of Ayyubid ruler Sultan al-Salih Najm al-Din Ayyub (reigned 1240–49) is built in Cairo.
- 1251 The Karatay *madrasa* in Konya, Turkey, is built by Anatolian Seljuk vizier Jalal al-Din Karantay.
- 1267–69 The Mosque of Mamluk Sultan Baybars (reigned 1260–77) is built in Cairo, Egypt.
- 1269 In what is now Somalia, the first Sultan of Mogadishu builds the Mosque of Fakhr al-Din. This is the oldest mosque in East Africa.
- *c.*1270 The second Ilkhanid ruler of Iran, Abaqa Khan (reigned 1265–82), builds the summer palace of Tahkt-i Sulayman in north-western Iran.
- 1284–85 The mausoleum and *madrasa* complex of Mamluk sultan Qalawun (reigned 1279–90) is built in Cairo. In 1284, Sultan Qalawun also builds the al-Mansuri Hospital in Cairo.
- *c.*1285 Ilkhanid ruler Arghun Uljaytu builds a new capital called Sultaniyya near Qazvin, north-western Iran.
- 1295–1303 The *madrasa* and Mausoleum of Mamluk Sultan al-Nasir Muhammad (reigned 1293–94, 1299–1309 and 1309–41) is built in Cairo, Egypt. It is begun by Sultan al-Adil Kitbugha (reigned 1294–96) prior to his deposition in 1296. Kitbugha installs the Gothic portal, brought from a crusader church in Acre (now Israel).
- 1309 The eighth Ilkhanid ruler of Iran, Uljaytu (reigned 1304–16), adds an exquisite stucco *mihrab* to the winter *iwan*, or hall, of the Friday Mosque in Isfahan, Iran.
- 1322–26 The ninth Ilkhanid ruler of Iran, Abu Said (reigned 1316–35), builds a congregational mosque at Varamin, Iran.
- 1327 The Djinguereber Mosque is built in Timbuktu, Mali, western Africa. It is the oldest of three ancient mosque-*madrasas* in the city; the others are the Sidhi Yahya and the Sankoré mosques, and the three together form the University of Sankoré.
- 1335–36 Mamluk Sultan al-Nasir Muhammad builds the Sultan's Mosque within the Citadel, Cairo.
- 1348–91 Nasrid sultans of Granada, Yusuf I (reigned 1333–54) and Muhammad V (reigned 1354–59 and 1362–91), expand the Alhambra Palace,

- building the Comares Palace and Palace of the Lions.
- 1356 Mamluk Sultan al-Nasir al-Hasan (reigned 1347–51 and 1354–61) commissions the building of his mosque and *madrasa* complex in Cairo.
- 1396–1400 Ulu Çami (the Great Mosque) is built in Bursa, north-western Turkey, by Ali Neccar on the orders of Ottoman Sultan Bayezid I (reigned 1389–1402).
- 1399–1404 Turkic ruler Timur (Tamerlane reigned 1370–1405) oversees the construction of the Bibi Khanum Mosque in Samarkand (now in Uzbekistan).
- 1403 Timur builds the celebrated Gur-e Amir tomb complex in Samarkand.
- 1415–20 The Mosque of Mamluk Sultan al-Muayyad Shaykh (reigned 1412–21) is built in Cairo. It is the last Mamluk congregational mosque of monumental dimensions.
- 1417–21 Ulugh Beg, grandson of Timur, (reigned 1411–49) builds a fine *madrasa* in Samarkand to complement the one he constructs in Bukhara at the same time.
- 1459–73 Mehmet II begins building the Topkapi Palace, also in Istanbul.
- 1463–70 Mehmet II builds the Mehmet Fatih Kulliye in Istanbul. It contains a mosque, mausolea, hospital, *caravanserai*, a bathhouse, two *madrasas*, a library and soup kitchen.
- 1515 The Great Mosque of Agadez in Niger, western Africa, is built by Askia Muhammad I, ruler of the Songhai Empire (reigned 1492–1528).
- 1539–40 Safavid Shah Tahmasp I (reigned 1524–76) commissions two very large Persian carpets for the dynastic shrine at Ardabil, Iran. Both are dated and signed by Maqsud Kashani.
- 1543–48 Ottoman architect Mimar Sinan (1489–1588) builds the Şehzade Mosque in Istanbul.
- 1550–57 Mimar Sinan builds the Süleymaniye Mosque in Istanbul for Sultan Suleyman I 'the Magnificent' (reigned 1520–66).
- *c*.1567–73 The young Emperor Akbar commissions an outsize manuscript of the romance *Hamzanama*, with 1,400 paintings.
- 1562 Mughal ruler Akbar (reigned 1556–1605) builds the Tomb of Humayan in Delhi to honour his father Humayan (reigned 1530–40 and 1555–56), second ruler of the dynasty.
- 1565–73 Akbar rebuilds the Red Fort of Agra, India.
- 1568–74 Ottoman architect Mimar Sinan builds the Selimiye Mosque in Edirne, Turkey.
- 1569 Akbar builds a new capital at Fatehpur Sikri, India.
- 1603–19 Safavid Shah Abbas I (reigned 1587–1629) builds the Lutfallah Mosque as part of his redevelopment of Isfahan, Iran. He also builds a Congregational Mosque on the same square, in 1611–30.
- 1612–14 The Tomb of Akbar (reigned 1556–1605) is built at Sikandra near Agra, India.
- 1609–16 Ottoman Sultan Ahmet I (reigned 1603–17) builds the Blue Mosque in Istanbul.
- 1632–54 Mughal Emperor Shah Jahan (reigned 1628–58) builds the Taj Mahal as a memorial shrine for his favourite wife, Mumtaz Mahal.
- 1656 Shah Jahan completes the building of the Jama Masjid Mosque in Delhi.
- 1678–82 The Ottoman Khan al-Wazir is built in Aleppo, Syria.
- 1706–15 The Shah Sultan Husayn mosque-bazaar complex is built on the Chahar Bagh in Isfahan.

Above The University of Qarawiyyin (founded 859) is important to Muslims as one of the best centres for education.

Above Shah Jahani-style, white marble buildings grace the terraced Shalimar Gardens, built in Lahore in 1642.

Above Figures greet each other in this 19th-century tile from the Golestan Palace, a Qajar palace in Tehran.

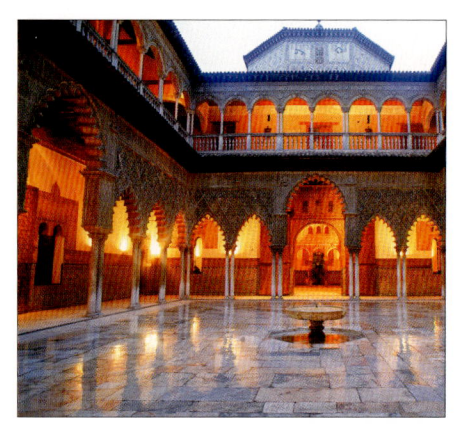

TIMELINE

Above A courtyard in the Alhambra, the 14th- and 15th-century residence of Muslim rulers in Granada.

Above Floral patterns feature on this 13th–14th-century Islamic dish, made during the Mongol period in Iran.

Above The Azadi Tower, built in Tehran in 1971, marked the 2,500th anniversary of the Persian Empire.

- 1749 Ottoman governor Asad Pasha al-Azem builds the Azem Palace in Damascus.
- 1836 In Istanbul, Krikor Balyan completes the Nusretiye Mosque for Ottoman Sultan Mahmud II (reigned 1808–39).
- 1848 Muhammad Ali Pasha, Wali of Egypt, completes the grand Muhammad Ali Mosque in Cairo.
- 1855 Architects Garabet Amira Balyan and Nigogayos Balyan complete the Dolmabahçe Palace in Istanbul for Ottoman Sultan Abdulmecid I (reigned 1839–61).
- 1961 The Dhahran International Airport in Saudi Arabia is completed, designed by American architect Minoru Yamasaki.
- 1971 The Shayad Tower ('Memorial of Kings') is built in Tehran, Iran. After the Islamic Revolution (1979) it is renamed the Azadi (Freedom) Tower.
- 1973 The Great Mosque of Niono in Mali, western Africa, is completed using traditional techniques and materials.
- 1984 The Freedom Mosque in Jakarta, Indonesia, is completed by Indonesian architect Frederick Silaban.
- 1986 The King Faisal Mosque is completed in Islamabad, Pakistan. The architect, Vedat Delakoy, is Turkish.
- 1989 Architect Abdel-Wahed el-Wakil completes the King Saud Mosque in Jeddah, Saudi Arabia.
- 1990 Architect Rasem Badran completes the King Abdullah Mosque in Amman, Jordan.
- 1993 The King Hassan II Mosque in Casablanca, Morocco, is finished. It is designed by French architect Michel Pinseau. Its minaret, at 210m (689ft), is the world's tallest.
- 1999 The Kingdom Tower office and retail complex in Riyadh, Saudi Arabia, is completed. It is 311m (1,020ft) tall. A rival Riyadh tower, the Al Faisaliyah Centre, is completed in 2000.
- 1999 The Burj al-Arab ('Tower of the Arabs') hotel is completed on a man-made island off Dubai.
- 2007 The Rose Tower built in Dubai. At 333m (1,093ft) tall, it is the world's tallest hotel.

Below The Islamic world extended across Africa, Europe and Asia.

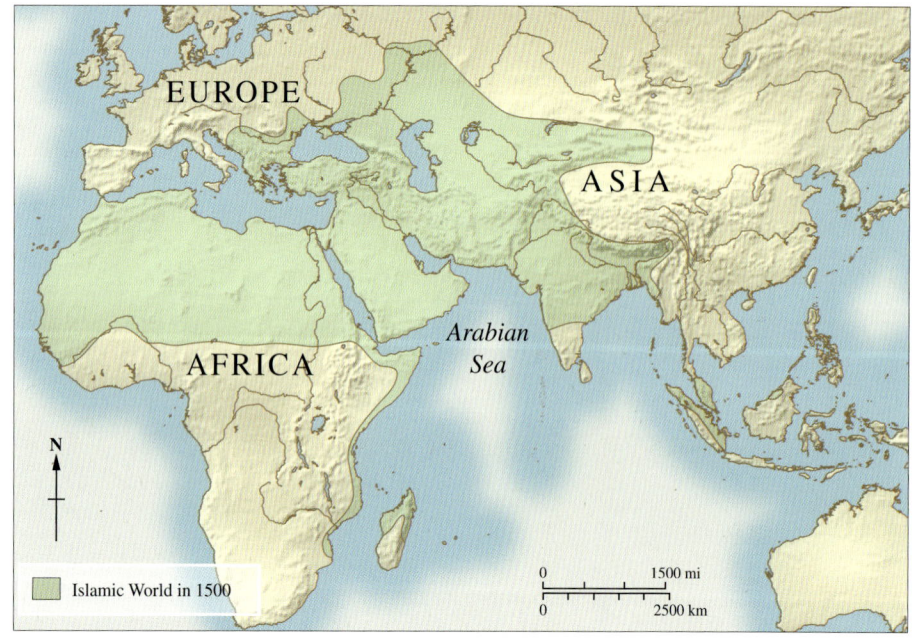

Opposite An illustration of the city of Baghdad, showing the famous bridge of boats across the Tigris, from a 1468 anthology by Nasir Bukhari.

14

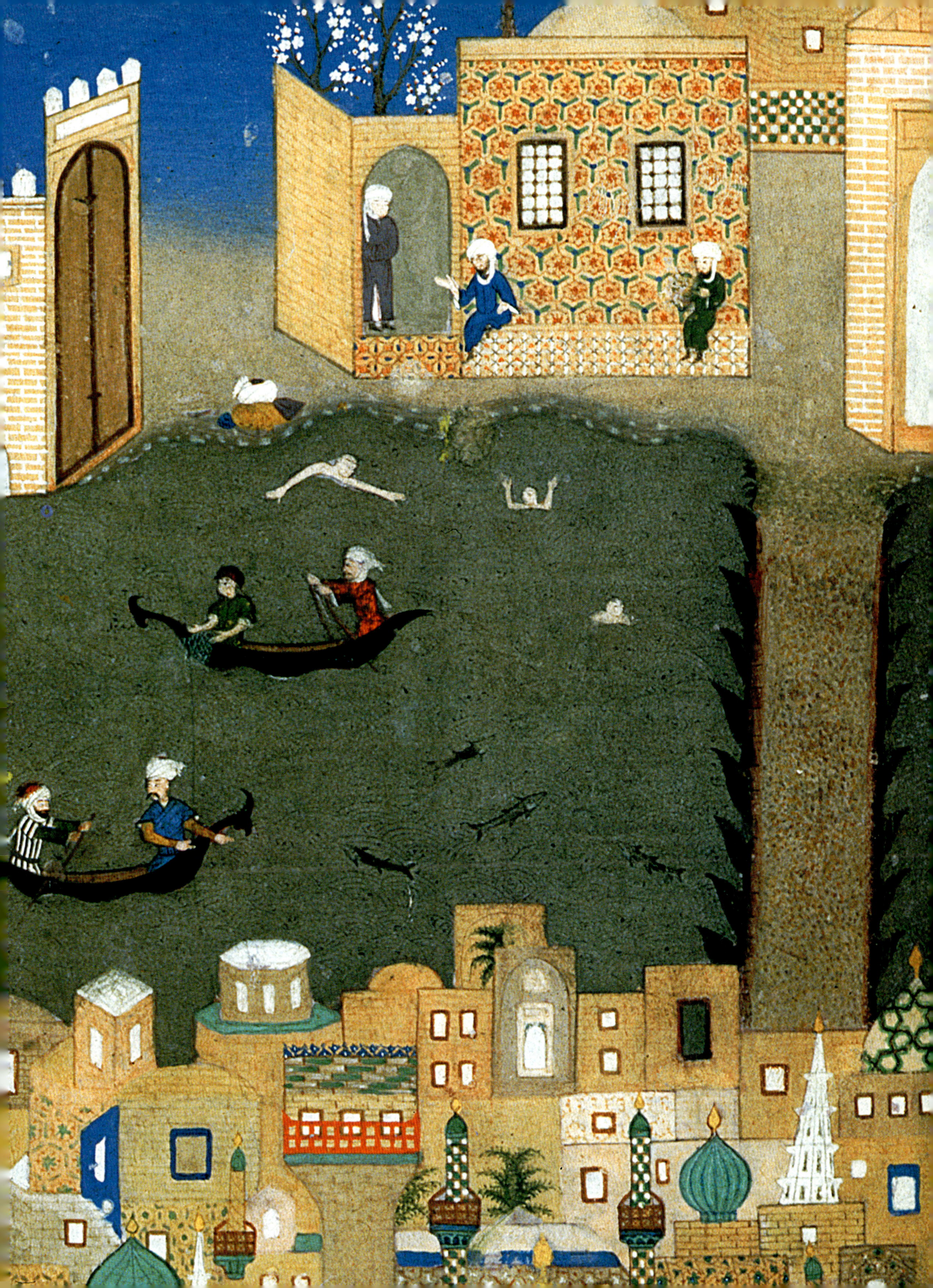

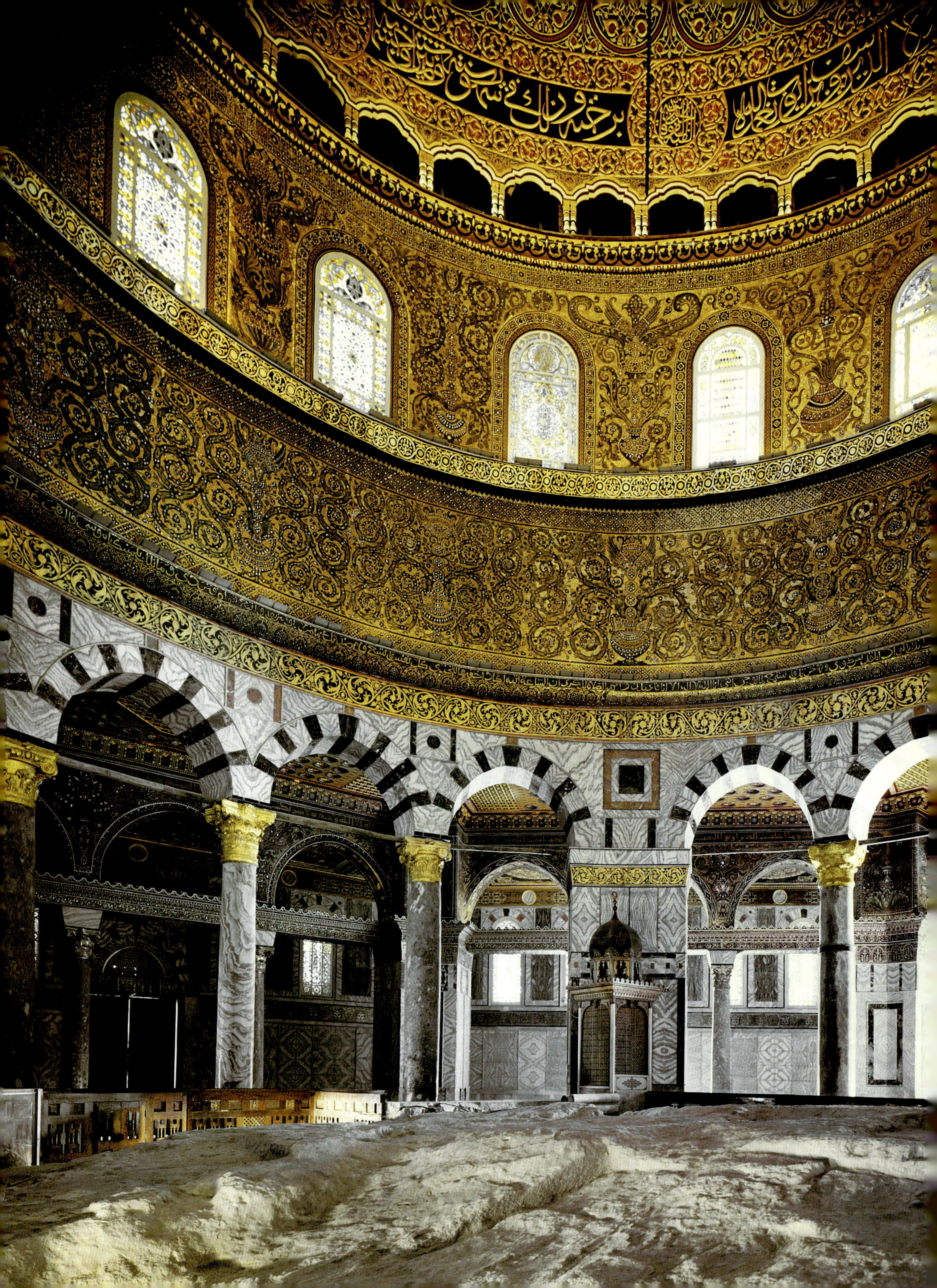

THE ARCHITECTURE OF THE ISLAMIC WORLD

The glorious architecture of Islam is found in many different cultures around the the world – from Spain to India, and Turkey to North Africa – each of which has at some time come under Muslim rule. The many types of Islamic structures include mosques, *qiblas*, *madrasas*, memorials for the dead, bazaars, buildings, courtyards, fortified walls, palaces and indeed whole cities. The splendid refinement of such architectural achievements signifies a longstanding culture of taste and discernment. The common factor in this great output from so many different cultures is the religion of Islam, for although the civilian populations of Western Asia and other parts of the Islamic world were never exclusively Muslim, they have long been ruled by caliphs, sultans, shahs and amirs who were. This chapter examines the main types of Islamic architecture, explaining the layout and purpose of each one.

Opposite *Beautiful mosaics, including prayers and quotations from the Quran, line the interior walls of the Dome of the Rock in Jerusalem. Pilgrims visiting the shrine follow the ambulatory around the sacred Rock at the centre.*

Above *Domes are clustered together at the Bayezid I Mosque complex (1390–95) in Bursa. The foundation includes a dervish lodge, hospital,* hammam, madrasa *and mausoleum for the sultan.*

THE MOSQUE

STARTING AS A SIMPLE HALL AND COURTYARD, THE MOSQUE DEVELOPED IN INCREASINGLY ELABORATE FORMS UNTIL IT REACHED THE GRAND, MANY-DOMED STRUCTURE BUILT BY THE OTTOMANS.

The original use for the mosque was as a place for Muslims to gather. They meet there to pray together, and also to perform communal, social and educational activities. The word 'mosque' derives from the Arabic *masjid*, meaning a 'place of prostration', where five times a day Muslims can bow their heads to the ground, thus making the act of submission in prayer to Allah that is required by their faith.

FIRST MOSQUES

The house of the Prophet in Madinah, built in 622, was the prototype for early mosques. Worshippers gathered in large numbers in its enclosed courtyard. The early courtyard mosques were based on this pattern: a flat-roofed prayer hall led to a *sahn*, or an open courtyard, which generally had arcades at the sides. In the centre of the courtyard was often a fountain at which worshippers performed ritual ablutions. A *mihrab*, or niche, in one wall indicated the direction of the *Kaabah* shrine in Makkah, toward which Muslims must face when praying. Gates or doorways were cut in any of the three walls, other than the *qibla* wall that contained the *mihrab*.

Tall towers called minarets were added to the mosque in the late 7th century. Among the first were the four built at the Great Mosque in Damascus, built in 706–15 under the Umayyad Caliph al-Walid I. The minarets were initially watchtowers in which lighted torches were kept – 'minaret' derives from the Arabic *manara*, meaning 'lighthouse' – but they became elevated positions from which the *muezzin* sent out the five daily calls to prayers.

ARAB-STYLE MOSQUES

The mosque developed in different styles. In Syria, and afterward in Spain and North Africa, mosques were built on a rectangular plan, with an enclosed courtyard and a vast rectangular prayer hall with a flat roof divided internally by rows of columns. Architectural historians call these Arab-plan, or hypostyle, mosques. They were typically built by early Arab Muslims. A hypostyle hall is an architectural term for a large building with a flat roof supported by rows of columns.

This design was followed in 706–15 in the Umayyad Great Mosque of Damascus, which has a prayer hall 160m (525ft) long with a wooden roof supported on

Left The Mosque of the Prophet in Madinah has changed from the simple courtyard and prayer hall that was the original prototype for mosques.

Above This illustration shows the 8th-century Great Mosque of Damascus, with its prayer hall facing a courtyard and an early example of the minaret.

columns and a great courtyard; the same pattern was used in 817–63 for the Great Mosque at Kairouan, Tunisia, where the prayer hall contains 8 bays and upward of 400 columns. At the Mezquita in Córdoba, Spain (begun in 784–86 under the Umayyad ruler Abd al-Rahman I), builders constructed a vast prayer hall containing 850 pillars that divide the hall into 29 aisles running east–west and 19 aisles north–south. Commentators note that the rows of columns in Arab-style mosques create a sense of limitless space.

FOUR-*IWAN* MOSQUES

In Iran, a new form was developed in the 11th century. It included four domed *iwans*, or halls, one in each of the walls surrounding the courtyard. Architectural historians call this the 'four-*iwan*' or cruciform design, because it creates a ground plan in the form of a cross. The form appears to have been introduced by the Seljuk Turks from central Asia, who took power in Baghdad in 1055. The Grand Mosque in Zavareh, Iran, built in

18

TYPES OF MOSQUE

Of the three types of mosque, the first one is the daily mosque, or *masjid*, a small building used by local people for the five daily prayers. The second is the *jami*, or congregational mosque, also known as the 'Friday Mosque'. This much larger type of mosque is used by crowds of people for Friday service. It contains a *minbar*, or pulpit, used for sermons in Friday prayer. The third type is a large outdoor place for assembly and prayer containing a *qibla* wall with *mihrab* niche to indicate the correct direction for prayer, but without other facilities. These are often built outside towns.

Above This delicate stucco mihrab, *commissioned by Ilkhanid ruler Uljaytu (reigned 1304–16), is in the Friday Mosque in Isfahan, Iran.*

1135–46, followed this design and is the earliest surviving four-*iwan* mosque. Behind the *qibla iwan* (the one aligned toward Makkah) there is another domed chamber containing the *mihrab*.

CENTRAL-DOME MOSQUES

In Turkey and the cities of their empire, the Ottomans developed the vast monumental mosque with a central dome surrounded by semidomes, often called 'central-dome' mosques. They were inspired by the local religious architecture of the Byzantine Empire, and in particular by the magnificent Hagia

Above The central dome in the Sultan Ahmet Mosque (1609–16) in Istanbul is decorated with calligraphy by Seyyid Kasim Gubari, who was the leading calligrapher of the period.

Sophia (Church of Holy Wisdom) in the Byzantine capital, Constantinople. Within days of Mehmet II 'the Conqueror' (reigned 1444–46, 1451–81) capturing Constantinople, he made the Church of Holy Wisdom into a mosque. Ottoman sultans and architects soon rose to the challenge of competing with the glorious Hagia Sophia.

Foremost among them was Mimar Sinan (1489–1588), chief Ottoman architect under sultans Suleyman I, Selim II and Murad III. Examples of magnificent central-dome mosques he built include the Şehzade Mosque (1543–48) and Süleymaniye Mosque (1550–57) – both in Constantinople – and the Selimiye Mosque (1568–74) in Edirne. The central-dome mosque was built at the heart of a complex of related buildings called a *kulliye*: the Selimiye Mosque, for instance, is surrounded by *caravanserais* (inns), schools, bathhouses, marketplaces, hospitals, libraries and a cemetery.

THE QIBLA

MUSLIMS ARE REQUIRED TO FACE TOWARD THE *KAABAH* SHRINE IN MAKKAH WHEN PRAYING DURING THE FIVE DAILY PRAYERS. THIS DIRECTION OF PRAYER IS CALLED THE *QIBLA*.

Within a mosque the *qibla* is indicated by a *mihrab*, a niche in a wall. The wall with the *mihrab* is known as the *qibla* wall. The word *mihrab* originally meant 'a special room'. In the Prophet's lifetime, he began to use the word for the room he used for prayer in his house in Madinah. He entered the mosque established in his house through this room.

Early Muslims prayed toward Jerusalem. It was Jewish custom to pray facing the Temple Mount, where the Jewish Temple stood (and also, subsequently, the location of the Dome of the Rock and the Al-Aqsa Mosque). One day during prayer in Madinah, the Prophet was inspired to turn toward the *Kaabah* in Makkah, a pagan sanctuary that Muslims claimed for monotheism. The revelation that he received, instructing him to change the direction of prayer, was recorded in the Quran (Surah al-Baqara: 144): 'We have seen the turning of thy face to Heaven (for guidance, O Muhammad). And now verily we shall make thee turn (in prayer) toward a *qibla*, which is dear to thee. So turn thy face toward the Inviolable Place of Worship, and ye (O Muslims), wheresoever ye may be, turn your faces (when ye pray) toward it…'

The place in which this event occurred is now called the Masjid al-Qiblatayn ('Mosque of the Two Qiblas'). It is unique in having two *mihrabs* to indicate the two directions of prayer, although at the time of the event Muslims were not yet indicating the direction of the *qibla* with a *mihrab*.

THE FIRST *MIHRAB*

The *mihrab* niche appears to have been introduced in the early 8th century. According to tradition, Caliph Uthman ibn-Affan (reigned 644–56) ordered a sign indicating the direction of the *Kaabah* in Makkah to be posted on the wall of the Mosque of the Prophet, at Madinah. When this mosque was renovated by Caliph al-Walid (reigned 705–15), a niche was made in the *qibla* wall and the sign made by Caliph Uthman

Above This *mihrab* within the Friday Mosque in Kerman, Iran, has a simple arch shape but is elaborately decorated with glazed ceramic tiles.

Left This 17th-century tile bears an illustration of Makkah with the black-draped *Kaabah* at its centre.

Right The mihrab *in the Mezquita, the former mosque of Córdoba in Spain, is especially notable because it is not aligned toward Makkah.*

placed within it. It became traditional for the *mihrab* niche to have the shape of a doorway, possibly to indicate that the worshipper can make a journey in spirit through the *qibla* wall to the *Kaabah* at Makkah. The arched *mihrab* shape can also be found on many objects, such as prayer mats, embroideries and tiles.

NOT FACING MAKKAH

A few *qibla* walls and *mihrabs* are not aligned toward Makkah. The most celebrated is that of the Mezquita (Spanish for 'mosque') in Córdoba, Spain, where the *mihrab* faces south rather than south-east (the correct direction for Makkah). Some historians believe that this is because the mosque was built on the remains of a Visigothic cathedral; others say that when building the mosque Abd al-Rahman I aligned the *mihrab* as if he were still at home in Damascus rather than in exile in Spain.

This *mihrab* was reworked under al-Hakam II, Caliph of Córdoba in 961–76, using skilled Byzantine craftsmen. Situated beneath a breathtaking dome, it is regarded as one of the greatest masterpieces of Islamic religious building. An inscription in Arabic begins 'Allah is the knower of all things, both concealed and apparent. He is full of power, and of pity, the living one…'

DETERMINING *QIBLA*

When building a mosque or when praying, Muslims had to determine the precise direction of Makkah. Their need to be able to do this inspired scientists to develop and improve scientific instruments, such as astrolabes. The astrolabe is an astronomical device that can be aligned with the position of the sun and other celestial bodies, such as the moon and planets, to determine latitude and local time. It was invented in the 1st or 2nd century BCE by the ancient Greeks. The first Islamic astrolabe was developed by the 8th-century CE Iranian mathematician Muhammad al-Fazari. Because they could be used to determine local time, they were also extremely valuable for setting the hours of prayer.

Above The astrolabe is a stereographic map of the night sky which can be set for one's exact date, time and latitude.

THE ARCHITECTURE OF THE ISLAMIC WORLD

THE MOSQUE INTERIOR

MOSQUES VARY GREATLY IN SIZE AND FORM. SOME FEATURES, SUCH AS THE *MIHRAB*, ARE PRESENT IN ALL MOSQUES, BUT OTHERS, INCLUDING THE *MINBAR*, ARE FOUND ONLY IN LARGER MOSQUES.

The essential elements found in a mosque are the *qibla* wall (indicating the direction of the *Kaabah* in Makkah), the *mihrab* in this wall and a fountain at which the faithful perform ablutions before prayer. A congregational mosque will also contain a pulpit called a *minbar*, from which sermons, proclamations and readings are delivered as part of Friday service. The *minbar* has always stood to the right of the *mihrab*.

PURPOSE OF THE *MIHRAB*

The holiest place in the mosque is the *mihrab* archway. It is often highly decorated and is usually made of part of the mosque wall. The imam or other prayer leader leads prayers in front of the *mihrab*. Today, his voice might be broadcast using microphones and speakers, but in pre-electronic times the opening of the *mihrab* amplified the imam's voice so that all present could hear him. The *mihrab* is often decorated with lamps, symbolizing the light of Allah's grace. A small window is sometimes cut in the wall above the *mihrab* to give a sense of the alignment outside the mosque.

MINBAR AND *MAQSURA*

The *minbar* is a free-standing structure, often carved from wood, to the right of the *mihrab*. In some traditions it is decorated, in others it is plain. Steps rise to the *minbar*: the *imam khatib* (preaching imam) who delivers the sermon stands on the lower steps – the top one is reserved in perpetuity for the Prophet Muhammad himself.

The first *minbar*, used by the Prophet, had three steps and was made from tamarisk wood; the Prophet stood on the top step, but the first caliph, or successor, Abu Bakr, would go no higher than the second one as a mark of respect and then the third caliph, Umar, used only the third step. Since that time, however, the preacher has stood on the second step from the top. In the early days of Islam, political and religious power were one: the Prophet and caliphs led prayers, and the governor first climbed the *minbar* to give a sermon, then descended to lead prayers in front of the *mihrab*.

In some early mosques, the *mihrab* and *minbar* were behind a carved wooden screen known as a *maqsura*. These screens were probably introduced to protect the caliph while at prayers after a rash of attacks on notables in mosques such as that on Caliph Umar, who was stabbed by a Zoroastrian slave as he led prayers in the mosque in Madinah in 644. However, over time the *maqsura*, which was often beautifully and lavishly decorated, functioned also as a statement of the ruler's power and wealth. Although the mosque belonged to the entire community of believers, the area beyond the *maqsura* was set aside for the prince or caliph as a celebration of his glory and the greatness of his rule.

Above A cantor kneels on the kursi, *or lectern, while reciting the holy words of the Quran in the Mosque of Sultan Barquq in Cairo, Egypt.*

Left A grand minbar *stands to the right of the* mihrab *in the eastern* iwan *of the Sultan Hasan Mosque in Cairo, Egypt.*

Right Some early maquras, *as in the Ibn Tulun Mosque, Cairo, were simple raised platforms with protective screens.*

RECITING THE QURAN

Most mosques have a *kursi*, or lectern, at which a cantor recites the Quran. The recitation of the Quran is a highly regarded art. Muslims believe that the Quran has the most profound impact on a believer's mind and heart when it is heard aloud. The *kursi* is a heavy but movable piece of furniture, often with a low platform on which the cantor kneels, facing the *qibla* wall, as he recites from the Quran.

Many larger mosques contained a *dikka*, a platform for the *muezzin* to sing the responses to the prayers chanted by the imam. It was usually aligned with the *mihrab*. Today, the prayers of the imam are heard through loudspeakers, but in large mosques in the days before amplifiers the responses of the *muezzin* on the *dikka* helped those at the rear of the mosque follow the service if they were unable to hear the prayers being chanted in front of the *mihrab*. Their task was also to adopt the positions taken by the imam so that those who could not see him were able to follow this part of the service. In most mosques today, the *dikka* is not used because the *muezzin* no longer stands on the platform during worship.

PRAYER RUGS

Mosques always contain prayer rugs, because worshippers kneel and lower their foreheads to the floor during prayers. They are also usually equipped with bookrests to support copies of the Quran and keep them off the floor, as well as containers to hold the Quran when it is not in use.

Right This 18th-century Turkish prayer rug bears an image of a mihrab *with two columns and a stylized hanging lamp.*

23

THE MADRASA

RELIGIOUS COLLEGES WERE OFTEN ATTACHED TO A MOSQUE, BUT THEY COULD ALSO BE INDEPENDENT INSTITUTIONS FUNDED BY HOSTELS AND MARKETS OR BY AN ENDOWMENT.

The Arabic word *madrasa* means 'a place where teaching and learning takes place', and refers to a religious school, university or college. The *madrasas* specialized in educating religious leaders and legal experts. Where they were funded by a *waqf* (religious endowment), the person who provided the endowment was usually buried in an associated mausoleum.

EARLY *MADRASAS*
In early Muslim communities, mosques were social centres in which a range of activities, such as teaching, took place. Informal teaching sessions were held by educated Muslims, who became known as shaykhs, and the *madrasa* is thought to have developed out of this custom.

The oldest known *madrasa* is in the Qarawiyyin Mosque (also known as the University of al-Qurawiyyin or al-Karaouine) in Fez, Morocco. It was established in 859 by Fatima al-Fihri, daughter of a wealthy merchant. Another early *madrasa* was the one at the al-Azhar Mosque in Cairo, Egypt, in 959; this became al-Azhar University.

SELJUK *MADRASAS*
In the 11th century, the Persian scholar and Seljuk vizier Nizam al-Mulk (1018–92) set up a series of *madrasas* in cities such as Isfahan and Nishapur (both now in Iran) and Balkh and Herat (both now in Afghanistan). These were well-organized places of higher education called *nizamiyyah* after Nizam, and they had a reputation for teaching throughout the Islamic world and even in Europe.

The *nizamiyyah* became the model for later *madrasas*. The first and most celebrated of these was al-Nizamiyya, set up in Baghdad in 1065. The widely admired Iranian Sufi mystic, philosopher and theologian al-Ghazali (1058–1111) was a teacher at al-Nizamiyya. It became common for Seljuk rulers to build and fund a *madrasa* attached to the mausoleum in which they would be buried.

Above Built in Konya (Turkey) in 1256 by Seljuk vizier Fakhr al-Din Ali, the Ince Minareli *madrasa is celebrated for its grand gateway.*

TYPES OF *MADRASA*
The *madrasa* came in a variety of forms. Some had a single large hall beneath a dome, but a typical configuration was the two-*iwan*, three-*iwan* or four-*iwan* plan, in which a central courtyard adjoins two, three or four large vaulted halls. *Madrasas* typically have grand gateways with imposing portals and towering minarets.

A splendid early example of a three-*iwan* design is the Mustansiriya *madrasa* built in Baghdad by the Abbasid caliph al-Mustansir in 1227–34. Standing beside the river Tigris, the large rectangular brick building is two storeys high and measures 106m by 48m (348ft by 157ft). Students travelled from far-flung parts of the Islamic world to this centre of learning, where they could study the Quran, theology, medicine, jurisprudence, mathematics and literature. It was the first of many *madrasas* to provide facilities for all four principal schools of Sunni Islam – the Hanbali, Shafii, Maliki

Left Three iwans *adjoin the courtyard at the Mustansiriya* madrasa. *It is one of the world's oldest centres of study.*

THE *MADRASA*

Right The Chahar Bagh complex in Isfahan, built by Shah Sultan Husayn in 1706–15, incorporated a caravanserai.

and Hanifi. Followers of each of the four schools had one corner of the *madrasa* to themselves.

Under later rulers, notably the Ottomans in Turkey and the Safavids in Iran, *madrasas* were built as part of a large complex centred on a grand mosque. In Iran, complexes often also contained a *caravanserai* (or inn) and a bazaar, and the commercial areas served to fund the educational and spiritual activities in the *madrasa*.

The Ottoman complexes were called *kulliyes*. Sultan Mehmet II built such a complex in Istanbul, the Mehmet Fatih Kulliye, in 1462–70. It had a hospital, kitchens, *caravanserai*, bazaar and several *hammams* (bathhouses), along with a *madrasa* 200m (656ft) in length for up to 1,000 students. Also in Istanbul, the Süleymaniye Mosque complex, built in 1550–57 by the great architect Sinan for Sultan Suleyman, contained, in addition to the superb mosque with its four minarets and dome, a hostel, a medical college, a school for boys, an asylum, a *hammam*, two mausolea and four *madrasas*.

THE SULTAN HASAN COMPLEX

In Cairo, Egypt, the Mamluks built many splendid *madrasas*. Of these, the most celebrated is probably the Sultan Hasan mosque and *madrasa* complex, commissioned in 1356 by Mamluk Sultan Hasan. The sultan intended it to house teachers of all four legal schools in Sunni Islam: it has four *iwans*, one for teachers and students of each school, adjoining a large central courtyard. Its façade is extremely impressive and measures 36m (118ft) high and 76m (249ft) long. Only one of the original two minarets is still standing, but at 84m (275ft) high it is the tallest of all the minarets surviving from medieval Cairo. The other minaret collapsed during construction and killed 300 people.

Left When it was established in 1356–62, the mosque and madrasa *of Sultan Hasan was the largest structure ever built in Cairo, Egypt.*

THE ARCHITECTURE OF THE ISLAMIC WORLD

Memorials for the Dead

ORTHODOX ISLAM DISCOURAGES LAVISH FUNERARY MONUMENTS, BUT FROM THE 10TH CENTURY ONWARD MANY MUSLIM RULERS LEFT EVIDENCE OF THEIR WEALTH IN GRAND TOMBS AND MAUSOLEA.

Some of the most spectacular Islamic architecture was created in memory of the dead.

FATIMID TOMBS

In the 10th–12th centuries, Ismaili Fatimid rulers of Egypt, North Africa and Syria (909–1171) created the earliest surviving group of mausolea in Islamic history. At least 14 Fatimid-era mausolea survive in Cairo, Egypt, compared to just 5 Fatimid mosques. Several generations of Fatimid caliphs were buried in a tomb in the Eastern Palace in Cairo, which is now lost.

In Aswan, Egypt, an entire city of mud-brick mausolea was built under the Fatimids. In the early years of Islam, elaborate mausolea were not permitted, because the Quran teaches that tombs should be humble. One way around the religious restriction on building fine tombs was to identify them as celebrations of warriors fallen in *jihad*: the cemetery at Aswan is called 'Tombs of the Martyrs' but historians do not know whether or not it actually contained the bodies of those killed fighting for the faith.

The Aswan cemetery contains about 50 tombs in different forms and sizes. Many are compact, square

Below The Tomb of Humayan in Delhi was a forerunner of the Taj Mahal. The main chamber is beneath its dome.

Above The tombs in the Fatimid cemetery at Aswan are mostly modest square buildings with small domes.

buildings topped with small domes; some have adjoining courtyards. One type is known as the *mashhad* ('site of martyrdom' or pilgrimage shrine), and is a small domed building with a walkway around it. Two notable mausolea in this form, the Mashhad of al-Qasim Abu Tayyib (c.1122) and that of

Yahya al-Shabih (c.1150), were built under the Fatimids in Cairo.

SELJUK INNOVATIONS

The style of mausolea was changed by Seljuk rulers, who built *turbe* (square domed buildings) or *gunbads* (tomb towers). A fine example of a *turbe* is the Gunbad-i-Surkh of 1147–48 in Maragha, Iran, decorated with mosaic faience tiles. Instead of being square, some *turbe* had 8, 10 or 12 sides, for example the decahedral (10-sided) mausoleum built for Seljuk Sultan Kilij Arslan II (reigned 1156–92) in the courtyard of the Ala al-Din Mosque in Konya (now in Turkey).

Most *gunbads* were tall towers with conical roofs: perhaps the finest of these is the Gunbad-i-Qabus built in 1006–7 in Gurgan, Iran, for Ziyarid ruler Shams al-Maali Qabus.

In the 14th century, the Ilkhanid ruler Uljaytu (reigned 1304–16), is commemorated at Sultaniyya near Qazwin, Iran, with a magnificent mausoleum. With an elegant dome 53m (174ft) tall, it stood in a vast complex of buildings raised by craftsmen from all over the Ilkhanid empire.

The breathtakingly beautiful Taj Mahal at Agra in India – perhaps the most famous Islamic building – was built in 1632–54 by the Muslim Mughal Emperor Shah Jahan (reigned 1628–58) as a shrine for his favourite wife, Mumtaz Mahal. The mausoleum is set in gardens divided into four areas, with waterways, designed to represent the Islamic paradise.

THE *CHAHAR BAGH*

A tomb placed in a walled, four-part garden with flowing waters, as at the Taj Mahal, was called a *chahar bagh*, from the Persian words *chahar* ('four') and *bagh* ('garden'). It was originally a Persian garden scheme, first used by the emperors of the Achaemenid Empire (550–330BCE) and by Emperor Cyrus the Great (reigned 576–530BCE) in Pasargadae (now an archaeological site in Iran).

In India, the *chahar bagh* design was first used for the Tomb of Humayan in Delhi, built to honour the second Mughal ruler Humayan (reigned 1530–40 and 1555–56) by his widow Hamid Banu Begum. Other lavish Mughal mausolea with *chahar bagh* designs include Akbar's tomb at Sikandra near Agra, built in 1612–14 by his son Jahangir (reigned 1605–27), and Jahangir's tomb, built c.1637 near Shahdara Bagh, Lahore, Pakistan.

At Sasaram, an ornate mausoleum commemorates Pashtun ruler Sher Shah Suri who briefly overcame the Mughals to rule in Delhi 1540–45. His domed red sandstone memorial stands 37m (121ft) tall and – like the Taj Mahal, which it rivals in beauty – is reflected in a lake.

OTTOMAN SPLENDOUR

The mausolea of the Ottomans were impressive structures in vast complexes centred on mosques. The Suleymaniye Mosque complex (built 1550–57) in Istanbul, for instance, contains two mausolea in the garden behind the mosque; these house the remains of Suleyman I (reigned 1520–66) and his family, and those of Suleyman II (reigned 1687–91) and Ahmet II (reigned 1691–95). Also in Istanbul, the beautiful Blue Mosque (built 1609–16) likewise contains the tomb of its founder, Sultan Ahmet I (reigned 1603–17).

SIMPLE BURIALS

For all the exuberance exhibited in the impressive tombs and mausolea, both the Quran and Islamic law call for simple burial of the dead and discourage the use of lavish funerary monuments. The preferred mode of burial is to inter the body wrapped in a shroud, rather than placed in a coffin, with the head facing toward Makkah. Graves of this sort were often left unmarked or identified with simple grave markers.

Above A woman prays at a cemetery in Iraq. Most Muslim graves are simple and unadorned.

Left Ten triangular flanges shoot up the sides of the tomb tower Gunbad-i-Qabus, at Gurgan, Iran.

THE ARCHITECTURE OF THE ISLAMIC WORLD

THE CITY

ISLAMIC RULERS MADE A PUBLIC DISPLAY OF THEIR POWER AND AUTHORITY BY BUILDING GREAT GATEWAYS, PALACES AND CITADELS – OR EVEN BY LAYING OUT ENTIRELY NEW CITIES.

Many major cities were established by Islamic rulers. In 762, the second Abbasid Caliph, al-Mansur, established Madinat as-Salam (the 'City of Peace'), now known as Baghdad, on the river Tigris in Iraq. The city was round and enclosed by three walls with a great gate at each of the points of the compass, which was named for the province or city that lay in that direction. Commercial and residential areas lay in the outer parts of the city, while at the centre of Baghdad stood the dynasty's imperial palace and mosque.

At Samarra, also on the Tigris in Iraq, al-Mansur's successor al-Mutasim (reigned 833–42) established a new royal capital in the years after 836. The city, which included several beautiful palaces as well as the inspiring Great Mosque, extended no less than 32km (20 miles) along the banks of the river Tigris. The name, according to medieval Islamic historians, meant 'A delight for he who sees it'. Samarra served as the capital city until Caliph al-Mutamid (reigned 870–92) returned to Baghdad.

Other examples of splendid new cities built to glorify rulers and dynasties include: Cairo in Egypt, founded in 969 by the Fatimid dynasty; Madinat al-Zahra near Córdoba in Islamic Spain, built in 936–40 by Umayyad caliph Abd al-Rahman III; and Sultaniyya in north-western Iran, built by Ilkhanid ruler Uljaytu (reigned 1304–16). Little remains of these early structures, but magnificent monuments and complexes that were built from the 15th century onward, notably in Iran, India and Turkey, have survived.

MUGHAL GLORIES

In India, Mughal Emperor Akbar built Fatehpur Sikri as a new capital in 1569 to celebrate the longed-for birth of a male heir – the future Emperor Jahangir – and raised the monumental Gate of Victory in front of the Courtyard of the Great Mosque. He built the city on the site of the camp previously occupied by Sufi mystic and saint, Salim Chishti (1478–1572), who had blessed Akbar and thereby apparently brought about the birth of Jahangir. The courtyard contains the Tomb of Salim Chishti, which

Above The Bab al-Amma in Samarra, Iraq, was once the gateway to the caliph's palace. The gateway stood at the top of steps that led up from the river Tigris.

Below The elegantly domed Shaykh Lutfallah Mosque, built 1603–19, stands on the eastern side of the vast Naqsh-e Jahan Square in Isfahan, Iran.

THE CITY

Left The Imperial Hall is part of the harem in the Topkapi Palace, Istanbul. The mother, wives, concubines and children of the Ottoman sultan lived in luxury in the harem's lavish quarters.

Akbar built in red sandstone but which was refashioned as a marble mausoleum. The city was largely abandoned later.

WONDERS OF ISFAHAN

In Iran, Shah Abbas I (reigned 1587–1629) built new monumental quarters in the city of Isfahan to demonstrate the greatness and prosperity of the Safavid dynasty. He built mosques, bathhouses, bazaars, parks, bridges and palaces. In the centre he laid out the palace, congregational mosque and Grand Bazaar around a vast open space known in Persian as Maidan-e Shah (now Maidan-e Imam). A popular phrase at the time was *Isfahan nesf-e jahan*: 'Isfahan is half the world', referring in part to its splendour and also to the presence of a large international community.

A CITY TRANSFORMED

In Turkey, the Ottoman emperors set about remaking the ancient Christian city of Constantinople as the capital of an Islamic empire, eventually renaming the city Istanbul. Mehmet II began the rebuilding after he conquered the city in 1453, making a bold statement of the greatness of the Ottoman sultan and his religion in the Grand Bazaar, the Topkapi Palace, the Fatih Mosque complex and the Eyyüp Sultan Mosque. A substantial part of the Ottoman rebuilding was carried out through the construction of complexes of buildings centred on mosques and containing hospitals, *madrasas*, *caravanserais* and other structures.

The Topkapi Palace, begun by Mehmet II in 1459, was not a single imposing building like a typical European palace, but instead consisted of a sequential system of small buildings, some plain and some practical, such as kitchens, but many splendid and lavishly decorated. The Topkapi Palace remained the residence of Ottoman sultans until 1853, when Sultan Abdulmecid I moved to the newly constructed, European-style Dolmabahçe Palace.

CITADELS

Set behind fortified walls the buildings of the Topkapi Palace are an example of an architectural feature unique to Islam – an enclosed city within a city, called a citadel. The Alhambra, built in Granada (southern Spain) by the rulers of the Nasrid dynasty in 1238–1358, is another well-preserved example of this feature.

The citadel in Aleppo, Syria, stands on a partly natural, partly man-made mound that dominates the city. The mound was fortified from ancient times, then the citadel was developed for military uses. Substantially rebuilt in the 12th century by Zangid rulers Imad al-Din Zangi and Nur al-Din, it was remade in the form in which it survives today by Ayyubid ruler al-Malik al-Zahir Ghazi (son of Salah al-Din) in 1186–1216. He strengthened the walls, redug the moat around the citadel, built the bridge across the moat and furnished the citadel with all the necessities of urban life, including granaries and cisterns.

Above At Aleppo, al-Malik rebuilt the entrance block in 1213 as part of his work on the citadel. The arches are those of the bridge across the moat.

Trade and Travel

THE MUSLIM TRADERS AND PILGRIMS WHO TRAVELLED VAST DISTANCES ACROSS THE ISLAMIC WORLD RELIED ON A NETWORK OF HOSTELRIES, CISTERNS, MOSQUES AND MARKETS.

From the early days of Islam, travellers made long trade journeys across western Asia. Travel and trade were part of their Islamic heritage: the Prophet Muhammad came from a trading family, and the wider Islamic world is strongly dependent on lively international trade. The Quran recorded Allah's blessing on mercantile transactions: 'It is no sin for you that ye seek the bounty of your Lord by trading' (Surah al-Baqarah: 198).

A WELL-TRAVELLED FAITH

The Islamic faith spread through military conquest, but it was also sustained by merchants and scholars who travelled. Most significant of all, thousands of Muslims set out for Makkah each year, obedient to the demand of their faith that they make a pilgrimage to the *Kaabah* at least once in their lifetime.

Because of all this traffic, trade and pilgrim routes were well trodden and well maintained; the great cities depended on the safe arrival of trade caravans and Islamic rulers invested in the necessary infrastructure. People generally travelled in camel caravans. Getting lost was not usually a danger, because there were some directional markers and watchtowers. However, people needed water and a safe place to rest. *Caravanserais* were secure roadside shelters along the route, where travellers could sleep, rest, wash, water themselves and also pray.

THE *CARAVANSERAI*

Typically, a *caravanserai* consisted of a square enclosure with a single gateway big enough to allow access to heavily laden camels

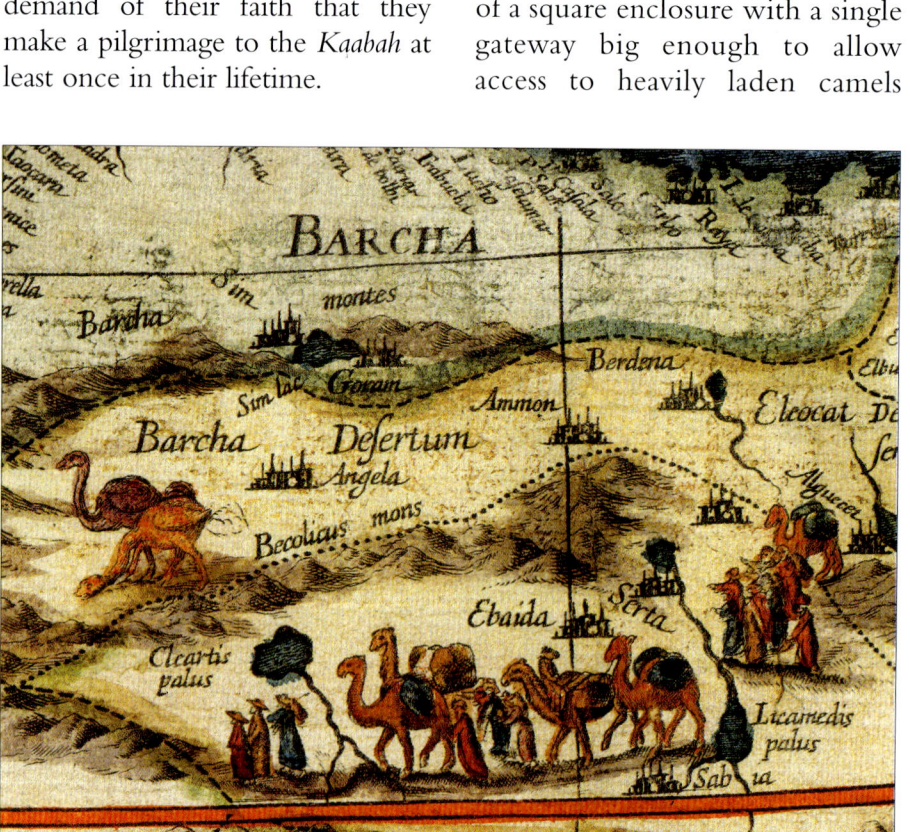

Above A *caravanserai* provides a haven, promising weary travellers a chance to recuperate, in this illustration from a 16th-century Ottoman manuscript.

and, within, individual rooms and stalls arranged around a large open courtyard; there were separate stables for the animals. There was a well or cistern to provide water for drinking and ritual washing; some *caravanserais* had bathhouses. There was also a mosque, usually a raised building in the centre of the courtyard with a fountain for ablutions beneath. There were shops or a market area for travellers to buy or sell supplies.

In Turkey, the Seljuks built a great network of *caravanserais*: around 100 survive today and there may once have been up to 400 on the trade routes across Anatolia. These were built with a large main gateway leading to an open courtyard, behind which there was a second gateway leading into a

Left A 17th-century detail from a map of Africa shows the camel train of a trade caravan making its way from one oasis to another across the Sahara.

TRADE AND TRAVEL

Above The mosque in the caravanserai built by Seljuk Sultan Ala al-Din Kaykubad I between Konya and Aksaray was raised above the courtyard on arches.

covered hall whose flat roof was used as sleeping space in summer. The grandest of these *caravanserais* were built near Konya by Seljuk Sultan Ala al-Din Kaykubad I (reigned 1220–37). One on the road between Konya and Aksaray, dated to 1229, has an elaborately decorated stone gateway and covers 4,900sq m (52,743sq ft). It is also the largest *caravanserai* in Turkey. The second, on the road between Kayseri and Sivas, was built in 1236.

In the Ottoman era, a number of *caravanserais* were built on the pilgrim route between Damascus and Makkah. Elsewhere, the Ottomans often built *caravanserais* as part of a *kulliye*, a complex of buildings centred on a mosque. The Tekkiye in Damascus, designed by the great architect Sinan for Sultan Suleyman I in the 1550s, is a fine example in which the *caravanserai* was used by *Hajj* pilgrims before they left for Makkah and after they returned.

KHANS

In urban centres, the equivalent of a *caravanserai* was a *khan*. This was more like a storehouse than a rest stop, and provided greater space for the storage of merchants' goods than for accommodation. Generally, the *khans* were built over several storeys, with the bottom and next floor up used for storage.

Several *khans* were established alongside *madrasas*, or religious colleges, and their profits paid for the religious and legal education of young Muslims. Examples include the splendid *khan* built by Mamluk Sultan Qansuh al-Ghuri in Cairo in 1504–5. It was laid out around a courtyard over five floors, with the lower two set aside for storage and the upper three rented out to merchants as accommodation; profits funded the sultan's adjacent *madrasa*. Similarly, the Khan Mirjan in Baghdad built in 1359 by Amin al-Din Mirjan, wali (or governor) of Baghdad under Shaykh Hasan-i Buzurg (founder of the Jalayirid dynasty of Iraq and central Iran), combined storage space below with extensive accommodation above and paid for the Mirjaniya *madrasa* (1357).

BAZAARS

Goods stored in the *khan* were sold in the market, known as *souk* in Arabic or *bazaar* in Turkish. In an Islamic town or city, the souk or bazaar typically consisted of a network of enclosed shopping streets, with a central secure area that could be locked at night, and one or more *hammams*, or bathhouses. It was located near the congregational mosque, which was at the centre of the community.

Major souks or bazaars survive in almost every great Islamic city, including Istanbul, Cairo, Isfahan, Damascus, Tehran, Delhi and Mumbai. The Grand Bazaar, or Kapali Carsi ('Covered Market'), in Istanbul contains 58 streets and 6,000 shops; the earliest of its two domed *bedesten* (secured areas) was raised in 1455–61 under Sultan Mehmet II 'the Conqueror'. The market was extended under Sultan Suleyman 'the Magnificent' (reigned 1520–66). In Cairo, the Khan al-Khalili souk has its origins in a *khan* built in 1382 by Amir Jaharks al-Khalili in the reign of Mamluk Sultan Barquq (reigned 1382–89 and 1390–99).

Above Merchants lay out their wares in a souk in Cairo in this 19th-century painting by David Roberts.

31

Hajj: Pilgrimage to Makkah

OVER THE CENTURIES, MILLIONS OF MUSLIMS HAVE MADE THE *HAJJ*, THE PILGRIMAGE TO MAKKAH THAT IS REQUIRED ONCE IN A LIFETIME OF ALL ABLE-BODIED MUSLIMS WHO CAN AFFORD IT.

Before the advent of railways in the 19th century, and of cars and aircraft flights in the 20th century, the *Hajj* often involved travelling in a camel caravan for months at a time, across deserts in punishing heat and under constant threat of attack by bandits.

The routes followed by Hajj pilgrims in earlier centuries can be traced by examining the intricate network of forts, caravanserais, mosques, paved roadways, cisterns, direction markers and milestones built to support them. A sense of the Hajj in medieval times can be gained from the writings of scholars such as the Moroccan traveller Ibn Battuta (1304–77), who made the Hajj four times, and by examining Ottoman travel guides and prayer books.

DESERT ROUTES

Hajj pilgrims came from all over the Islamic world and they made the last part of their journey across Arabia to Makkah following set itineraries. There were six main routes. One went from Damascus in Syria, one from Cairo in Egypt by way of the Sinai Desert and one from Baghdad through Basra in Iraq. For those arriving by boat across the Arabian Sea south of the Arabian peninsula, there were three routes: two from Yemen, one along the coast and one inland, and one from Oman.

THE WAY FROM DAMASCUS

The principal routes were those from Iraq, Syria and Egypt, and of these the oldest was the one from Damascus, capital of the Umayyad Caliphate. Major sites on the route through Jordan include the city of Humayma, the square fortress and mosque of Khan al-Zabib, and palaces at Ma'an and Jize, which seem to have been used by leading Umayyads when on pilgrimage and perhaps as *caravanserais* to host passing dignitaries. Both were near large ancient Roman reservoirs.

The route lost importance after the capital moved from Damascus to Baghdad in the 8th century, but

Above The pilgrims' goal is the shrine of the Kaabah *in Makkah. This illustration of Muslims at the* Kaabah *is from the 15th-century Persian classic* Haft Awrang *(Seven Thrones).*

Left The main Hajj *pilgrimage routes to Makkah. The most used early route was from Damascus.*

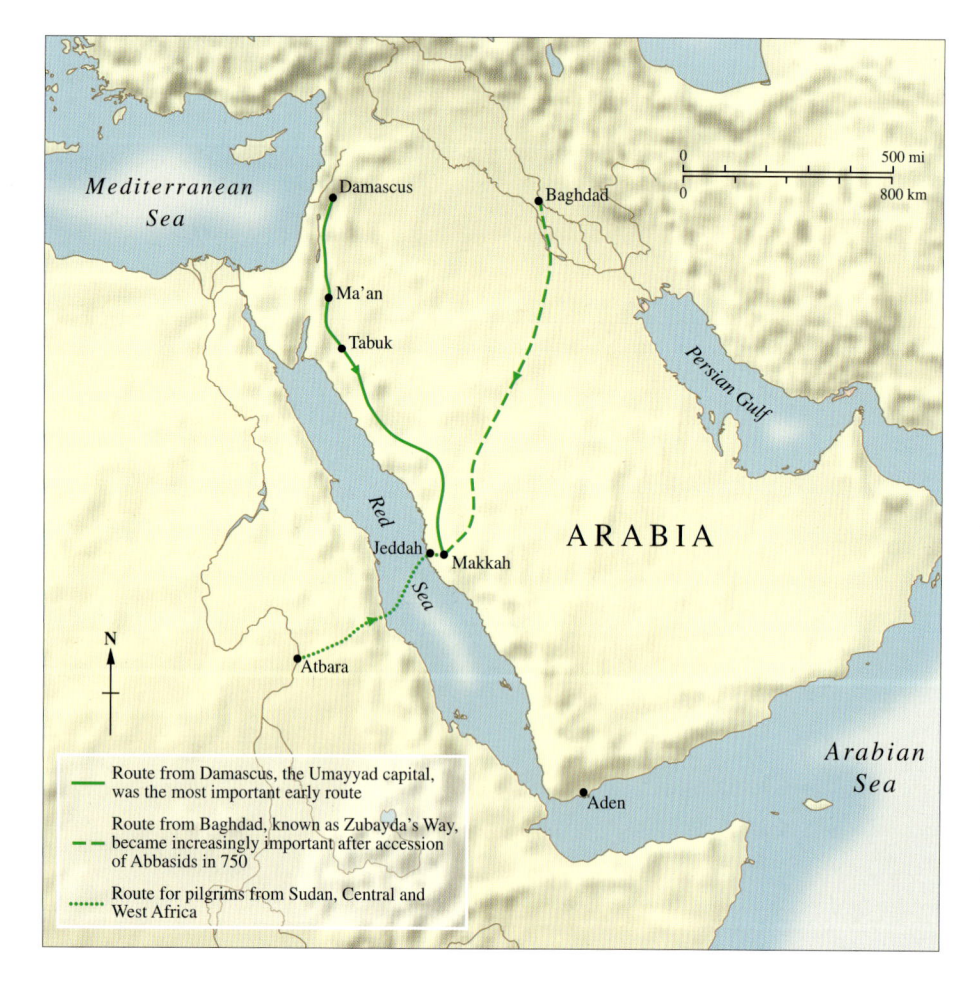

it remained in use for many centuries. The Mamluks built forts along it, such as those at Zerka and Jize. In the 14th century, Ibn Battuta followed this route on his first *Hajj* journey, taking the inland route parallel to the western coast of the Arabian peninsula. With the aid of a large camel caravan, he travelled the 1,350km (840-mile) journey from Damascus to the holy cities in about 50 days.

On Ibn Battuta's first *Hajj* pilgrimage, and typically for that era, a desert caravan was like a travelling city, a group bound by a common geographical and religious goal that stayed together for six or seven weeks. There was a *muezzin* to call the travellers to prayer, Imams to lead the prayers and *qadis*, or judges, to provide resolution when disputes arose. Soldiers and guides travelled with the caravan to provide protection from desert bandits.

The position of the leader of the caravan had great political importance and in some cases he could rise to a role in government.

FORTS AND CISTERNS

Under the Ottomans, forts and cisterns were built along the Damascus–Madinah/Makkah route and garrisoned with troops. The forts guarded the cisterns and provided protection for pilgrim camps alongside them against attacks by Bedouin raiders. The Ottomans upgraded these facilities in the 18th century and again in the early 20th century, when a railway was laid along the entire Damascus to Madinah route, with new forts to protect key sites.

Right In a Hajj *caravan, people from many backgrounds lived together for weeks at a time. This Ottoman illustration is based on a 13th-century painting.*

BAGHDAD TO MAKKAH

From the earliest Islamic period, the road from Baghdad to Makkah was an important trade and pilgrimage route. With the transfer of the capital to Baghdad in the 8th century, it became the major route to the holy cities. Zubayda bint Jafar, wife of Caliph Harun al-Rashid (reigned 786–809), is known to have ordered the construction of a network of wells, reservoirs and buildings along the road to provide pilgrims and travellers with water and shelter; thereafter the road became known as Darb Zubayda ('Zubayda's route'). Several Arab geographers have described how the road was renowned both for its safety and the evenness of its surface, which was tarred and kept free of sand and stones. Archaeologists have identified more than fifty stopping points on the route; these included a cistern for watering camels and drinking water for pilgrims, a fort or palace, plus a residential area and a mosque. Several caliphs are known to have built palaces to stay in as they made the pilgrimage. Harun al-Rashid is known to have made the Hajj nine times during his reign, more than once on foot.

Above This fort at Qatrana in Jordan was built in 1559, one of the network of forts built by the Ottomans along the Hajj *route from Damascus to Makkah.*

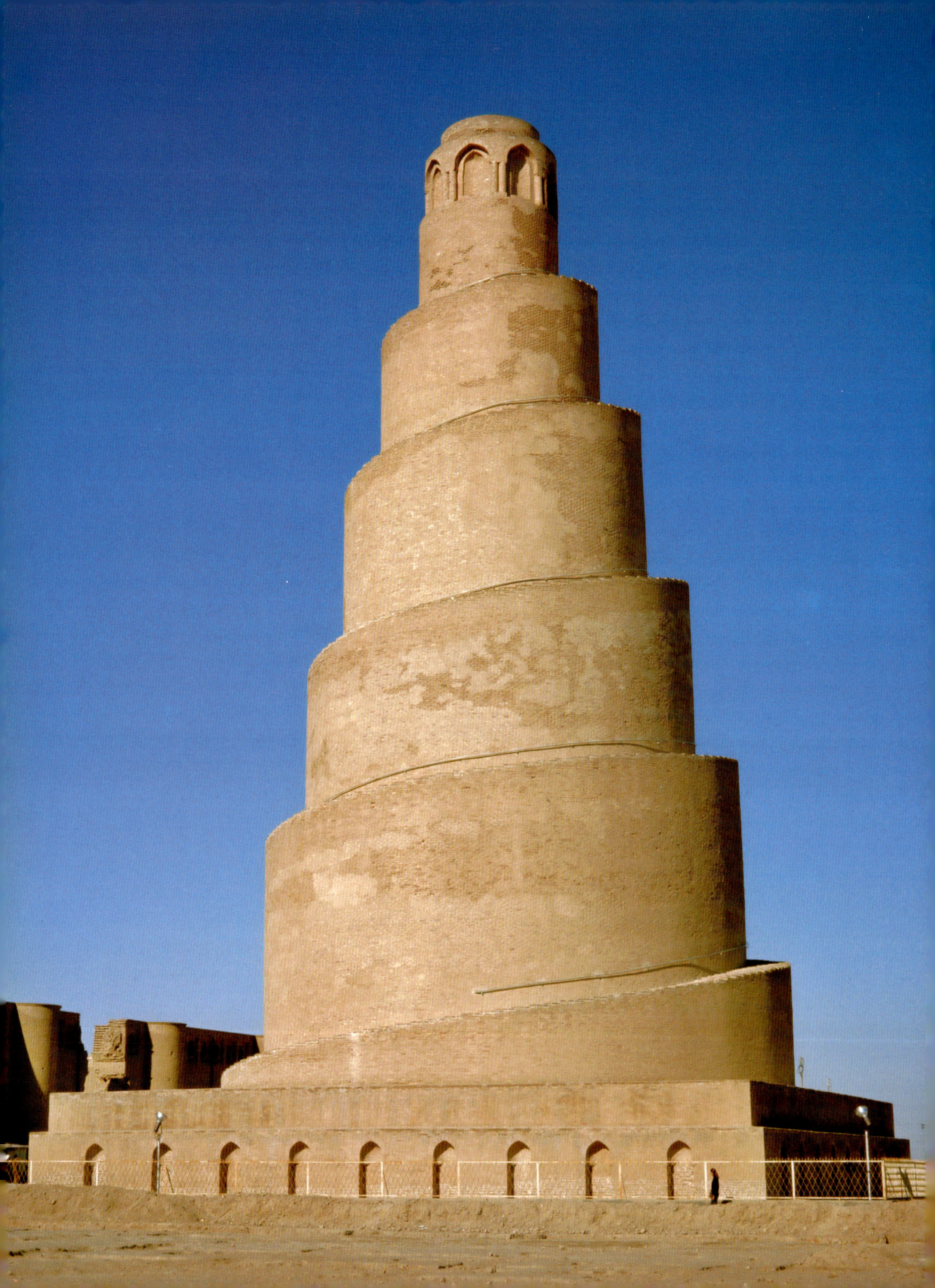

ISLAMIC ARCHITECTURE THROUGH THE CENTURIES

The first caliphal dynasty of the Islamic empire was founded by al-Muawiyah of the Umayyad clan in 661 and lasted for 90 years. Beginning with the dynasty of these first Umayyad rulers, this chapter covers Islamic architecture through the centuries and in different cultures. There are special features on the Dome of the Rock in Jerusalem, the Great Mosque of Damascus, Islamic architecture in Africa, Samarkand tombs in Uzbekistan, the Taj Mahal at Agra, and Topkapi Palace in ancient Constantinople. To this day, world-famous icons of modern architecture continue to be built in Muslim countries, particularly the Arabian peninsula, and the book concludes with examples of modern mosques, state-of-the-art commercial buildings and even international airports in locations such as Pakistan, Jakarta, Tehran, Saudi Arabia and Dubai.

Opposite The striking 52-m (170-ft) tall minaret of the Great Mosque of Samarra was built in the new imperial capital in 848–52 by the Abbasid Caliph, al-Mutawakkil.

Above Dramatic turquoise, yellow and blue tiles cover the dome of the Gur-e Amir ('Tomb of the King') in Samarkand. Many Timurid mausolea and mosques have slender ribbed domes with bright blue tiles.

THE UMAYYAD PERIOD

THE UMAYYADS WERE THE FIRST ISLAMIC RULERS TO ESTABLISH A DYNASTY (661–750). THEIR BUILDINGS PROMOTED THE AUTHORITY OF THE REIGNING FAMILY, AS WELL AS THE YOUNG FAITH OF ISLAM.

The first member of the Umayyad family to become caliph was Muawiyah I, a provincial governor who challenged the authority of Ali ibn Abi Talib, the Prophet's cousin and son-in-law, as ruler of the Islamic world.

Muawiyah did not take power until 29 years after the Prophet Muhammad's death, in 632. Abu Bakr, a companion of the Prophet and an early convert to Islam, had been chosen as the caliph, or successor, to be both religious leader of Muslims and political ruler of the Islamic world.

Shortly before his death in 634, Abu Bakr nominated Umar ibn al-Khattab as the next ruler. In 644, Umar's successor as caliph, Uthman ibn-Affan, was elected by a committee of religious elders. On Uthman's murder in 656, Ali ibn Abu Talib, one of the elders who had elected Uthman, assumed control. However, Ali struggled to impose his authority, and the *ummah*, or Islamic religious community, had its first great schism. Muawiyah was among those who did not accept Ali's authority.

RULERS FROM MAKKAH

Like Muhammad himself, the Umayyad family belonged to the powerful Quraysh tribe of Makkah. They had initially opposed Muhammad but accepted his rule and converted to Islam when the Prophet took control of Makkah in 630. Muawiyah then fought in the Arab Islamic army in Syria against the Byzantine Empire, and in 640 he was appointed Governor of Syria

Below At its peak, c.750, the Umayyad Empire stretched from Spain in the west to Persia in the east.

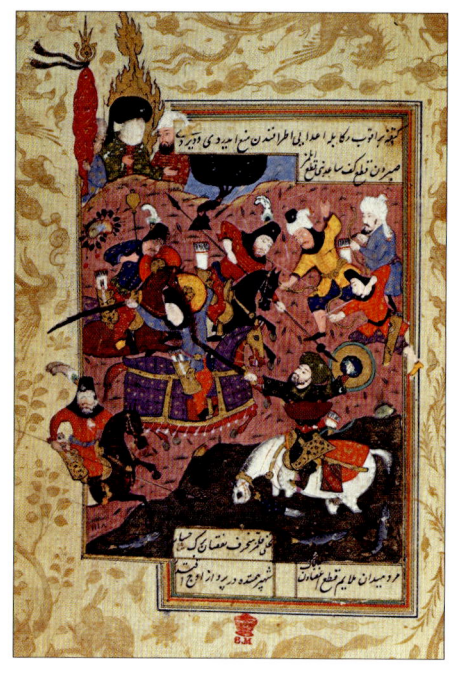

Above Husayn ibn Ali is attacked during the Battle of Karbala as he tries to obtain water from the Euphrates.

by the second caliph, Umar ibn al-Khattab. Throughout the reign of Ali ibn Abu Talib, Muawiyah maintained his independence and expanded the Umayyad power base by taking military control of Egypt. When Ali was murdered in 661, Muawiyah seized power and forced

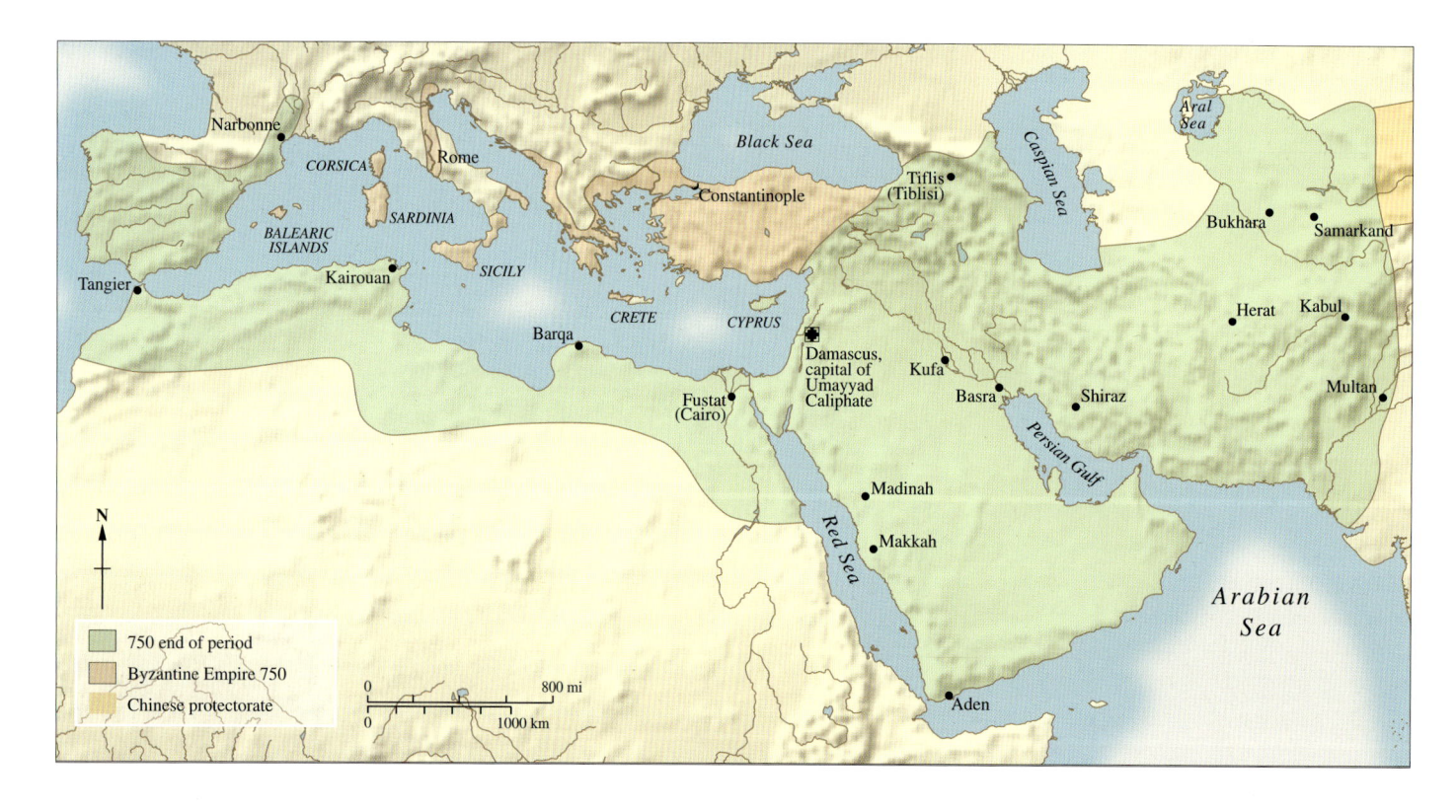

Ali's son Hasan to abandon his own claim to be caliph. Muawiyah declared himself *amir al-mumineen* ('Commander of the Faithful').

Ali's principal power base had been the city of Kufa in Iraq, built as a garrison town following the Arab victory over the Byzantines at the Battle of Yarmouk in 636, but Muawiyah established Umayyad rule in the ancient city of Damascus in Syria. Such had been the military expansion under the first four caliphs that by 661, when Muawiyah took power, the Islamic Empire already stretched from Iran in the east to Egypt in the west.

Muawiyah held these disparate landholdings together through ties of personal loyalty. Government was strong under his rule: he developed bureaucracies on a Byzantine model; in Syria, he appointed Christians – many with experience of government under the Byzantines – to key positions.

SHIAH OPPOSITION

Muawiyah established the first dynasty in Islamic history when he passed the Caliphate to his son Yazid I in 680. This created further conflict: Husayn ibn Ali, son of Ali and, through his mother Fatima, a grandson of the Prophet, claimed the right to rule, but he was killed by Yazid's troops at the Battle of Karbala on 10 October 680.

The Prophet's descendants continued to oppose the authority of the Umayyad rulers: in particular, they never forgave the Umayyads for Ali's death at Karbala. Gradually the group of followers, or Shiah, of Ali grew. In 750, when members of the Hashim clan, who were descended from Muhammad's uncle al-Abbas, led a revolt against

Right The courtyard of the Great Mosque of Damascus, built on the site of the Christian Church of St John the Baptist in 706–15.

the Umayyads, they were supported by several Shiah groups. The Hashim were successful and their leader, Abu al-Abbas, became the first of the Abbasid caliphs.

ARCHITECTURAL GLORIES

The Umayyad rulers, especially Abd al-Malik (reigned 685–705), al-Walid I (reigned 705–15), Sulayman (reigned 715–17), Hisham (reigned 724–43) and al-Walid II (reigned 743–44), financed an imperial building programme, primarily in Syria. They established a splendid court in Damascus and built a series of grand palaces on country estates nearby. In Damascus, they lived in a palace south of the Great Mosque: from contemporary descriptions it is known that the building had a green dome, and included a pool. They also invested heavily in an infrastructure to promote agriculture across Syria, building vast numbers of dams, wells, canals and gardens. Syria became a prestigious place to live.

In these years, Damascus was the capital and Syria the centre of an empire in which a variety of pre-Islamic architectural and artistic traditions still existed. To the east were Iraq and Iran, where the Assyrians, Babylonians, Achaemenids and Sasanians had ruled; to the west,

Above Caliph Hisham built Qasr al-Hayr al-Gharbi in the Syrian desert in 728. It was a palace complex with a bathhouse and caravanserai.

south-west and north were lands that had once been part of the Byzantine Empire, where Graeco-Roman traditions were strong. To the south, in the deserts of Arabia, was the birthplace of Islam. The Umayyads summoned craftsmen from every part of this diverse empire to work on their building projects. Documents found in Upper Egypt provide evidence that a local governor was required to send workers to labour on the Great Mosque of Damascus, built under al-Walid I. These workmen applied their local styles and skills to Umayyad mosques and palaces, such as Coptic carving from Egypt and Persian stucco work.

ISLAMIC ARCHITECTURE THROUGH THE CENTURIES

DOME OF THE ROCK

THE IMPOSING DOME OF THE ROCK IN JERUSALEM, COMPLETED IN 691–92 BY UMAYYAD CALIPH ABD AL-MALIK, IS THE WORLD'S OLDEST SURVIVING ISLAMIC SACRED BUILDING.

By building the Dome of the Rock, Abd al-Malik made a bold statement of the power of the Umayyad caliphs and the wealth of the spreading Islamic empire. He diverted the entire taxation revenue of Egypt for seven years to pay for the project. Moreover, he chose a position and form of building that would give Islam a highly visible and spiritually resonant presence in Jerusalem, challenging the two rival Abrahamic faiths of Judaism and Christianity.

Neither a mosque nor a mausoleum, the Dome encloses an area of rock, known as the Foundation Stone, that is sacred in Islam because of its associations with prophets before Muhammad and because Muslims believe that it was the place from which Muhammad rose to heaven in the course of his blessed Night Journey in 620. Muslims call the precinct *Haram al-Sharif* ('The Noble Sanctuary').

BYZANTINE FORM

Abd al-Malik built the Dome to commemorate the sacred rock beneath it, overseeing the design of the octagonal domed structure with its double walkway, or ambulatory, centred on the Foundation Stone.

Above The interior of the dome is decorated with applied stucco work.

Below The Umayyads understood the effect grand and prominent structures, such as the Dome of the Rock, had in promoting the new faith.

A SACRED SITE

The Dome of the Rock stands on the area known to Jews as Har HaBayit ('Temple Mount'), which is believed to have been the site of their historic First and Second Temples (957 BCE and 537 BCE). The Mount is regarded by Jews as the world's most sacred spot, the place from which the planet expanded into the form that is seen today, where God took the dust with which he made the first man, Adam. The Dome is built around a large rock known as the Foundation Stone, which is believed to have been the site of the Holy of Holies within the Jewish temples and the place at which Abraham prepared to sacrifice his son Isaac to God, and where Jacob dreamt of a ladder connecting the earth and heaven.

In terms of Jerusalem's cityscape, the building's overall form and its grand dome were a challenge to the city's most sacred Christian structure, the Church of the Holy Sepulchre, which had a grand dome and was also built around an area of rock – Calvary – the hill on which Christ was crucified, and the tomb in which he was buried.

The 10th-century geographer al-Maqdisi made explicit the competition with the Church of the Holy Sepulchre: he declared that Abd al-Malik worried that Muslims would be 'dazzled' in their minds by the greatness of the Church of the Sepulchre, so he had the Dome of the Rock erected in a prominent and ancient sacred position, where it could be an equally imposing holy building for Muslim followers.

The Dome's builders appear to have based their calculations on a close study of the Church of the Holy Sepulchre, because the Dome of the Rock's dome is 20.2m (66ft 3in) in diameter and 20.48m (67ft 2in) high, compared to dimensions of 20.48m (67ft 2in) in width and 21.05m (69ft) in height for the dome of the Church of the Holy Sepulchre. Although the Dome of the Rock was, marginally, the smaller of the two buildings, it occupied a highly visible position on ancient and holy ground outside the city walls.

The wooden dome, which is mounted on an elevated drum, stands above a circuit of 12 columns and 4 piers within an octagonal walkway of 16 columns and 8 piers. The walkway is matched by 8 outer walls, each around 18m (59ft) wide and 11m (36ft) high, in an octagonal formation. The dome is filled with light, which enters through 16 windows in the drum and 40 windows in the octagonal lower part. Building and dome together rise a full 30m (98ft) above the Foundation Stone within.

GRAND DECORATION

According to al-Maqdisi, around 100,000 gold coins were melted down and used to cover the dome's exterior. As a result, he wrote, it glittered so that no one could look at it for long in bright sunlight. In the 16th century, the ancient mosaics on the outside of the building were replaced by exquisite Iznik tiles in a seven-year redecoration project ordered by Ottoman Sultan Suleyman I 'the Magnificent' (reigned 1520–66). During 1960–64, the Dome was covered with a bronze-aluminium alloy, and this covering was renewed in 1998 using 80kg (176lb) of gold.

The interior of the Dome is still lavishly decorated with the original glass mosaics from the 7th century. Many of the images – including trees, bejewelled vases and chalices, and beautiful plants – recall Sasanian and Byzantine imagery and are thought to refer to Islam's victory over these two great empires.

Around the interior walls is a gold mosaic frieze, 240m (more than 785ft) in length, bearing a *kufic* inscription proclaiming the message of Islam, including '*la sharik lahu*' ('God is without companions'), which is repeated five times. Although Jesus (or Isa) is mentioned here as an honoured prophet, the inscription also confronts the Muslim objection to the Christian doctrine of the Trinity, as explained in the Quran (Surah Maryam: 35) – 'It befitteth not (the Majesty of) Allah that He should take unto Himself a son.' The inscription is dated 72H (691 or 692), which historians take to be the date of construction of the Dome.

Above During the 20th century, the Iznik tiles added in the 16th century by Ottoman Sultan Suleyman 'the Magnificent' were replaced with replicas.

Above The mosaic decoration above the dome's arcade is part of the original 7th-century building programme.

THE GREAT MOSQUE OF DAMASCUS

CONTEMPORARIES HAILED THE UMAYYAD MOSQUE IN DAMASCUS AS ONE OF THE WONDERS OF THE WORLD. THEY PRAISED ITS GRAND PRAYER HALL, COURTYARD AND GOLDEN MOSAICS.

The sixth Umayyad caliph, al-Walid I, built the Great Mosque in Damascus in 705–15, when the empire he controlled was expanding fast in size, power and wealth. In 711, during the construction of the monumental mosque, Islamic armies crossed from Africa into the Iberian peninsula, swept away the power of the Visigothic rulers and extended Islam and Umayyad power into Spain. In Damascus, al-Walid set out – like his father Abd al-Malik, builder of the Dome of the Rock – to make an impressive statement of Umayyad rising imperial power and to promote Islam as a major world religion.

To build the Great Mosque in Damascus, al-Walid I took over the city's principal sacred place, once the site of an ancient Aramaic temple to the storm god Hadad, then of a Roman temple to Jupiter and most recently a Christian basilica dedicated to John the Baptist. After the conquest of Damascus by Arab Muslims in 661, the church was shared by Christians and Muslims. But al-Walid purchased the site and planned a grand congregational mosque, retaining only the original Roman exterior walls and columns.

DESIGN OF THE MOSQUE

Using the model of the Prophet's Mosque in Makkah, which was the prototype for all early mosques, the builders laid out a vast enclosed courtyard with a prayer hall along its southern side, containing a *mihrab* wall arch, indicating the required direction of prayer toward the *Kaabah* in Makkah. They filled the temple area of the ancient Roman temple: the mosque and courtyard measured 100m by 157.5m (328ft by 517ft). At each corner of the enclosure they raised a minaret, or watchtower – these were initially lookout towers, but in time they were used for calling the faithful to prayer.

Within the prayer hall, the space was divided into three aisles by two rows of columns with Corinthian capitals, spaced well apart so that worshippers could see clearly across the prayer hall and obtain a good view of the *mihrab* niche in the *qibla* wall, so they knew the direction of prayer. The division of space into aisles with columns was an essential element in the layout of a Byzantine basilica, but in the Damascus mosque the columns ran parallel to the *qibla* wall, so the building's orientation (toward the *qibla* wall) is at right angles to the long rows of columns. At the centre of the prayer hall and opposite the *mihrab* they built a great vaulted dome; originally the *maqsura*, behind which the caliph was set apart from his people when praying, was beneath it. Light entered the mosque through windows in the dome and high in the side walls of the prayer hall.

Above The courtyard façade was rebuilt and redecorated after a major fire damaged the mosque in 1893.

JOHN THE BAPTIST

The mosque contains a shrine to John the Baptist, who is revered in the Islamic tradition under the name Yahya b. Zakariyya as one the prophets. It is within the main prayer hall of the mosque and the shrine is still in place today. Christians visit the mosque to pray at the shrine and in 2001, when Pope John Paul II entered the mosque for this purpose, he became the first pope ever known to have entered a mosque.

Right The shrine that reputedly holds the head of St John the Baptist is in the centre of the mosque.

THE GREAT MOSQUE OF DAMASCUS

Right The Great Mosque's treasury survives on its original eight classical columns in the inner courtyard. The mosaics on the upper part date from the late 20th century.

This was the first prayer hall in Islamic history in which the *mihrab* was given a particular prominence by raising a dome before it. The design was to be highly influential.

The builders constructed a single-aisle ambulatory around the other three sides of the courtyard. In the centre of the courtyard they raised a fountain, at which the faithful could wash themselves before worship, and in the northwest corner a domed treasury.

IMAGES OF PARADISE

The interior of the Great Mosque was decorated with Byzantine-style mosaics. The lower parts of the walls were faced with veined marble slabs, above which there was a band of gold glass mosaics. The mosaic decorations depict large landscape scenes of trees, classical palaces, pavilions and bridges along a riverbank.

These mosaics have been interpreted as representing the palaces and gardens of paradise, a world at peace under Islamic rule, or the luxurious palaces of the Umayyads themselves along the Barada river in Damascus.

The golden decorations inside and outside the mosque originally covered 4,000sq m (43,000sq ft) and were one of the reasons the building was viewed with such awe by contemporaries.

LATER ADDITIONS

The Great Mosque of Damascus is Islam's oldest extant monumental mosque. However, the three

Right The beautiful mosaic decoration of tall trees and classical buildings is on the inner west wall of the prayer hall.

minarets standing today are not survivors of the original four, but are later replacements – the Minaret of the Bride (9th–12th centuries); the Minaret of Jesus (13th–18th centuries), so-called because many Muslims believe that Jesus will appear here just prior to the end of the world; and the Minaret of Qayt Bey (16th century). The building has survived several disasters over the centuries, including Timur's invasion of Damascus in 1401, an earthquake in 1759 and a serious fire in 1893. It was heavily restored in 1970.

Desert Palaces

THE FINEST SURVIVING EXAMPLES OF SECULAR BUILDINGS FROM THE UMAYYAD ERA ARE THE *QUSUR*, OR DESERT PALACES, SUCH AS QUSAYR AMRA IN JORDAN AND QASR AL-HAYR AL-GHARBI IN SYRIA.

Although called 'desert palaces', the qusur, were built alongside agricultural land or oases. While some stood on trade routes and incorporated *caravanserais* (travellers' lodgings), and others were perhaps used as hunting lodges, they were principally country houses at the centre of farming estates.

FRESCOES AT QUSAYR AMRA

The small palace of Qusayr Amra was probably built under Caliph al-Walid I in 712–15, and stands beside an oasis in semi-arid land around 80km (50 miles) east of Amman in Jordan. The remains of a castle, tower, waterwheel and well have been uncovered, but the principal surviving buildings are a rectangular throne room and audience chamber and a bathhouse. The internal walls of both are decorated with remarkable frescoes.

One fresco in the audience chamber shows a ruler, probably Caliph al-Walid I, grandly enthroned in the Byzantine fashion beneath a canopy. He faces a fresco in which six kings stand in line as if paying homage. Other subjects include the pleasures of life at the Umayyad court, such as a royal hunt and scenes of relaxation in the bathhouse, together with some of the many crafts activities carried out under the Caliph's patronage. The vaulted ceiling is divided into rectangular sections and also shows craftsmen working.

The walls of the three rooms in the bathhouse are decorated with musicians and dancing girls, and scenes of animals, including gazelles, camels, donkeys, and even a

Below The abandoned complex of Qusayr Amra was rediscovered in 1898 by Czech orientalist Alois Musil.

Above Hunters and maidens cavort in a detail from the wall frescoes at Qusayr Amra. These are the largest surviving group of early medieval frescoes.

bear playing a musical instrument. The domed ceiling in one room is painted with the main constellations of the northern hemisphere – the oldest surviving representation of the stars of the night sky on a domed surface.

The wonderful images at Qusayr Amra are confidently drawn and delicately coloured, using methods and iconography from the classical worlds of Greece and Rome. They are part of a princely propaganda attempt to establish the Umayyad rulers and their court on an equal footing with other imperial rulers and establishments past and present.

FINE STUCCO WORK

Qasr al-Hayr al-Gharbi was built by Caliph al-Hisham about 60km (37 miles) west of Palmyra, a caravan trade city on the road from Damascus. The complex includes a palace, bathhouse and *khan* (travellers' lodge), together with agricultural land, all surrounded by a protecting wall set with semicircular towers. An irrigation system is fed by underground canals that connect to an ancient Roman dam at Harbaqa, 16km (10 miles) to the south.

Within the enclosing wall, the *khan* is laid out around a courtyard. The palace is square in shape with sides measuring 70m (230ft). It originally had two storeys, although only the lower one survives, and a monumental gateway with carved stucco decoration – the oldest Islamic example of this type of decoration, which was derived from the work of Sasanian craftsmen. The stucco work is now in the National Museum, Damascus.

The palace complex at Khirbat al-Mafjar in the Jordan Valley near Jericho in Palestine was built in the years before 743 by Caliph al-Hisham. Set within a protective wall, the grouped buildings include a two-storey palace, a mosque, and a great domed bathhouse with audience room, together with a large courtyard with central fountain and circular colonnade. The very grand bathhouse and audience room contain a bathing pool and a second plunge pool that reputedly once held wine, as well as a latrine with space for 33 guests at once. The bathhouse floor consists of no fewer than 39 adjoining mosaic panels decorated with geometric designs; together these form the world's largest floor mosaic still surviving from antiquity. Another striking mosaic panel, located in the audience hall, depicts a lion attacking a gazelle.

The palace at Mshatta, built in 743–44 by Caliph al-Walid II around 32km (20 miles) south of Amman in Jordan, was seemingly intended to be the grandest of all the Umayyads' royal buildings, but work was abandoned when the Caliph was killed in a battle against rebels in 744. The unfinished square complex, built in limestone and brick, includes a mosque, entrance hall, audience hall and residential quarters covering a vast 144sq m (1,550sq ft). Its splendid stone façade reveals many influences: it is decorated with Sasanian-style solar rosettes divided by a zigzag band moulding of a kind often seen in Christian Syrian buildings and backed by a detailed classical-style relief of animals and vines.

Above A detail from the stone façade of the palace at Mshatta in Jordan (743–44) shows Sasanian-style rosettes.

Above This beautifully decorated doorway is part of the Umayyad desert palace of Qasr al-Hayr al-Gharbi, built under Caliph al-Hisham in Syria.

SASANIAN INFLUENCE ON METALWORK

The earliest Islamic metalwork shows the artistic influence of the Sasanians, the pre-Islamic Iranian dynasty who ruled in 226–651. The Umayyad metalworkers shared the Sasanian taste for decorative birds, animals and composite creatures, such as the winged griffin and the senmurv, a creature from Persian mythology that combined a dog's head and front paws with wings and a peacock's tail.

A bronze ewer was part of a cache of objects discovered at Abu Sir in Egypt, where the last Umayyad caliph Marwan II (reigned 744–50) was reputed to have been killed by the Abbasids. Now kept in the Museum of Islamic Art in Cairo, its spout is cast in the form of a rooster and water would have been poured in through the creature's open beak. The inscription – on a silver and copper inlaid bronze figure of a bird of prey, dated 796–7 and signed by Sulayman – indicates that it is the earliest, firmly dated bronze item from the Islamic period. Unusually, the bird was not made to function as a container and its precise use is unknown. The engraved decoration on both objects recall the stucco carvings found in the palaces of Khirbat al-Mafjar and Mshatta.

BAGHDAD

ONE OF THE WORLD'S MOST POPULOUS AND WEALTHY CITIES, ABBASID BAGHDAD WAS A GREAT CENTRE OF LONG-DISTANCE TRADE AND AN INTELLECTUAL AND ARTISTIC CAPITAL.

In 762, the Abbasid Caliph al-Mansur founded a great city called Madinat as-Salam ('The City of Peace'), or Baghdad as it soon became known, beside the river Tigris in Iraq. This was a vast project: according to the 9th-century Arab historian al-Yaqubi, an army of labourers 100,000 strong was drafted in to build the city.

The city was laid out in a vast fortified circle centred on the caliph's palace and a great *jami*, or Friday Mosque. In choosing the circular layout, al-Mansur was following ancient local tradition going back at least to the foundation of the Assyrian city of Dur Sharrukin in the 8th century BCE, and evident in the city of Ghur (modern Firuzabad) established by the Sasanian Shah Ardashir I (reigned 226–41CE).

FORTIFIED CITY
Little remains of the early structures of Baghdad, but contemporary written accounts enable experts to build up a picture of its design. The Round City was 2.7km (1.68 miles) in diameter and stood within a double set of mud-brick walls and a moat flooded from the Tigris. Four gates led to and were named after Basra (at the south-east), Kufa (south-west), Khurasan (north-east) and Damascus (north-west). Each gate had a zigzag entranceway to make it easier to defend against charging attackers, and each stood beneath a chamber accessed by a ramp or stairs. These chambers had a domed roof topped with a weathervane shaped like a horseman.

From the gates, long vaulted and arcaded avenues ran into the centre of the city. Along the inside of the defensive walls was an outer circuit of buildings used as residences for the caliph's family and members of the court. Key government buildings, including the treasury and the weapon store, were part of an inner ring of buildings. In the centre of the city were a building for guards as well as the mosque and palace.

MOSQUE AND PALACE
The central mosque was a square hypostyle design, its sides 100m (330ft) long and enclosing an open courtyard. Next to it, the palace covered four times the area of the mosque. A vaulted reception hall, with sides measuring 15m by 10m (50ft by 33ft), led into an audience chamber with sides 10m (33ft) long.

A second audience hall had a dome called Qubbat al-Khadra ('Green Dome'), which was 40m (130ft) tall and topped with a weathervane shaped like a warrior on horseback holding a spear. This figure was celebrated as a symbol of Abbasid power: wherever he faced he looked out over lands ruled by the caliph. According to tradition, the caliph learned of rebellions, as well as of meteorological storms, from the movements of this figure. The dome and the horseman collapsed in 941. This was an ill omen, as just four years later the Buyids established themselves as de facto rulers of the empire, leaving the caliphs in only nominal control.

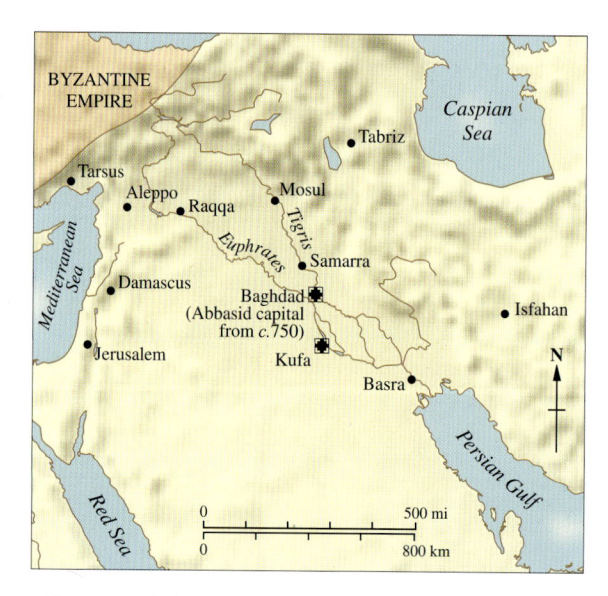

Above The Tomb of Zumurrud Khatun was built c.1193. It is celebrated for its tall cone-shaped muqarnas dome.

Above Baghdad became the Abbasid capital in 762. Kufa was the original capital.

PALACE OF UKHAYDIR
The buildings of Baghdad owed much to local tradition, marking a shift from Umayyad style. No traces of the original city survive in Baghdad itself, but the nearly contemporary fortified desert palace of Ukhaydir, built in c.775 near Kufa, about 200km (125 miles) south of Baghdad, gives experts an idea of the likely appearance of the Round City. This vast

Above The original buildings of Baghdad resembled Ukhaydir Palace, near Kufa, built c.775.

complex stands within walls 19m (62ft) tall and in a slightly elongated square measuring 175m by 169m (574ft by 554ft). It contained courtyards, halls, a mosque and a bathhouse. It is characteristic of the Abbasids' preference for surrounding audience chambers and palatial buildings with fortifications – they combined a commitment to grand ceremonial with security.

ARTS AND LEARNING

Baghdad was a centre for luxury arts, attracting artisans from all over the Islamic Empire while exporting its metropolitan style far and wide. This was an important phase in Islamic art and architecture. Baghdad, and later Samarra, drew in eastern influences from Iran and passed these westward as part of an identifiable Abbasid style: in al-Andalus (Islamic Spain), artisans copied the textiles of Baghdad, and in Egypt architects used decorative stucco as found in Samarra. Under these influences, Islamic artisans and architects moved away from Graeco-Roman and Byzantine styles.

Baghdad was also an intellectual capital, where scholars contributed to the highly influential 'Translation Movement', translating into Arabic ancient Greek works of philosophy, medicine, mathematics and astrology by classic authors, such as Aristotle (384–322BCE), Galen (129–216CE) and Ptolemy (c.100–161CE), and Indian texts by the mathematicians Sushruta (6th century BCE) and Aryabhata (476–550CE).

HARUN AL-RASHID

Harun al-Rashid (reigned 786–809), the fifth Abbasid caliph, ruled Baghdad at the height of the city's prosperity and prominence as a centre of art and learning. He was a poet and scholar and a great patron who invited intellectuals to his court from far and wide. His own fame reached as far as Western Europe: he exchanged a series of ambassadors and gifts with Charlemagne, King of the Franks (reigned 747–814). In return for gifts of hunting dogs and Spanish horses, Harun sent Charlemagne an elephant called Abdul-Abbas, chessmen made of ivory and a mechanical clock that astonished all who saw it at the court of the Franks in Aachen (now western Germany). He even features as a character in the world's most celebrated piece of literature in Arabic, *Alf laylah wa laylah* ('The Thousand and One Nights'), which began as an oral tradition.

Left A detail from a 15th-century manuscript from Nizami's Khamsa (five poems or 'Quintet'), showing Harun al-Rashid in a bathhouse.

SAMARRA

THE CITY OF SAMARRA IN IRAQ WAS THE ABBASID IMPERIAL CAPITAL FOR JUST OVER 50 YEARS, 836–92. ITS NAME REPUTEDLY DERIVED FROM THE PHRASE *SURRA MAN RA'A* ('A JOY FOR HE WHO SEES IT').

In Baghdad, Abbasid caliphs lived in their vast palace complex isolated from their people. As their authority began to wane in the 9th century, they became increasingly dependent on their Turkish slave troops from Central Asia. In 836, violent clashes in Baghdad between the slave troops and local citizens persuaded Caliph al-Mutasim to move the imperial capital to Samarra 125km (78 miles) north of Baghdad.

In Samarra, al-Mutasim and his successors raised a huge city, which extended for 50km (30 miles) along the banks of the river Tigris and covered 150sq km (60sq miles); it included several sprawling palaces, grand boulevards, extensive barracks and lush gardens, as well as the Great Mosque of Samarra, at the time the world's biggest mosque. Outside the city limits were large hunting parks and three tracks for horseracing. Samarra remained capital of the Abbasid Empire until 892, when Caliph al-Mutamid moved the administration back to Baghdad.

HOUSE OF THE CALIPH

The main palace at Samarra was the Dar al-Khilafa ('House of the Caliph'), a huge assembly of courtyards, chambers, apartments and pools that covered 70ha (173 acres). The structure dwarfed the relatively small palaces of the Umayyad era.

A bank of steps rose from the Tigris to the main public entrance, the Bab al-Amma, which had three large brick archways. The principal audience chamber was a domed hall at the centre of four vaulted *iwans*, or halls, and opening on to a garden overlooking the river Tigris. In the audience hall, the caliph held public audiences on a Monday and Thursday. Nearby and within the palace complex was a field used for polo matches and parades.

THE GREAT MOSQUE

In 848–52, al-Mutasim's son and successor al-Mutawakkil built the Great Mosque, which measured 239m by 156m (784ft by 512ft) and was protected by tall walls supported by 44 semicircular towers. The whole was set within an enclosure of 444m by 376m (1,457ft by 1,234ft).

The mosque originally had colonnaded arcades halls around a courtyard: the flat roof of the sanctuary on the south wall was supported by 24 rows of 9 brick-and-stone columns. The *mihrab*, or prayer niche, was decorated with gold glass mosaics with two rose-coloured columns of marble on

Above The outer walls of the Great Mosque in Samarra, restored by Saddam Hussein.

Below Qasr al-Ashiq in Samarra, on the right bank of the river Tigris, was built by al-Mutamid (reigned 870–92).

each side. Little remains of the mosque's interiors, except for its distinctive spiral minaret known as al-Malwiya. It stands on a square base, from which a round tower rises 55m (180ft) above ground. A spiral ramp runs counter-clockwise around the outside of the tower to a pavilion at the top. This particular form of minaret appears to have been inspired by ancient Mesopotamian ziggurats, or temple towers.

OTHER PALACES

In addition to the Great Mosque, al-Mutawakkil built as many as 20 palaces, leaving the Abbasid treasury badly depleted by the end of his reign. In the 850s, he laid out a new area north of Samarra, called Jafariya, that contained a vast palace called the Jafari, as well as a second grand congregational mosque (now called the Mosque of Abu Dulaf), built in imitation of the Great Mosque and with a similar spiral minaret, but on a smaller scale.

The building of large palaces set behind high walls probably reflected the development of a more hierarchical society in the Abbasid era, when the caliphs adapted Persian ideas of kingship. At the same time, religious and political authority, once united in the person of the caliph, began to diverge, and the mosque became more the preserve of the *ulama*, or religious legal scholars.

Although most of the buildings, even the palaces, were built of only mud brick, they were lavishly decorated, with glass mosaics and elaborate wood or marble panelling. The setting was one of high luxury: glass objects, gold and silver dishes and lustreware have been excavated.

STUCCO DECORATION

A distinctive type of carved and moulded multicoloured painted stucco decoration was developed and made popular in Samarra, and from there spread throughout the Islamic Empire. The decoration appears in three distinct styles.

The first was derived from the vegetal carving of the Umayyad period: a surface was divided into compartments by roundels and filled with curling vine tendrils. In the second style, the compartments contained carved plant decoration so stylized that it could no longer be associated with plants; in some, the contemporary Chinese symbols for the properties of yin and yang appeared. In the third, the compartments contained abstract decorative motifs, such as palmettes, bottle shapes and spirals. Known as the 'bevelled style', this was made with a shallow cut using moulds in symmetrical patterns that could be repeated as far as required, so it could be applied quickly across wide areas of wall. The third style had an important influence on later Islamic art as it led to the development of arabesque decoration.

The walls were also decorated with paintings, including naturalistic images of human figures. These included hunting scenes with wild animals and naked women. A wall painting from the Dar al-Khilafa shows two serving girls dancing while pouring wine into goblets.

Above The first style of Samarran stucco wall decoration uses curling plants; this example is from Qasr al-Ashiq.

Below This is an example of the third Samarran style, made with a shallow cut and using symmetrical designs.

MAJOR ABBASID CALIPHS
Abu al-Abbas al-Saffah (750–54) Dynastic founder
al-Mansur (754–75) Founded Baghdad
Harun al-Rashid (786–809) Great patron
al-Mutasim (833–42) Moved to Samarra
al-Mutawakkil (847–61) Great builder in Samarra
al-Mutamid (892–902) Moved capital back to Baghdad
al-Mustasim Billah (1242–58) Final Baghdad caliph

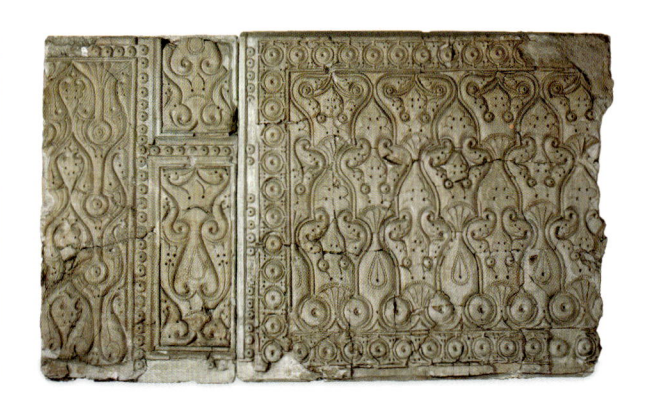

ISLAMIC ARCHITECTURE THROUGH THE CENTURIES

THE FATIMID CALIPHATE

THE FATIMID CAPITAL OF AL-QAHIRA (THE VICTORIOUS), NOW KNOWN AS CAIRO, WAS A WALLED PALACE CITY CENTRED ON THE CALIPH'S RESIDENCE AND A CONGREGATIONAL MOSQUE.

The Fatimids emerged as an Ismaili sectarian movement in Tunisia. There, in 909, Ubayd Allah declared himself the Mahdi, or Holy One, and founded a Fatimid Caliphate in their temporary capital, Raqqada. The dynasty claimed sacred descent from Ali, the Prophet's son-in-law, and his wife Fatima, the Prophet's daughter – from whom the name Fatimids derives.

Supported by missionary activity around the Islamic world, the Caliphate quickly grew, and in 921 Ubayd Allah built the splendid palace city of Mahdia on the Tunisian coast. He was succeeded as ruler by al-Qaim (934–46), al-Mansur (946–53) and al-Muizz (953–75). During al-Muizz's reign, the Fatimids moved eastward to conquer the Ikhshidid governors of Egypt, and in 969 al-Muizz ordered General Jawhar al-Siqilli to found a new dynastic capital on the Nile, to be called al-Qahira 'the Victorious' and now known as Cairo.

This walled settlement was a proud statement of the power and ambition of a youthful dynasty. The walls, which had eight gates set into them, enclosed a large area measuring 1,100m by 1,150m (3,610ft by 3,773ft).

TWIN PALACES

A broad street called Bayn al-Qasrayn ('between the two palaces') ran through the middle of the city. Across this street, two royal palaces faced each other; the Eastern Palace larger than the more secluded Western Palace. The Bayn al-Qasrayn was a parade ground where elaborate processions and public ceremonies were held to celebrate religious holidays and other significant dates, such as the start of the agricultural year.

According to contemporary accounts, these palaces were beautifully planned and furnished, with cloisters of marble and rooms bedecked with the finest textiles. The gardens, which were set within high walls, had artificial trees carved from precious metal with

Above An 11th-century wall painting from a bathhouse near Cairo depicts a young man drinking wine. In secular settings, figurative art was common.

Below At its greatest extent, the Fatimid Caliphate stretched across North Africa and into the Arabian peninsula. Sicily was also part of the Caliphate.

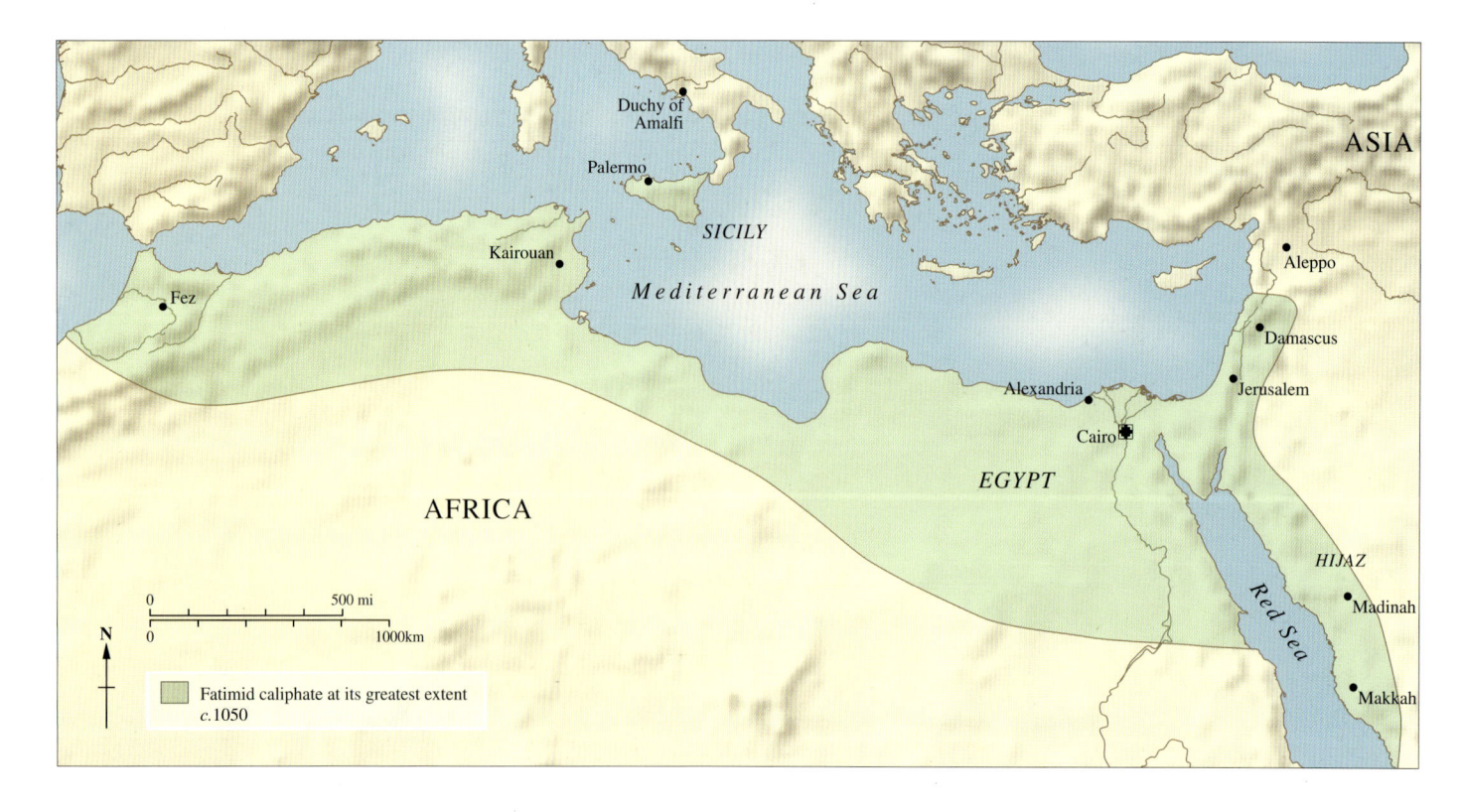

clockwork singing birds. The 11th-century Persian traveller Nasir-i Khusrau visited the Western Palace in 1049, and reported seeing a raised dais carved with hunting scenes and fine calligraphy, a golden balustrade and silver steps.

During a financial crisis in 1068, the unpaid Fatimid army rose up and looted the Fatimid treasury, where they found huge numbers of precious luxury items – and promptly sold them on the open market to the great astonishment of the Cairo public.

MOSQUES

The magnificent Mosque of al-Hakim was begun in 990, under the rule of Caliph al-Aziz, and finished in 1012, by Caliph al-Hakim (reigned 996–1021). Four arcades enclose a courtyard. Within the prayer hall there are five bays: the bay before the *mihrab*, or prayer niche, and, unusually, the two corner bays at each end of the *qibla* wall that indicates the direction of prayer are domed. The outer walls are surmounted by battlements, and there is a three-part façade with a monumental entrance gateway, plus a spectacular minaret at each end – one circular and one square. The design of the façade was derived from that of the Great Mosque (916) in Mahdia.

UNDER THE VIZIERS

In the late 11th and 12th centuries, the power of the Fatimid caliphs weakened. Cairo was governed by its viziers, or ministers. One of these was Badr al-Jamali, vizier to Caliph al-Mustansir (reigned 1036–96), who rebuilt and extended the city walls. The splendid fortified gates of Bab al-Nasr and Bab al-Futuh are from this period. Bab al-Futuh has twin towers 8m (26ft) high, rising to a battlement with a parapet. It was built with the latest defensive features, such as machicolation (small

Above Bab al-Futuh (the Gate of Victories) was built in 1096 for vizier Badr al-Jamali by Armenian builders.

openings through which to drop missiles to enemy forces).

Mamun al-Bataihi, another vizier of al-Mustansir, founded the remarkable Aqmar Mosque in Cairo in 1125. This mosque has a decorated façade with a central porch bearing a medallion inscribed with the names of Muhammad and Ali – who is revered by Shiahs as the first Imam – at its centre.

A distinctive aspect of Fatimid architecture in Egypt is the building of lavish mausolea. The Fatimids and their fellow Shiah contemporaries in Iran, the Buyids, were the first rulers in Islamic history to build funerary monuments. Shiah Islam encourages religious devotions at the tombs of saints and Imams, while orthodox Sunni Muslims are discouraged from venerating any human forebears. For this reason, the building of mausolea was initially found

FATIMIDS IN JERUSALEM

In 969, the Fatimids captured Jerusalem. They rebuilt the citadel, and in 1035 Caliph al-Zahir rebuilt the al-Aqsa Mosque, which had been destroyed by an earthquake two years earlier, in the form in which it survives today. Deciding to promote Jerusalem as a pilgrimage site to rival the holy cities of Makkah and Madinah, Fatimid rulers encouraged writers to create works about the beauties of Jerusalem, and a new genre came into being: *Fada'il al-Quds* (Songs in Praise of Jerusalem).

more in the Shiah tradition than in Sunni Islam. The Fatimid caliphs were buried in a splendid dynastic tomb in the Eastern Palace, but their wealthier subjects built many tombs, principally to celebrate Shiah martyrs and saints in large cemeteries at Aswan and Cairo.

SICILY

ARTISTS FROM THE FATIMID EMPIRE WORKED FOR THE NORMAN LORDS OF SICILY IN THE 11TH AND 12TH CENTURIES, MOST PROMINENTLY IN THE CAPPELLA PALATINA (PALATINE CHAPEL).

At the start of the Fatimid era in 909, the island of Sicily was largely under the control of the Aghlabid amirs of Tunisia. They had first attacked Byzantine-held Sicily in 827, but the conquest of the island took almost 140 years, until 965. Under their rule the island thrived: Palermo replaced Syracuse as capital and became one of the great cities of the Islamic Mediterranean world. Architects converted Palermo's basilica into a great mosque and made the former citadel into a splendid royal palace.

Infighting made the amirate vulnerable, and Norman warlord Robert de Hauteville (also known as Guiscard), with his brother Roger, conquered Sicily in 1072. Roger reigned as Count of Sicily in 1072–1101 and was succeeded by his sons Simon (count in 1101–05) and Roger II, who was count from 1105 and then, with papal backing, was crowned King of Sicily in Palermo on Christmas Day 1130.

His glorious coronation mantle made of red silk interwoven with pearls and gold thread must have been made after his coronation, because it bears an inscription with the Hijra date 528, which corresponds to 1133–34. This unique textile depicts two mirror-images of a lion attacking a camel. At this time, the products of the textile workshop in Roger's palace became famous far beyond Palermo.

THE PALATINE CHAPEL

Muslim craftsmen served at the Christian court of Roger II. In 1132–40, Roger had a magnificent chapel built at the royal palace. Dedicated to St Peter, the Palatine Chapel has splendid floors, elegant Byzantine wall mosaics and a grand wooden ceiling painted in tempera in a style similar to frescoes in the 9th-century palaces of Abbasid Samarra and contemporary paintings in royal buildings in Fatimid Cairo. There are almost 1,000 paintings covering a profusion of *muqarnas* (small vaults arranged in tiers). They mainly depict the pleasures of life at an Islamic court, with images of kings served by attendants, noblemen playing backgammon or chess, dancers, wrestlers, courtiers drinking wine, elephants, beasts of prey and exotic birds, processions, and scenes of racing and hunting. The architectural backgrounds to the images are mostly the arcades and domed roofs of an Islamic palace city.

There are also scenes associated with the zodiac and mythology, such as sirens, griffins and sphinxes. The pictures have beaded edgings and the bands between the images contain *kufic* inscriptions that wish fame, great power and charity on the chapel patron. Other rooms in the palace are as magnificent. The Roger Hall has mosaics depicting

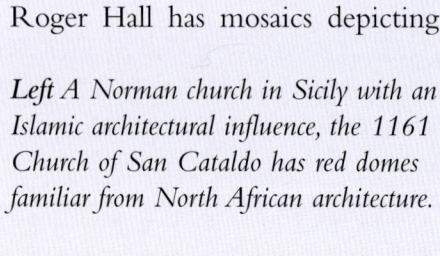

Above Water flowed down the shadirwan *at the summer palace of La Zisa in the Jannat al-Ardh hunting grounds.*

Left A Norman church in Sicily with an Islamic architectural influence, the 1161 Church of San Cataldo has red domes familiar from North African architecture.

Above In the Palatine Chapel, fine Byzantine mosaics adorn the end and side walls, while Fatimid-style paintings decorate the ceiling above the nave.

stylized landscapes that feature lions, peacocks, palm trees and leopards.

The co-existence of Christian and Muslim iconography is striking in the Palatine Chapel. The scenes of Fatimid court life in the *muqarnas* suggest that Fatimid culture and the magnificent city of Cairo were the primary reference point in the Mediterranean for those who aspired to courtly splendour. Furthermore, it is noteworthy that Roger II, who was seeking to enhance the dignity of his position by building an impressive sacred space, turned to Fatimid artists and architects.

MEDIEVAL WORLD MAP

Roger was also a patron of great Islamic scholars and writers, such as the geographer Muhammad al-Idrisi (1100–66), who worked at the court in Palermo for 18 years and drew a celebrated world map in 1154, probably the most accurate made in the medieval period. Known as the 'Tabula Rogeriana', the map shows all of Eurasia and northern Africa. Al-Idrisi also wrote a geographical work named the *Nuzhat al-Mushtaq*, which appears to contain an account of Muslim sailors crossing the Atlantic and landing in the Americas, where they encountered natives 'with red skin'. He also made a silver planisphere, a circular device for demonstrating the shift of the constellations and the signs of the zodiac.

SUMMER PALACES

The Norman lords hunted in the Jannat al-Ardh ('Paradise of the Earth'), the Kalbid estates outside Palermo's city walls. They laid out summer palaces which, like the Umayyad desert palaces, were set within agricultural fields, in this case, of date palms, citrus and olive trees. The summer palace of La Zisa was built in the last years of the Fatimid era, in 1166.

As was typical of country palaces in the Islamic world, water played a major role at La Zisa: the building had pools around it, and an elegant *shadirwan*, or fountain room.

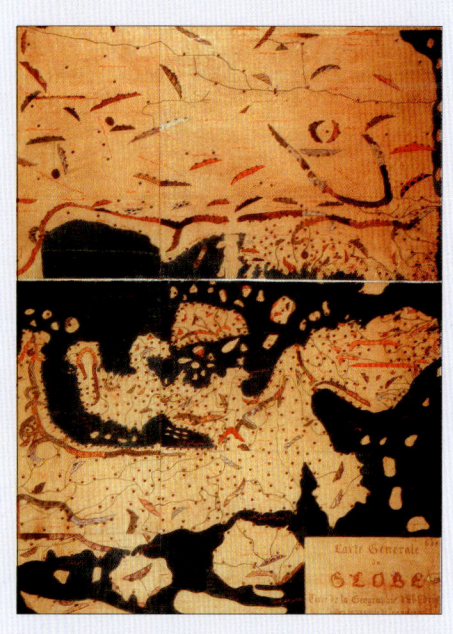

Right Muhammad al-Idrisi's world map, known as the 'Tabula Rogeriana', was the most accurate map of its day. North is at the bottom.

THE SAMANID DYNASTY

THE SAMANID RULERS FOSTERED AN IMPORTANT REVIVAL OF PERSIAN CULTURE – IN POTTERY, CALLIGRAPHY, METALWORK AND TEXTILES, FOR EXAMPLE – DURING THE 9TH AND 10TH CENTURIES.

The Samanids first rose to prominence as local governors in Transoxiana (a province spanning modern-day Tajikistan, Uzbekistan and Turkmenistan) under the Tahirids, who served the Abbasid caliphs in Baghdad. The dynasty took its name from Saman Khuda, an 8th-century feudal aristocrat from the province of Balkh in Afghanistan who had served the Abbasid governor of Khurasan. According to many accounts, Saman was a Zoroastrian who converted to Sunni Islam.

In the early 9th century, Saman's grandsons Ahmad, Nuh, Yahya and Elyas helped to defeat an uprising against Abbasid Caliph al-Mamun (reigned 786–833) and in return were given the provinces of Ferghana, Samarkand, Shash and Herat. The Samanids reached the peak of their power under Ahmad's son Ismail Samani (reigned 892–907). Ismail defeated Amr, the Saffarid ruler of Khurasan, in 900, and the following year defeated Muhammad b. Zaid, ruler of Tabaristan, thus conquering new territory across northern Iran to add to the provinces of Khurasan and Transoxiana. Ismail made his capital at Bukhara (now in Uzbekistan).

The Samanids were staunch Sunni Muslims and were opposed to, and tried to repress, the Ismaili strand of Shiah Islam promoted by their Fatimid contemporaries. Under Samanid rule thousands of Turkish tribesmen converted to Islam. The dynasty claimed descent from the pre-Islamic Sasanian shahs, and were keen sponsors of Persian culture, overseeing a renaissance in art, architecture and literature and the emergence of New Persian as a literary language.

SAMANID ARCHITECTURE

The finest monument of the Samanid era is the mausoleum in Bukhara. It is traditionally associated with Ismail Samani, but may also have been used as a tomb for later Samanid princes. It takes the form of a tapering cube built from bricks topped with an elegant hemispherical dome rising from a flat roof with a small cupola at each corner. Both within and without, the mausoleum is notable for its intricate brickwork and the symmetry of its design.

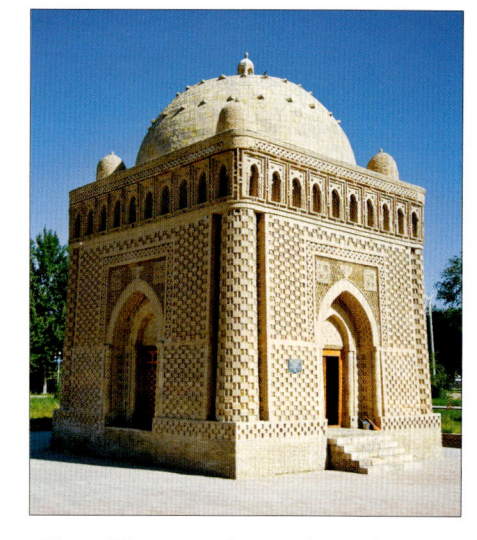

Above The mausoleum of Ismail Samani and the Samanid rulers in Bukhara now stands alone but was once at the centre of a substantial complex.

PERSIAN CULTURE

The wealth and sophistication of this period survives in the luxury objects that are known today. Samanid potters produced fine work in the cities of Samarkand and Nishapur, reviving ancient Persian imperial iconography, such as bulls' heads, mounted horse riders, birds and lions, but also courting Islamic culture through the use of pithy Arabic calligraphy. Metalwork of the period also made self-conscious reference to Sasanian artistic traditions, as did textiles. A remarkable pictorial silk fragment, depicting elephants, camels and peacocks, generally known as the St Josse silk, was made for an amir of Khurasan, Abu Mansur Bukhtegin, in c.955.

Left Nuh-Gunbadh Mosque, now in ruins, was one of 40 mosques built in Balkh in the 9th century. This fine example of Samanid architecture was influenced by earlier styles.

THE SAMANID DYNASTY

Left The Samanid mausoleum is a masterpiece built in brick. Each arch in the arcade around the top of the outer walls has a slightly different decoration.

Ghaznavid patronage. Another great poet of the era was Rudaki (859–c.941), who served at the court of Samanid ruler Nasr II (reigned 914–43). He is celebrated as one of the founders of modern Persian literature and reputedly wrote more than 1.3 million verses.

FALL FROM POWER

From c.950 onward, the rulers of the vast Samanid empire began to lose their power, challenged by palace rebellions and external threats from the Qarakhanid Turks to the east. The Samanids were finally defeated by the Ghaznavids, who ruled from Ghazni (modern-day Ghazna in Afghanistan, south of Kabul) and had previously served them as governors.

First, Mahmud of Ghazni (998–1030) led a revolt, deposed Samanid ruler Mansur II (reigned 997–99), and took Khurasan to found the Ghaznavid Empire, which eventually extended as far east as the border with India. The final Samanid ruler was Ismail II, who failed to counter Mahmud and was killed in 1005.

THE FAME OF BUKHARA

Bukhara was a major city and centre of learning under the Samanids. With a population of more than 300,000, it was the largest city of central Asia and, for a period, rivalled Córdoba, Baghdad and Cairo as one of the foremost cities of the world. It was a principal centre of Sufi Islam, particularly of the Naqshbandi Order.

Bukhara is known for its scholars. It is the birthplace of Muhammad al-Bukhari (810–70), revered by Sunni Muslims as the author of *Sahih Bukhari*, a collection of *hadith*, or sayings, of Muhammad that is considered the most authentic of all extant books of *hadith*. The great polymath ibn Sina (980–1037) was born near Bukhara in the Samanid era. Known in the West as Avicenna, he was a major philosopher as well as the author of the *Canon of Medicine*, used as a textbook for medical students in European universities until the 17th century.

The national poet of Iran, Firdawsi (c.935–c.1020), was born and worked under the Samanid rulers, although he completed his masterwork, the *Shahnama*, under

Above This detail of the St Josse silk shroud shows a pair of elephants and part of an inscription praising an amir of Khurasan who died in 961.

ISLAMIC ARCHITECTURE THROUGH THE CENTURIES

THE GHAZNAVID AND GHURID DYNASTIES

DURING THE 10TH CENTURY, THE GHAZNAVIDS QUICKLY ESTABLISHED A BROAD EMPIRE AND MADE INROADS INTO NORTHERN INDIA. IN THE 12TH CENTURY, THEY WERE SUPPLANTED BY THE GHURIDS.

By the 10th century, the political cohesion of the Islamic world was beginning to disintegrate. In the east, the Ghaznavids eventually became the dominant power, ruling from 962 until 1186. This Turkic dynasty originated from a corps of slave-guards who had served the Samanids and eventually supplanted them. From their capital at Ghazni in Afghanistan, they built up a considerable empire, which, at its height, included most of Iran, Afghanistan, Khurasan and parts of northern India.

GHAZNAVID BUILDINGS
The royal strongholds built by the Ghaznavids seem to have been modelled on those in Abbasid Samarra, in Iraq. This is certainly obvious in Lashkari Bazaar (Qalah-i Bust), a meandering complex of 11th-century palatial buildings that stretched for several miles along the banks of the river Helmand in south-western Afghanistan. These are now largely in ruins, although the remains of the winter palace, with its four *iwans* (vaulted halls) and its painted frieze of bodyguards, are still impressive.

The most tangible surviving reminders of Ghaznavid power can be seen in a number of remarkable towers. In Ghazni itself are the lower sections of two imposing, early 12th-century minarets. One was built by Masud III (reigned 1099–1114) and the other by his son, Bahram Shah (reigned 1118–52). Constructed in a similar style on a star-shaped plan, the minarets are decorated with inscriptions and geometric patterns created in brickwork. More impressive still is the Gunbad-i-Qabus, the best preserved of all the Islamic tomb towers. Located in north-eastern Iran, the tower was commissioned by a local Ziyarid ruler, Qabus ibn Wushngir. Cylindrical in shape, the tower has ten triangular flanges around the exterior and a very striking and austere appearance.

Nominally at least, the tower was meant to be Qabus's tomb, but at over 60m (197ft) high the sheer size of the structure ensured that it was also an affirmation of his political strength. It is not clear if Qabus was ever buried there, but a medieval account claims that his body was placed in a glass coffin suspended from the roof.

Above Dating from 1007, the tower of Gunbad-i Qabus was a potent symbol of power. Its stark, brick surface was adorned with just two bands of kufic *script.*

Above A story from the Shahnama *is depicted on this 13th-century Kashan stonepaste cup.*

FIRDAWSI
The poet Firdawsi (*c*.935–*c*.1020) is one of the most celebrated figures in Iranian culture. His masterpiece is the 60,000 couplet epic *Shahnama* (Book of Kings), a monumental account of Persia's early history. Firdawsi is said to have laboured on the project for more than 30 years, beginning it under the Samanids in 977, but only completing it in the Ghaznavid era in 1010. Drawn from earlier accounts and oral sources, the *Shahnama* describes the kings, queens and heroes of pre-Islamic Iran. This beguiling mixture of history and legend provided Islamic artists with a fertile source for illustration in manuscript copies of the stories and in other media.

THE GHURIDS
In 1186, the Ghaznavids were displaced by the Ghurids, who took their name from their native

province (Ghur) in Afghanistan. Like their predecessors, they extended their control over large swathes of Afghanistan, Iran and northern India. They owed much of their influence to the military success of Muhammad of Ghur (1162–1206), who conquered Lahore in 1186.

The Ghurids are associated with two famous minarets, both of which are registered as World Heritage Sites by Unesco. The oldest of these is the Minaret of Jam, which dates back to the 12th century. It is hidden away in a remote Afghan valley – in fact, it is so remote that the tower was forgotten by the authorities until a boundary commission rediscovered it in 1886. Jam stands close to the river Hari Rud. The leaning shaft of the minaret is liberally adorned with decorative panels of calligraphy that cite all of Surah 19 of the Quran.

The purpose of this isolated minaret has been the source of considerable speculation. It is possible that it stands on the site of Firuz Kuh, the ancient summer capital of the Ghurids, and was once associated with a mosque there. Alternatively, it may have been built as a symbol of Islam's victory and never used for calling the faithful to prayer.

The huge minaret of Qutb Minar in Delhi was constructed on an even grander scale. Built on the site of an old Jain temple, it was attached to the Quwwat al-Islam ('Might of Islam') Mosque, the first great Muslim foundation on the Indian subcontinent. The 73m (240ft) high minaret dates from 1202, with many subsequent additions, and is made of red sandstone. The fluted columns of the tapering shaft owe much to local architectural traditions, but the decoration is truly Islamic, consisting of carved ornamental bands of floral, geometric and calligraphic designs.

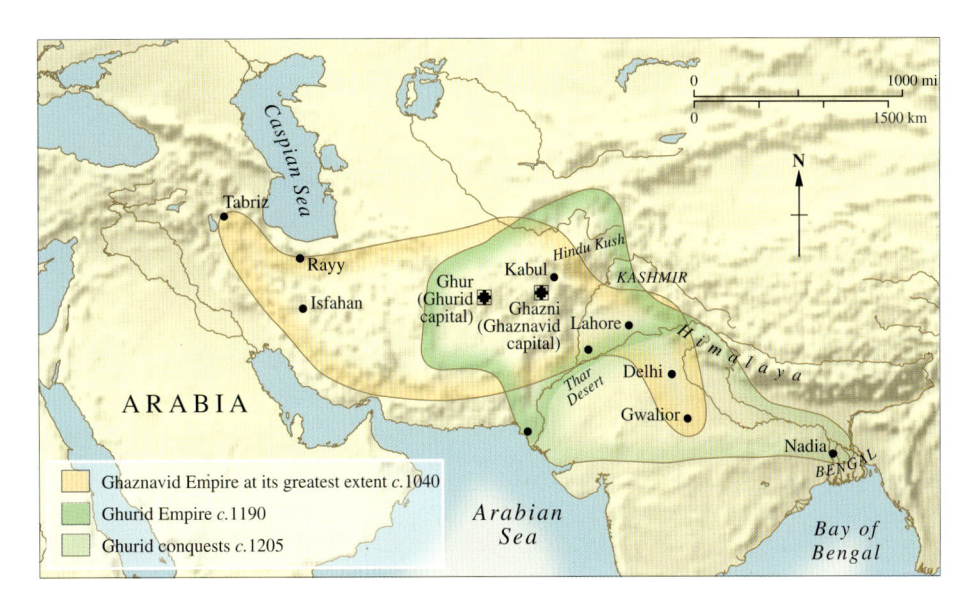

Above The Ghaznavid Empire reached its peak in c.1040 and stretched into most of Iran. The Ghurids displaced the Ghaznavids and by c.1205 had conquered most of northern India.

Below The Minaret of Jam is the finest surviving example of Ghurid architecture. Built for Ghiyath al-Din (1153–1203), it is over 60m (197ft) high and decorated with glazed-brick inscriptions.

THE GREAT SELJUKS

THE SELJUK TURKS WERE GREAT BUILDERS WHO REVIVED EARLY IRANIAN TRADITIONS, SUCH AS USE OF THE DOMED *IWAN* (VAULTED HALL), IN THEIR MOSQUES, MAUSOLEA AND *MADRASAS* (COLLEGES).

The Seljuks were Oghuz Turks from the steppes, who converted to Sunni Islam in the 10th century under their leader Seljuk, after whom they are named. They entered the Islamic world as auxiliary troops, used by various dynasties in north-eastern Iran, but established an independent sultanate of great power, with several regional branches. One of Seljuk's grandsons, Toghrul Beg, defeated the Ghaznavids in 1040, conquered western Iran, Azerbaijan and Khuzestan, and marched into Baghdad in 1055 to oust the Buyids and take control of the Abbasid Caliphate. He described the war as one in support of religious orthodoxy, to free the Sunni Muslim caliph from the Shiah Buyids.

Toghrul Beg was succeeded by his nephew Alp Arslan (reigned 1063–72), who defeated the Byzantine Empire in the Battle of Manzikert (1071). Both Alp Arslan and his son, Malik Shah, were served by the outstanding vizier, or minister, Nizam al-Mulk, who imposed centralized control over the vast empire. This branch of the dynasty are known as the Great Seljuks to distinguish them from the Anatolian Seljuks, descendants of Kutalmish, Alp Arslan's cousin, who established the independent Anatolian Seljuk Sultanate.

THE ISFAHAN MOSQUE

Alp Arslan's successor, Malik Shah, selected Isfahan in Iran as the imperial capital, and in his reign the congregational, or Friday, Mosque originally built there under the Buyids was developed into a masterpiece. The Abbasid mosque had been built with an enclosed courtyard and hypostyle prayer hall containing the *mihrab*, a niche indicating the direction of prayer. Malik Shah's vizier Nizam al-Mulk raised a grand domed chamber in front of the *mihrab*. An inscription on the base of the dome states that it was raised by Malik Shah and Nizam al-Mulk; it has been dated to 1086–87. Historians believe that the chamber was a tribute to the dome at the Great Mosque of Damascus, which Nizam had visited in 1086, and that Nizam al-Mulk intended it to be a *maqsura*, a reserved area for the sultan. At the time of its construction, it was the largest dome ever built.

A second domed pavilion was built by Taj al-Mulk, the imperial chamberlain and a rival of Nizam al-Mulk, in 1088. It was aligned with the first dome, but was originally outside the mosque precincts. The purpose of the second dome may have been ceremonial, intended to mark the procession of the sultan into the mosque. Later Seljuk builders added four *iwans*, or vaulted halls, one on each side of the courtyard and opening on to it. This work was probably carried out some time in the first half of the 12th century.

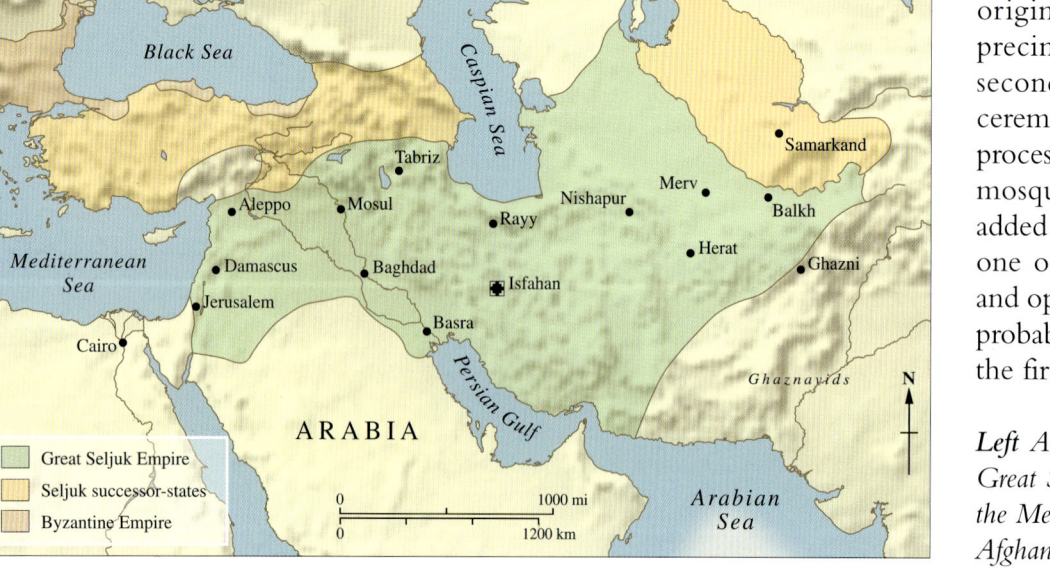

Above The iwan *on the south side of the courtyard in the 11th–12th-century Friday Mosque in Isfahan has minarets that were added under the Safavids.*

Left At its greatest extent in 1092, the Great Seljuk Empire stretched from the Mediterranean in the west to Afghanistan in the east.

The design of the Isfahan mosque, combining four *iwans* with a domed chamber containing the *mihrab*, became the standard Seljuk design for large congregational mosques. The four-*iwan* plan had roots in early Iranian architecture; the Seljuks applied it to *madrasas* and *caravanserais* (rest places for travellers). The design appears to have been well suited to the climate of Iran, because the southerly *iwan*, which was attached to the domed chamber with the *mihrab*, opened north on to the courtyard and would not receive direct sunlight for most of the year, while the other *iwans* would have been in sunlight all day.

THREE-PART MOSQUES

Another mosque design used by the Seljuks, known as the 'three-part mosque', combines a square, domed chamber with two domed side aisles. A fine example is the 11th-century Talkhatun Baba Mosque at the oasis city of Merv in Central Asia (today in Turkmenistan). All four façades are decorated with intricate brickwork. Another example is the memorial mosque beside the tomb of poet, philosopher and Sufi saint Hakim al-Termezi in Termez, which has three rooms, the central one containing a *mihrab*. The Seljuks also built small single-chamber domed mosques, often beside the tombs of saints to provide a place for the pilgrims to pray.

SELJUK MINARETS

The Seljuks developed a new, cylindrical form of minaret that contrasted with the square minaret towers in North Africa. The Seljuk minarets were set on multi-sided plinths; they were tall, and decorated with beautiful brickwork featuring geometric patterns and bands of carved inscriptions. One of the finest examples is the minaret of the mosque at Saveh, Iran, which dates to 1010; it features beautiful brick patterns and inscriptions in *naskh* and *kufic* scripts. Another fine Seljuk minaret rises above the Tari Khana Mosque at Damghan. Dated to 1026–27, its minaret inscription is the oldest surviving tile work in Islamic architecture.

Below The Imam Mosque in Isfahan, built in the 17th century under the Safavids, is based on the four-iwan layout formalized by the Seljuks.

Above The tomb tower of Pir-e Alamdar in Damghan (1026–27) was built by government official Abu Harb Bakhtiyar for his father.

MONUMENTS AND MADRASAS

THE GREAT SELJUKS DEVELOPED TWO STYLES OF MAUSOLEA, THE *GUNBAD*, OR TOMB TOWER, AND THE SQUARE OR POLYGONAL DOMED MAUSOLEUM. FEW OF THEIR MANY *MADRASA* COLLEGES SURVIVE.

The Seljuk period was a time of major development in the field of architecture: builders working for Seljuk sultans were innovative and highly skilled. Distinctive styles emerged in the lands governed by the Seljuks, and examples of these styles are described as 'Seljuk architecture' even when they were built by successive regimes.

Of all the Seljuk buildings the finest are the mausolea. These were built as memorials in cemeteries or were added to mosques, *madrasas* (religious colleges) or *caravanserais* (travellers' lodges). The mausoleum commemorated the ruler whose legacy had funded the mosque, *madrasa* or *caravanserai* alongside it, or it would be raised in memory of a major religious scholar or saint.

The spread of mausolea was closely associated with that of Sufism, because it was common practice among Sufis to visit the graves of their teachers and saints. Under the Seljuks, Sufism became established in Persia and Anatolia. Officially, Islam did not permit praying at these memorials, and (unlike those in Egypt, for example) the Central Asian mausolea built by the Seljuks did not have *mihrabs*, or niches in the *qibla* wall to indicate the direction of prayer, and were generally not aligned to Makkah. A memorial mosque was often built near the mausoleum to provide a place for devotions.

PRE-SELJUK PROTOTYPES

The earliest Seljuk mausolea in Persia and Central Asia were tomb towers. They were influenced by a celebrated forerunner, the Gunbad-i-Qabus of 1007 in Gurgan, Iran, which was built for a pre-Seljuk king – Ziyarid ruler Qabus ibn Wushngir. A similar circular tower encircled with flanges was built for Seljuk Sultan Toghrul Beg at Rayy, near Tehran. This tomb had a grand entrance porch of the kind known as a *pishtaq*.

The domed square tomb of the Seljuks also derived from that of earlier rulers, notably the 10th-century Samarid mausoleum at Bukhara. The Gunbad-i-Surkh in Maragha, western Iran, was seemingly built on this model in 1147–48; it has a square chamber topped with an octagonal drum. This structure once supported an eight-sided dome.

MAUSOLEUM OF SANJAR

Another similar square-domed mausoleum was that of Seljuk Sultan Muizz al-Din Sanjar at Merv, built in *c.*1152. The four sides of the main chamber were each

Above The 12th-century tomb tower of Seljuk ruler Toghrul Beg at Rayy in Iran is 20m (66ft) tall. The conical dome, that was originally on the top collapsed during an earthquake.

Left The Mausoleum of Seljuk Sultan Sanjar at Merv (now Turkmenistan) was once connected to a mosque within a large complex.

27m (89ft) long, beneath a large octagonal dome. According to contemporary reports, originally there was an outer dome, decorated with beautiful turquoise tiles of such size that the dome could be seen by trade caravans while still a full day's travel from the city. The interior had stucco decoration, and the outside was of geometric brickwork (which has now mostly disappeared). The mausoleum was part of a palace complex, and was also attached to a mosque. Contemporaries regarded this as the world's biggest building.

MADRASAS

From contemporary accounts, there is evidence that during the Seljuk period a network of *madrasas*, or religious colleges, was established across the empire. Nizam al-Mulk, who was vizier from 1065 until 1092, during the reigns of Alp Arslan (reigned 1063–72) and Malik Shah (reigned 1072–92), was the driving force behind the building of these religious colleges as part of his efforts to help the promotion of Sunni orthodoxy. He attempted to cut the ties between Sufism and Shiah Islam and to integrate Sufism into Sunni Islam.

Like Seljuk mosques, these *madrasas* typically had a four-*iwan* format, with the four *iwans*, or vaulted halls, arranged around and leading on to a central courtyard. The *iwans* were used as teaching spaces, while the other buildings enclosing the square or rectangular courtyard held kitchens and accommodation. The design also usually included a splendid portal or gateway that was flanked by two halls.

Right *These octagonal tomb towers were built at Kharraqan in Iran in 1067 and 1093. Since this picture was taken they have suffered serious structural damage in an earthquake.*

As was the case in other areas of architecture, this *madrasa* layout, sometimes proposed as a Seljuk invention, was derived from earlier examples. The ruined Khwaja Mashhad *madrasa* at Shahritus, in Turkmenistan, was built in this form as early as the 9th century. The two halls here were a mosque and a mausoleum, and the main focus was a courtyard with the four *iwans* built around it. The *madrasa* was functioning in the 10th century, and among its students was Nasir-i Khusrau, a celebrated Tajik poet who was a major force for the local spread of Islam. It is believed that Khwaja Mashhad *madrasa* is the oldest *madrasa* in Central Asia.

NIZAMIYYAS

The *madrasas* established by Nizam al-Mulk were known as *nizamiyyas* in his honour. He took charge of appointing the professors and teachers, while personally ensuring that each establishment was well supplied and funded. The first *madrasa* that Nizam al-Mulk set up was built in Baghdad in 1065. He appointed philosopher-theologian Muhammad al-Ghazali – the greatest Muslim intellectual of the medieval period – to teach there,

Above The Sircali *madrasa of 1242 in Konya, built by Muhammad of Tus, is typically arranged over two storeys around an open courtyard. The entrance is through a wide, decorated stone portal.*

and the renowned Persian poet Shaykh Saadi (1184–1291) was a pupil. This network of religious colleges included institutions in Balkh, Basra, Damascus, Ghazni, Herat, Isfahan, Mosul, Merv and Nishapur, but few of these colleges survive.

CARAVANSERAIS

THE SELJUKS BUILT A NETWORK OF *CARAVANSERAIS* ALONG TRADE ROUTES. THESE SHELTERS PROVIDED SECURE ACCOMMODATION, FOOD AND WATER FOR TRADERS, TRAVELLERS AND THEIR ANIMALS.

A complex of buildings could typically be found inside a *caravanserai*, often with an imposing, decorated gateway as an entrance leading to a courtyard surrounded by lodging and stables, with a fountain and mosque and normally a bazaar or trading area. These *caravanserais* became important trade centres and were often fortified. The usual layout of Seljuk *caravanserais* was of four *iwans*, or halls, surrounding the courtyard.

A traveller was typically allowed to stay for three days without paying because the *caravanserais* were built as an expression of the Muslim duty of charity toward travellers. Local rulers built the entrances in a very grand style to signal their wealth and generosity. Some *caravanserais* were built as part of a complex attached to a mausoleum and paid for by a legacy from the deceased.

The Seljuks built *caravanserais* in Iran, across Afghanistan and Central Asia toward India and Russia, and in Anatolia, where they were usually known as *hans*. (*Han* is simply the Turkish word for *caravanserai*.) They were also known as *ribats*. The *caravanserais* were positioned approximately every 30km (19 miles) along the road.

GRAND PORTAL

One typical *caravanserai* of the early Seljuk period is the Ribat-i Malik in Uzbekistan, built on the road between Bukhara and Samarkand in 1078–79 by the Qarakhanid Sultan Nasr (reigned 1068–80). The sultan was a son-in-law to Seljuk sultan Alp Arslan (reigned 1063–72) and a client ruler under Seljuk overlordship. The splendid portal gateway of the *caravanserai* still stands, bearing an inscription in Persian declaring that it had been

Below The Rabat Sharaf caravanserai near Mashhad in Iran was built in 1128. Behind its tall and elegant entrance portal, it has two courtyards.

Above This portal, all that remains of a caravanserai in Uzbekistan, on the road from Samarkand to Bukhara, would have been a welcome sight for any traveller seeking respite.

raised by the 'sultan of the entire world' and that within, by God's grace, the setting would be like that of paradise. Archaeological excavations have determined that the *caravanserai*'s layout was square and that it was surrounded by sturdy walls that were set with semicircular towers.

Some later *caravanserais* were built with two courtyards, leading into each other. The 11th-century Akcha Qala near Merv (now in

Right The courtyard of the Aksaray Sultan Han covers approximately 2,250sq m (24,220sq ft).

Turkmenistan) and the Rabat Sharaf *caravanserai* built on the road between Nishapur and Merv in 1114–15 are examples. In these, the first enclosure was reserved for stables for camels and areas for storing goods, while the second was used for lodging. This double-enclosure layout was used in the Seljuk-era *caravanserais*, or *hans*, in Anatolia, except that in these complexes the second courtyard was usually covered by a roof.

CARAVANSERAIS IN ANATOLIA

Two particularly grand *caravanserai* were built near Konya by the Anatolian Seljuk Sultan Ala al-Din Kayqubad I (reigned 1220–37). The larger of the two, the Aksaray *caravanserai* on the road from Konya to Aksaray, was built in 1229. With great walls, a large projecting portal almost 50m (164ft) wide and 13m (43ft) tall, 6 corner towers and 18 side towers, it has the look of a castle. However, it is also beautifully finished with elegantly carved marble side panels on the portal, featuring polygonal geometric patterns along with naturalistic representations of flowers.

The portal faces south-west. It leads into an entrance room beneath a star-shaped vault, flanked by office rooms. The courtyard has a colonnade along its western side, which was used for stabling and storage; rooms used for kitchens, dining rooms and bath facilities are ranged along its eastern side. Beyond the courtyard a large, nine-aisled, barrel-vaulted hall provided living and sleeping areas for the winter months; in summer, residents slept outside on the roof. The hall covers about 1430sq m (15,400sq ft).

The *caravanserai* found on the road between Kayseri and Sivas (on the route from Konya eastward to Iran and Iraq) was built slightly later, in 1232–36. Like the one at Aksaray, it has an entrance way flanked by guard or office rooms. This leads into a courtyard with stables and storage areas along one side and accommodation, kitchens and bathhouse facilities along the other. Beyond, as at Aksaray, is a covered hall.

KIOSK MOSQUE

In the centre of the courtyards at both the Aksaray and Kayseri Sultan Hans is a free-standing mosque. The mosque at Aksaray is lifted above the ground on four arches, accessed by steps on the south side, beautifully decorated with stone carving without, and with a fine *mihrab* niche within. Known as a 'kiosk mosque', this kind of structure was typical of Seljuk *caravanserais* in Anatolia. There are similar kiosk mosques in the *caravanserais* in Agzikara (built 1231–37, near Konya) and Sahipata (1249–50), between Afyon and Aksehir.

Above The Incir caravanserai *was built near Bucaq, between Isparta and Antalya (now in Turkey), in 1238 by Sultan Keyhusrev II (reigned 1238–46).*

THE ANATOLIAN SELJUKS

THE RULERS OF THE INDEPENDENT ANATOLIAN SELJUK EMPIRE BUILT MOSQUES WITH THREE OR MORE DOMES AND GRAND *MADRASAS* AND *HANS* (*CARAVANSERAIS*) WITH CARVED GATEWAYS.

The Seljuks became established in Anatolia in the wake of Sultan Alp Arslan's devastating defeat of the Byzantine Empire at the Battle of Manzikert in 1071. Anatolia is the region formerly known as Asia Minor, bound by the Mediterranean Sea to the south, the Aegean Sea to the west and the Black Sea to the north; it was part of the Byzantine Empire and fell to Seljuk troops that came in the wake of Alp Arslan's army.

Under Suleyman bin Kutalmish, the Seljuks took the Byzantine cities of Nicaea (modern Iznik) and Nicomedia (modern Izmit) in 1075. In 1077, Suleyman declared himself ruler of the independent Seljuk sultanate of Rum (so-called from the medieval Islamic word for Rome, because the territories had been part of the Byzantine or eastern Roman Empire).

The Seljuk state in Anatolia survived in various forms until the early 14th century, when the region became a province of the Ilkhanid empire established by the successors of Mongol invaders who had captured Baghdad in 1258. The Seljuk capital, initially at Nicaea, was at Konya for most of this time, after being moved there by Sultan Kilij Arslan II (reigned 1156–92) in 1181. The greatest of the Anatolian Seljuk rulers was Ala al-Din Kaykubad I (reigned 1220–37), who presided over a glittering court, expanded the boundaries of the empire and oversaw a great age of building in his territories.

Right The Anatolian Seljuk Empire at its greatest extent c.1240 occupied most of modern-day Turkey.

Many more Seljuk-era buildings survive in Anatolia than in Central Asia. The Anatolian Seljuks built congregational mosques, *madrasas* (religious colleges), *caravanserais* (resting places on travellers' routes), palaces, monasteries, tombs and mausolea, bathhouses and hospitals. In addition, they pioneered the construction of building complexes typical of the Ottomans; known as *kulliye*, these incorporated mosque, *madrasa*, *caravanserai* and mausoleum in one setting. A Seljuk example is the Huand Hatun complex of 1238 in Kayseri, which includes a mosque, *madrasa*, mausoleum and *hammam* (bathhouse). It was built by Mahperi Hatun, the wife of Sultan Ala al-Din Kaykubad.

MOSQUES

The congregational mosque was called the *ulu çami* by the Anatolian Seljuks. They did not follow the four-*iwan* plan used by the Great Seljuks, but instead used variations, for example the 'basilican' design – so called due to its similarity to

Above The Gök madrasa in Sivas, built in 1271, has a dramatic entrance portal. The entrance is behind a niche within a stone frame, flanked by minarets.

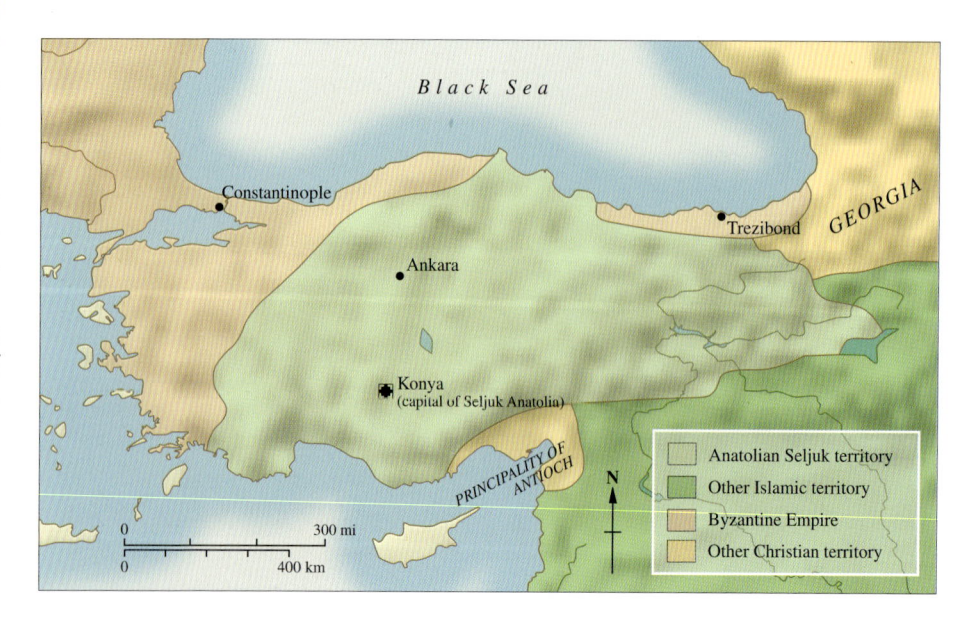

church architecture – used three domes. In some mosques, such as the Ala al-Din Çami of 1223 in Nigde, the three domes were aligned above three bays in front of the *qibla* wall that indicates the direction of prayer; in others, such as the Burmali Minare Çami of 1237–46 in Amasya, the three domes were arranged above the length of the hall at right angles to the *qibla* wall. In another design, used at the Gök Çami *madrasa* of c.1275–1300 at Amasya, the two options were combined, so that three domes ran parallel to the *qibla* wall and three also ran at right angles. These mosques were a direct influence on Ottoman mosque architecture.

The Anatolian Seljuks also built mosques based on the hypostyle mosque of Syria and Arabia, in which the prayer hall's flat roof was supported by rows of pillars. In many of the Anatolian examples, architects used wooden rather than stone pillars. The Sivrihisar Ulu Çami of 1232, the Afyon Karahisar Ulu Çami of 1272 and the Arslan Hane Çami of *c*.1290 in Ankara are all examples of this type.

MADRASAS

The Anatolian Seljuks built some *madrasas* on the model of those built by the Great Seljuks, with four *iwans* arranged around a courtyard, but more typically in Anatolian *madrasas* the courtyard was covered with a great dome, while a single *iwan* was built in the centre of the rear wall with one domed room to each side of it, and lines of smaller rooms arranged along the sides of the courtyard.

The two most celebrated surviving Seljuk *madrasas*, the

Above The dramatic façade of the Karatay madrasa *in Konya (1252) features patterns created by alternating light and dark stone, a sign of Syrian influence.*

Karatay *madrasa* of 1251 and the Ince Minareli *madrasa* of 1258, both in Konya, follow this plan. In the Karatay *madrasa*, which was built by Jelaleddin Karatay, vizier to Sultan Izzeddin Kaykavus, the dome, decorated with turquoise, white and black mosaic tiles and calligraphic inscriptions, rises to an open top that admits daylight, and a pool beneath catches rainwater.

MAUSOLEA AND *CARAVANSERAIS*

Like their counterparts in Iran and Central Asia, the Anatolian Seljuks built tomb towers and square-domed mausolea. The Anatolian tombs are different, in that they generally have two levels – a vault used for burial and a prayer room above – while the tombs of the Great Seljuks were single-storey, without a vault. Moreover, despite the fact that prayer was not permitted at mausolea and tombs in orthodox Islam, many of the Anatolian mausolea have *mihrabs* – niches that indicate the direction of prayer.

The Anatolian Seljuks built a network of *caravanserais*, along the trade routes that ran east–west and north–south across their territories. Most were built under Ala al-Din Kaykubad I and Ghiyath al-Din Kay Khusrau II (reigned 1237–47).

The typical design, seen in the surviving *caravanserais* of Aksaray and Kayseri, had an imposing portal, a large courtyard and a vast covered hall.

VARQA AND GULSHAH

The 10th-century Persian poet Ayyuqi wrote the *Romance of Varqa and Gulshah*, his masterpiece, in 997, in the era of Sultan Mahmud of Ghazni, founder of the Ghaznavid Empire. In *c*.1250, Abd al-Mumin al-Khuyyi created a magnificent illustrated manuscript of this tragic story. The artist, who signed the manuscript, was probably working in Konya, the capital of the Anatolian Seljuks. The manuscript paintings run across the middle of the page, with the poem continuing above and below. This unique manuscript is now in the Topkapi Palace Museum in Istanbul.

Left Here, the couple embrace in a garden before fate separates them. Their union is echoed by the presence of a cockerel and hen.

THE ZANGIDS OF MOSUL

THE TURKISH ZANGID RULERS OF NORTHERN IRAQ AND SYRIA IN 1127–1222 WERE CHAMPIONS OF SUNNI ISLAM. THEY WERE ALSO PATRONS OF THE ARTS, ESPECIALLY IN MOSUL.

Imad al-Din Zangi, the son of the governor of Aleppo under the Seljuk sultan Malik Shah, was the founder of the Zangid dynasty. Zangi's father, Aq Sunqur al-Hajib, was executed for alleged treason against his Seljuk masters in 1094, and thereafter Zangi was raised in Mosul by the city's governor Karbuqa. Zangi established himself as governor of Basra in 1126, Mosul in 1127 and Aleppo in 1128.

In seeking to extend his authority farther, he fought against both Muslim enemies and the Christian crusaders who had established the 'crusader states' (the County of Edessa, the Kingdom of Jerusalem, the Principality of Antioch and the County of Tripoli) during and after the First Crusade of 1095–99.

FIGHTING THE ENEMY

Zangi won a major victory over the crusaders when he captured the capital of the County of Edessa on 24 December 1144. This shocked the Christian world and led directly to the Second Crusade, which was called for by Pope Eugenius III on 1 December 1145 and mounted in 1147–49.

After Zangi's untimely death in 1146 (he was murdered by a slave), his territories were split between two sons: Nur al-Din Mahmud (reigned 1146–74) ruled Syria from Aleppo, while Sayf al-Din Ghazi I (reigned 1146–49) ruled northern Iraq from Mosul. Nur al-Din, like his father, proved a scourge of the crusaders and personally led the army that broke the Second Crusade by relieving the Siege of Damascus in 1149. Thereafter, Nur al-Din took control of Damascus in 1154, and in doing so he created a united Muslim Syria.

Subsequently, the Zangids came into conflict with the nascent Ayyubid Empire that was established in Cairo by Salah al-Din, who was the nephew of Nur al-Din's general Asad al-Din Shirkuh. The Zangid rulers of Mosul twice survived attacks by Salah al-Din (in 1182 and 1185), but they were forced to accept his overlordship. The Zangid dynasty came to an end in Mosul with the rule of Nasir al-Din Mahmud (reigned 1219–22). He was ousted by his former slave Badr al-Din Lulu, who governed the city until 1259, when it was captured by the Mongols under Hulagu Khan.

Left Remains of the castle built by Nur al-Din at Mosul (northern Iraq) stand against sheer rock. Here, the Zangids were twice besieged by Salah al-Din.

Above Nur al-Din commissioned this richly carved minbar for the Al-Aqsa Mosque in 1169. It stood beside the prayer niche from 1187 until it was destroyed in an arson attack in 1969.

PROMOTING THE FAITH

Nur al-Din was a zealous promoter of the idea of *jihad*, or holy war, against the Christians in Syria and Palestine. He had tracts read out in mosques praising the beauties of al-Quds (Jerusalem) and the Muslim sanctuaries in the Haram al-Sharif (Noble Sanctuary), the area known as Temple Mount by the Jews. Reports circulated that the crusaders, who had captured Jerusalem in 1099 at the peak of the First Crusade, were desecrating the Dome of the Rock and the Al-Aqsa Mosque in the Noble Sanctuary. Recapturing Jerusalem for Islam became a focus of *jihad*.

As a statement of his confidence that Islamic armies would regain the city, Nur al-Din had a fine new *minbar* (pulpit) made for the Al-Aqsa Mosque by five craftsmen from Aleppo in 1169. The cedarwood pulpit had exquisite intarsia (coloured wood inlay) and panelling in its side walls and was inscribed with a declaration of Islam's superiority and victory over rival faiths. As it turned out, the richly decorated *minbar* could not be installed in Nur al-Din's lifetime, but it was fitted in the Al-Aqsa Mosque after Ayyubid ruler Salah al-Din took Jerusalem from the Christians in 1187.

BUILDING IN ALEPPO

Nur al-Din was a great builder, responsible for refortifying Aleppo's city walls and citadel, as well as for repairing the aqueduct. Within the city, Nur al-Din ordered work on the markets and the Great Mosque. Perhaps to establish his credentials as a proponent of *jihad* or possibly through religious fervour, he promoted orthodox Sunni Islam by building a network of *madrasas* (religious colleges), which were designed to combat the influence of Shiah Muslims in Syria. He also built a string of *khanqas* (institutions like monasteries) for Sufis.

PATRONS OF MOSUL

From the late 12th and early 13th centuries, there survive a number of illustrated manuscripts linked with court production at Mosul. One of these is an 1199 copy of a late classical work on toxicology, *Kitab al-Diryaq* (Book of Antidotes). The manuscript's frontispiece depicts a central, seated figure holding up a large lunar crescent. A pair of entwined dragons coil around this central figure. Four attendant angels, or genies, hover at the corners. In Mosul, this seated figure is the characteristic heraldic image for the Zangid dynasty and is also used on their coinage and other metalwork.

A mid-13th-century copy of the same text was also made in Mosul, but the frontispiece shows a ruler at his court enjoying a reception. Although the exact patron is not known, the style is a close match to depictions of Badr al-Din Lulu made for frontispieces in a multi-volume set of the great poetic anthology, *Kitab al-Aghani* (Book of Songs), produced in Mosul *c.*1216–20. The frontispieces show the typical Seljuk costume – most notably, the *sharbush*, or fur-lined bonnet.

Above The Nur al-Din Mosque, built in Hama, Syria, in 1172, is celebrated for its fine square minaret.

Left An illustration from Kitab al-Aghani (Book of Songs), c.1216–20, by Abu al-Faraj al-Isfahani, showing a ruler listening to musicians.

The Ayyubid Dynasty

OF KURDISH DESCENT, THE SUNNI MUSLIM AYYUBID DYNASTY RULED EGYPT, SYRIA, YEMEN AND PARTS OF IRAQ IN THE 12TH–13TH CENTURIES.

Salah al-Din (known in the West as Saladin), the most celebrated of Muslim generals, established Ayyubid rule in Cairo in 1169. He was hailed for both his strategic brilliance and chivalrous bearing by the European crusaders he fought, and was acclaimed throughout the Muslim world for his triumph in recapturing the holy city of al-Quds (Jerusalem) from the Christians on 2 October 1187. The dynasty Salah al-Din founded was named after his father Najm al-Din Ayyub ibn Shadhi, a Kurdish soldier in the service of the Seljuk Turks who became governor of Damascus.

A NEW EMPIRE

Salah al-Din came to Egypt with his uncle Shirkuh, the principal general of the Zangid ruler of Syria, Nur al-Din. He campaigned in Egypt alongside Shirkuh three times – in 1164, 1167 and 1168–69 – and on the final occasion took power after killing the Fatimid Egyptian vizier Shawar (Shirkuh died of natural causes). Salah al-Din abolished the Ismaili Fatimid Caliphate on the death of Caliph al-Adid in 1171 and declared Cairo to be under the authority of the Sunni Muslim Abbasid Caliph in Baghdad, al-Mustadi. He created an empire, taking power in Syria after the death of Nur al-Din in 1174, then winning control in northern Iraq, as well as the Hijaz and Yemen.

Salah al-Din was a champion of Sunni orthodoxy. As a proponent of the *jihad*, or holy war, he was named 'Protector of the holy sites of Makkah and Madinah' by the Abbasid caliph in Baghdad, and he waged an intermittent war against the crusader kingdoms, which culminated in his victory at the Battle of the Horns of Hattin in July 1187 and the capture of Jerusalem three months later.

On Salah al-Din's death in 1193, the empire was divided among his brothers and other relatives and thereafter was weakened by internal feuding. Nevertheless, the Ayyubids had survived more than 50 years, until the establishment in 1250 of the Mamluk Sultanate by the Ayyubids' former slave soldiers.

CAIRO WALLS AND CITADEL

On taking power in Cairo in 1171, Salah al-Din began work to extend the city walls, uniting the Fatimid royal capital of Cairo (founded in 969) to the older garrison town of Fustat (founded in 641). This task was not completed, but as part of the project Salah al-Din built a citadel and made it the centre of government. Known as the Citadel, it was raised on the Muqattam Hill in 1176–83.

Muqattam Hill had been the site of a pavilion known as the 'Dome of the Wind', built by Hatim ibn Hartama, the city's governor, in 810; Fatimid rulers and nobility had used it to enjoy the breezes and the views of the city. Salah al-Din, however, saw its military significance as a site for a fortified base from which to defend the city at a time when crusader armies were frequent and unwelcome visitors to Egypt. The

Above The great Ayyubid ruler Salah al-Din built his citadel on Muqattam Hill in Cairo in 1176–83.

Left The towers of the Citadel in Cairo were enlarged in 1218–38 by Ayyubid Sultan al-Kamil.

citadel raised by Salah al-Din had walls 10m (33ft) high and 3m (10ft) thick with rounded towers from which defenders could fight off an attacking force. Within, Salah al-Din's engineers dug a great well 87m (285ft) deep through solid rock and with a long ramp so that animals could be led down into the depths to drive machinery needed to lift water such a great height.

After Salah al-Din's death, Sultan al-Kamil (reigned 1218–38) greatly enlarged a number of the citadel's towers — notably those known as the Blacksmith's Tower and the Sand Tower, which overlooked the narrow pass between the citadel and hills alongside. He added square towers on the wall perimeter; three of these, 30m (98ft) wide and 25m (82ft) tall, are still standing, overlooking the area today used for parking cars outside the walls. Sultan al-Kamil also built a palace within what is now the citadel's southern enclosure in 1218; this building is no longer standing.

MADRASAS IN EGYPT

As part of a programme to counter the influence of Shiah Islam and establish Sunni orthodoxy, the Ayyubids built the first *madrasas* (religious colleges) in Egypt, principally in Cairo. Their design was based on *madrasas* built by the Seljuks of Anatolia: they had long courtyards lined with accommodation and two *iwans* (halls) at each end. In Cairo, Salah al-Din built five *madrasas* and a mosque, and imported Sunni professors from Syrian legal schools to teach there.

The best surviving Ayyubid *madrasa* in Egypt, however, is the Madrasa of Sultan al-Salih Najm al-Din Ayyub, built by the sultan of that name toward the end of the Ayyubid era in 1242–44, on part of the site once occupied by the Fatimid Eastern Palace in the centre of Cairo. Like the Mustansiriya *madrasa*, built in Baghdad in 1234 by Abbasid Caliph al-Mustansir, this was designed to house all four Sunni Muslim schools of legal thought — the Maliki, Shafii, Hanifi and Hanbali — with one *iwan* each.

The last of the Ayyubid sultans, al-Salih Najm al-Din Ayyub, died in 1249 and his mausoleum was added to the complex by his powerful widow, Shajar al-Durr, in 1250.

Above A seated ruler represented on this silver coin, made in south-eastern Anatolia in 1190–91.

Below Parts of the Madrasa of Sultan al-Salih Najm al-Din Ayyub, built in Cairo in 1242–44, still survive.

ALEPPO AND DAMASCUS

THE SYRIAN CITIES OF ALEPPO AND DAMASCUS WERE KEY STRONGHOLDS FOR THE AYYUBIDS. IN BOTH LOCATIONS, AYYUBID RULERS UNDERTOOK MAJOR BUILDING PROJECTS.

Both Aleppo and Damascus had been important bases for Zangid ruler Nur al-Din in his war against the Christian crusaders. Later Ayyubid work complemented building begun by the Zangids: the Ayyubids refortified the citadel, built or rebuilt mosques and founded numerous *madrasas*.

THE ALEPPO CITADEL

Salah al-Din conquered Aleppo in 1183, and his son al-Malik al-Zahir Ghazi was soon made governor (1186–1216). Ghazi set to work refortifying the citadel: his men regraded the sides of the mound on which the citadel stood, re-excavated the moat, built a bridge, strengthened the ramparts and raised a gateway flanked by towers. Within the citadel they built a weapon store, dug a deep well and reservoir, erected palaces and bathhouses and added gardens.

Ghazi also renovated the Mosque of Abraham built by Nur al-Din. According to tradition, the patriarch (and Islamic prophet) Abraham stopped on the mound that became the citadel on his voyage from Ur to the Promised Land and milked his cows there; Nur al-Din's mosque was raised on the spot where Abraham was said to have milked the creatures.

Archaeologists have excavated what they believe to be the remains of Ghazi's principal palace within the citadel, the Dar al-Izz ('Palace of Glories'), which had a grand central courtyard paved in marble with an octagonal fountain at its centre and was surrounded by four *iwans* (halls). The northern *iwan* contained an indoor *shadirwan*, or fountain, running into a pool.

MADRASA AL-FIRDAUS

Daifa Khatun, who was Ghazi's wife, founded two notable buildings in Aleppo: one a *madrasa* (religious college), the other a *khanqa* (Sufi monastery). The Madrasa al-Firdaus (College of Paradise) was laid out around a courtyard paved with marble and centred on an octagonal fountain and pool decorated with a cloverleaf pattern; on the northern side was an *iwan*, with student quarters behind it, while on the southern side was a three-domed mosque between mausolea, and to east and west were halls probably

Above A half-dome of muqarnas rises above a grand entranceway to the palace in the Aleppo citadel.

Left The Mosque of Abraham in the Aleppo Citadel once contained a fine wooden mihrab donated by Nur al-Din.

ALEPPO AND DAMASCUS

Above Ayyubid Sultan Al-Malik al-Zahir Ghazi added the bridge and fortified gateway to the Aleppo citadel.

used for teaching. The 1237 Khanqah al-Farafra also has an *iwan*, mosque and accommodation built around a fountain in a courtyard.

This arrangement of buildings around a courtyard with octagonal fountain was typical of Ayyubid buildings in Aleppo. In palaces, the courtyard was usually surrounded by four *iwans*, and religious buildings always had the mosque on the southern side. The mosques had a dome raised above the bay in front of the *mihrab* (niche). Their *mihrabs* were often adorned with a stonework pattern of interlinking knots, which inspired Mamluk and Ottoman architectural decoration.

Ayyubid buildings were usually made of dressed stone and left undecorated on the outside, except for entrance portals ornamented with *muqarnas* (stalactite-styled vaulting) or niches. Different types of stone were combined in some buildings, for example, by laying alternating horizontal bands of light and dark stones to create a design. Known as *ablaq*, this technique was an established one in Syria, having been used in the Great Mosque of Damascus, but it may have been inspired by the Byzantine tradition of using alternate bands of white ashlar and reddish baked brick.

IN DAMASCUS

Following the death of Nur al-Din in 1174, Salah al-Din became ruler of Damascus. Under Ayyubid rule, the citadel was strengthened, notably under al-Malik al-Adil in 1208–9. A number of mausolea and *madrasas* were built there, including the Madrasa al-Adiliya, which had been begun by Nur al-Din.

The Salihiyya quarter was established outside the city walls, where the al-Muzaffari Mosque was raised in *c.*1202–13. This historic treasure is the second oldest mosque surviving in Damascus. It contains a fine *mihrab* beneath a semidome adorned with *muqarnas* vaulting and on its right a *minbar* (pulpit) carved with geometric and floral designs, the oldest surviving *minbar* in Syria. Its design was based on the Umayyad Great Mosque of Damascus, with a plain façade, arcaded courtyard and rectangular prayer hall with three aisles on the south side of the courtyard.

Above The mihrab in the Madrasa al-Firdaus, Aleppo, is made from marble set in a beautiful interlacing pattern.

The Mamluks

FORMER SLAVE-SOLDIERS FOUNDED THE MAMLUK SULTANATE, WHICH RULED EGYPT, SYRIA AND THE HIJAZ FROM 1250 TO 1517. MAMLUK SULTANS EMBARKED ON A MAJOR BUILDING PROGRAMME IN CAIRO.

Izz al-Din Aybak, amir (military commander) for the Ayyubid regime, took control in Cairo in 1250. After the last Ayyubid sultan al-Salih Ayyub died in late 1249, his son and successor Turanshah was murdered and his widow Shajar al-Durr (meaning 'Tree of Pearls') seized the throne and briefly ruled as sultana. She did not receive the backing of al-Mustasim Billah, the Abbasid caliph in Baghdad, who had originally given her to al-Salih as a slave girl. So, to consolidate her position, Shajar al-Durr married her Mamluk military commander, Izz al-Din Aybak, and then passed the throne to him. Aybak founded the Bahri Mamluk Sultanate (1250–1382), subsequently replaced by the Burji Mamluks (1382–1517).

The Mamluks swiftly established themselves as the defenders of Islam and of Sunni orthodoxy. They won a series of military victories against Mongol invaders, beginning with the great Battle of Ain Jalut in Palestine in 1260, after which they took control of Syria, and also drove the Christian settlers from Palestine and Syria in 1291.

THE MAMLUK CAPITAL

Cairo had been a great city under the Fatimids and Ayyubids, but with the rise of the Mamluks it replaced Baghdad as the centre of Sunni Islam, especially after the Mongols killed the last Abbasid caliph in Baghdad in 1258. Cairo also benefited from the exodus of Iraqi and Iranian craftsmen escaping the advancing Mongols. These men were at the centre of a growth in metalwork and fine tiling in Egypt and introduced the ribbed dome into Egyptian buildings. Both Cairo and Damascus became established as centres for a wide-ranging international trade, with mercantile connections to the emerging city-states of Italy, southern Russia, the steppes of Eurasia, India and South-east Asia.

Above The Mosque of al-Maridani in Cairo was built in 1338–40 for Amir Altunbugha, who served as cup-bearer to Sultan al-Nasir Muhammad.

The Mamluks maintained their court in a grand style, with colourful pageantry and ceremony. In Cairo, their architecture also placed emphasis on style, with grand façades competing for attention on the major streets, such as the former square between the Fatimid Eastern and Western palaces and the main road leading to the Saladin Citadel. As the most highly prized locations became built up, it was a challenge for architects to fit their complexes into enclosed spaces. New buildings could not be aligned as was traditional on the *qibla* wall that faces the direction of prayer; the façades were treated separately, while the *qibla* orientation was achieved in the building's interior.

MAMLUK MOSQUES

The Mamluk sultans built several courtyard mosques on the model of the first Arab hypostyle designs, but

Left Cairo's mosque of Sultan al-Muayyad, built in 1415–20, has a magnificent dome carved with chevrons, placed behind the great entrance portal.

Above A large ablution fountain sits at the centre of the marble courtyard of the Sultan Hasan mosque and madrasa complex, built in 1356–62 in Cairo.

Below Many of the decorative elements of the Sultan Hasan mosque survive – including the gold and multicoloured marble design of the qibla wall.

with a vast dome above the *maqsura* (a private area in the prayer hall) before the *mihrab* (niche). Sultan al-Zahir Baybars (reigned 1260–77) built the first of these, in the newly developed area of Husayniyya, outside the northern gates in Cairo's city wall in 1266–69. Its courtyard was surrounded on three sides by arcades and on the fourth by a prayer hall. Contemporary sources claim the large dome before the *mihrab* was based on that of the Mausoleum of Imam al-Shafii, built by the Ayyubid sultan al-Kamil in 1211 – up to that date the grandest mausoleum built in Cairo.

Later courtyard mosques of this type included the Sultan's Mosque within the Citadel, built by al-Nasir Muhammad in 1335–36. Many congregational courtyard mosques, all with large domes, were built by al-Nasir Muhammad across Cairo. His son-in-law Amir Altunbugha built another mosque of this type, the Mosque of Amir Altunbugha al-Maridani, in 1338–40, on the road running to the citadel from the gateway of Bab Zuwayla.

The final substantial Mamluk congregational courtyard mosque was the Mosque of Sultan al-Mu'ayyad Shaykh (reigned 1412–21) built in 1415–20. Its south-east end stands against Bab Zuwayla and the Fatimid-era towers of this gate are the base for the mosque's minarets.

FOUR-*IWAN* MOSQUES
Many mosques were built on the four-*iwan* plan imported from Iran by way of Syria, in a cross-shape with four *iwans* (halls) arranged around a courtyard. These mosques were often included in complexes with *madrasas* (religious colleges). Major examples include the mosque and *madrasa* of Sultan Hasan which was built in 1356–62 and combined *madrasas* for the four leading schools of Sunni legal thought, a four-*iwan* congregational mosque, and a mausoleum.

MAMLUK MAUSOLEUM COMPLEXES

COMPLEXES BUILT BY MAMLUK RULERS IN CAIRO BETWEEN THE LATE 13TH AND EARLY 16TH CENTURIES GROUPED MOSQUES AND RELIGIOUS COLLEGES WITH MAUSOLEA AND FOUNDATIONS.

The Mamluks were responsible for creating charitable building complexes that also incorporated the mausoleum of the founder. These foundations included mosques, *madrasas* (religious colleges) and sometimes hospitals. One example is the complex of Sultan Qalawun, regarded as the most ambitious – and visually impressive – of the projects built by the Mamluks in Cairo.

QALAWUN COMPLEX

The complex of Sultan Qalawun was built in 1284–85 on al-Muizz Street, on the site of and using building materials salvaged from the Fatimid Western Palace. It stands behind a grand street façade that runs for almost 70m (230ft) and contains a superb mausoleum and *madrasa* and originally also had a hospital based on a four-*iwan* (hall) courtyard, although little of this last building survives.

Below The tall, ribbed domes of the complex of amirs Salar and Sanjar al-Jawli are visible from street level.

Above The madrasa *complex of al-Nasir Muhammad has a Gothic marble portal, removed from a crusader church.*

Instead of the usual square-dome design used for such buildings, the mausoleum features an inner octagon supported on four piers and four granite columns on which stands a high drum containing windows beneath a superb dome. The octagonal shape is a tribute to the design of the 7th-century Dome of the Rock in Jerusalem. The interior of the building is opulently decorated. The *madrasa* was laid out with two *iwans* at either end of a square courtyard, and rooms for accommodation or teaching space placed along the sides; in the *qibla iwan* (orientated to the direction of prayer), there were three naves.

GOTHIC PORTAL

Standing alongside the *madrasa* complex of Sultan Qalawun, the Madrasa and Mausoleum of al-Nasir Muhammad of 1295–1303 was in fact begun by al-Adil Kitbugha prior to his deposition in 1296. Kitbugha was responsible for the building's most celebrated feature – a Gothic marble portal, carried to Cairo by Sultan al-Ashraf Khalil (reigned 1290–93) from a crusader church in Acre (now in Israel) and installed in the façade;

Above Rooms around the courtyard of the Sultan Qansuh al-Ghuri's wikala *in Cairo provided rest for merchants.*

it was intended as a statement of Islamic triumph over Christianity, as the word 'Allah' was added at the portal's apex by Sultan al-Nasir. The complex was completed by Muhammad, who added the widely admired minaret with its lace-like stucco decoration on the lower square shaft; the upper octagonal part of the minaret was added at a later date. Within the complex, little remains except the beautiful carved stucco prayer niche.

OTHER COMPLEXES

The mausoleum complexes of the amirs Salar and Sanjar al-Jawli, dating to 1303–4, have a number of interesting features: the ribbed, pointed brick domes of the mausolea are raised on high drums well above the façade for maximum visual effect, and the minaret is an early example of the 'pepperpot' shape that became standard in Mamluk Cairo, combining square, octagonal and circular sections. Behind the mausolea is a hall topped with what is probably Cairo's first stone dome. The mausolea and adjoining hall are orientated toward Makkah, but the attached two-*iwan* courtyard that was either a *madrasa* or *khanqa* (Sufi monastery) is not. This is an example of Mamluk builders having to adapt their layout to a constrained urban site – or perhaps, in this case, making use of the building structures that were already in place. The courtyard contains open arches with carved stone screens.

Built in the late Mamluk period, the complex of Sultan Qansuh al-Ghuri (reigned 1501–16) is an example of the architecture of the period at its most expansive. The complex occupies sites on both sides of al-Muizz Street, with the mausoleum and *khanqa* on the eastern side and a large *madrasa* and congregational mosque on the western side. Its façades are set back from those of the rest of the street, forming a wider area resembling a square. Income raised by stalls and shops set into the lower façades would have helped to pay for the upkeep of the complex. The large mausoleum once had an elegant dome coated with blue faience.

Nearby, the same sultan built an impressive 'wikala' or urban *caravanserai* in 1504–5: this was centred on a great courtyard lined on all sides by storerooms on the two lower storeys, and on the upper floors, three-room apartments to be rented to merchants, pilgrims and travellers. In the centre of the courtyard was originally a kiosk mosque.

MAMLUK HERALDRY

The buildings and all the associated furnishings and regalia of the Mamluk military elite were typically marked with the owner's personal identity. Until the mid-14th century, this was done with heraldic blazons, a system with a symbol assigned to each Mamluk amir, which represented his household role when he had been a slave-soldier. From their adolescence, all Mamluk amirs and sultans had passed through a system of education, training and service as a slave. On manumission, each became an amir with slaves of his own. Deeply loyal, each was proud of his service role and, from then on, used it as a heraldic badge – for example: a pen box emblem for the secretary; a cup for the cup-bearer; and a sword for the sword-bearer. The blazons were gradually replaced by emphatic calligraphy in the late 14th century.

Above Amir Tabtaq's heraldic blazon – a cup – was inlaid on to the neck of this 14th-century Mamluk ewer.

THE UMAYYADS OF SPAIN

THE MUSLIM CONQUEST OF IBERIA IN 711 WAS CONSOLIDATED BY THE LONE SURVIVOR OF THE UMAYYAD CALIPHATE OF DAMASCUS, WHO FOUNDED A DYNASTY THAT RULED THE PENINSULA UNTIL 1031.

In 711, an army of Arabs and Berbers, unified under the Umayyad Caliphate of Damascus, invaded the Christian Visigothic Kingdom of the Iberian Peninsula. During the eight-year campaign, the entire peninsula, except for Galicia and Asturias in the north, was brought under Muslim control. The conquered territory, under the Arabic name al-Andalus, became part of the Umayyad Empire.

ESTABLISHING A DYNASTY

When the Umayyad Caliphate of Damascus was overthrown by the Abbasid revolution in 750, the only member of the Caliphate to survive the subsequent massacre of the royal family, Abd al-Rahman I, escaped from Syria and fled to North Africa, reaching southern Spain in 755. Welcomed by Syrian immigrants loyal to his family, he re-established the Syrian Umayyad dynasty in Spain, which was to last for two and a half centuries. Nonetheless, nostalgia for Syria was a key theme in Spanish Umayyad culture. At his capital of Córdoba, he began the construction of the Great Mosque, which was later enlarged by his successors.

During his 32-year reign, Abd al-Rahman I had to contend with numerous uprisings, some of which were supported by the Abbasids and one by Charlemagne. His successor, Abd al-Rahman II, was a poet and patron of the arts whose rule was marked by peace and prosperity. He brought scholars, musicians and poets from all over the Islamic world to Córdoba. The brief reign of his son Muhammad I was a period of crisis, but his successor, Abd al-Rahman III (912–61), was to reign for half a century. Abd al-Rahman III was the first Spanish Umayyad to declare himself caliph in 929, openly challenging the Abbasids in Baghdad and countering Fatimid claims from Cairo. Under his rule, and that of his son al-Hakam II (961–76) – a great patron of the arts and bibliophile – Umayyad Córdoba was a worthy and aspiring competitor to the great courts of Byzantine Constantinople, Abbasid Baghdad and Fatimid Cairo. Art, poetry, philosophy and science flourished. Works in the 'courtly love' tradition were carried by troubadours (from an Arabic word meaning 'to be transported with joy and delight') into southern France. Al-Andalus became a centre for the translation of Arabic works (via Spanish) into Latin and Greek, and for innovations in music. Court culture followed sophisticated codes of manners for gastronomy, cosmetics, perfumes, dress codes and polite behaviour. Luxury objects, such as carved ivory boxes, bronze statues of animals and richly patterned silks, adorned the palaces, which were decorated with ornate capitals and marble fountains.

Above With its double tier of horseshoe arches, the Great Mosque at Córdoba, begun by Abd al-Rahman I in 784, is one of the great medieval buildings.

Left This gilt silver casket, dating from 976, bears the name of the Umayyad Caliph al-Hisham II. Luxurious silver caskets like this one were commissioned by caliphs to demonstrate their wealth and royal authority.

TECHNICAL INNOVATIONS

The introduction of new farming methods and the improvement of the Roman irrigation system turned the Guadalquivir Valley, the wetlands of the Genil and the fluvial areas of the Mediterranean

Above The diminutive mosque, Bab al-Mardum, in Toledo has an inscription on the façade saying it was built in 999 by Musa ibn Ali.

coast into fertile orchards and fields. Among the crops that were introduced into the region are pomegranates, apricots, peaches, oranges, rice, sugar cane, cotton and saffron. Andalusian products were sold in Baghdad, Damascus and Makkah and as far away as India and Central Asia.

Al-Hakam II's son, al-Hisham II, was usurped by al-Hisham's opportunistic chamberlain, Muhammad ibn Abi Amir, who adopted the title of al-Mansur, or 'the Victorious One'. Al-Mansur carried out more than 50 punitive expeditions against the Christians of northern Spain. It was during one such expedition that the Basilica of Santiago de Compostela, the most famous Christian sanctuary in Spain, was sacked. However, these victories only served to unite the Christian rulers of the peninsula against al-Mansur. In 1002, he was succeeded by his son Abd al-Malik, known as al-Muzaffar, who ruled until 1008.

CIVIL WAR

After Abd al-Malik, Sanchuelo, his ambitious half brother, took over. However, his attempt to take the Caliphate for himself plunged the country into a devastating civil war leading to the end of the Umayyad Caliphate in Spain. The region then fragmented into a few weaker, rival *taifa* kingdoms who were unable to resist Christian powers that were encroaching from the north.

Left This impressive water wheel was built on the site of a Roman mill, during Abd al-Rahman II's reign (822–52), to raise water from the Guadalquivir river to the Caliphal Palace, Córdoba.

UMAYYAD TIMELINE

Below are the main dates important to this dynasty:

711–18	Umayyad conquest of Spain
750	Umayyad Caliphate of Damascus taken over by Abbasids
755	Abd al-Rahman I arrives in Spain
756–88	Abd al-Rahman I reigns
786	Construction of the Great Mosque, Córdoba, begins
788–96	Hisham I reigns
796–822	al-Hakam I reigns
822–52	Abd al-Rahman II reigns
852–86	Muhammad I reigns
886–88	al-Mundhir reigns
888–912	Abdallah ibn Muhammad reigns
912–61	Abd al-Rahman III reigns
929	Abd al-Rahman III declares himself Caliph
936	Building starts on Madinat al-Zahra
947	Government of Umayyad Caliphate is transferred to Madinat al-Zahra
961–76	al-Hakam II reigns. A noted bibliophile, his library was reputed to contain 400,000 books.
976–1008	al-Hisham II reigns
997	al-Mansur sacks Santiago de Compostela
c.1010	Madinat al-Zahra sacked
1010–12	al-Hisham II (restored)
1010–13	Civil War
1026–31	al-Hisham III, last Umayyad Caliph of Córdoba

Córdoba

UNDER THE UMAYYAD CALIPHATE, CÓRDOBA BECAME ONE OF THE MOST WONDERFUL CITIES OF THE WORLD, ITS OPULENCE AND CULTURE UNRIVALLED THROUGHOUT WESTERN EUROPE.

Situated along the Guadalquivir river, Córdoba had half a million people living in 113,000 houses scattered among 21 suburbs at the height of its prosperity. There were 1,600 mosques, 900 public baths and more than 80,000 shops. The Spanish Umayyad caliphs followed the pleasure-loving ways of their Syrian ancestors, and the elegance of life at court depicted on the ivory caskets was one of the specialities of Córdoba's skilled craftsmen.

During the caliphate of al-Hakam II, one of the most scholarly caliphs, Córdoba became the most cultured city in Europe. The library of al-Hakam is believed to have held 400,000 manuscripts. A great state institution, al-Hakam's library was a hub for a range of intellectual activities on an international level.

THE GREAT MOSQUE

With its complexity of design, decorative richness and delicacy of its superimposed arches, the Great Mosque at Córdoba is the finest surviving monument of Umayyad Spain. Its construction was begun by Abd al-Rahman I in 784, reportedly on the site of a Roman temple and a Visigothic church. Subsequent Umayyad rulers extended and embellished the Great Mosque, creating a truly remarkable building.

The mosque interior is a deep hypostyle hall, featuring a dense forest of arched columns. Set on salvaged classical stone columns, the double arches are striped in red brick and white stone voussoirs, and mounted in pairs. This gives a dazzling visual result, heightening the hall and emphasizing the effect of receding perspective.

In 962, al-Hakam II added a new *mihrab* (niche) area, a small domed room exquisitely decorated in gold glass mosaic and carved stucco panels. Many aspects of the Great Mosque of Córdoba may be deliberate evocative references to the architecture of Umayyad Damascus.

Above This ornate doorway, with its horseshoe arch, is part of the additions made by al-Hakam II to the exterior of the Great Mosque at Córdoba.

Left The dome in front of the mihrab in Córdoba's Great Mosque is decorated with Quranic inscriptions and flowing designs of plant life.

MADINAT AL-ZAHRA

The splendid palace-city of Madinat al-Zahra, about 5km (3 miles) east of Córdoba, was modelled after the old Umayyad palace in Damascus, and it served as a symbolic tie between Caliph Abd-al-Rahman III and his Syrian roots. Only ten per cent of this remarkable city has so far been excavated, but a palatial complex of great luxury has come to light. Its construction began in 936 and continued for 25 years. Built in three large terraces on the hillside at the base of the Sierra Morena, with the caliph's palace at its highest point, the city was visible for miles around. In 941, the city's mosque was consecrated, and by 947 the government had transferred there from Córdoba.

At its zenith, Madinat al-Zahra was said to have a population of 12,000 people. The city was a vast and luxurious complex of buildings and irrigated gardens, including the caliph's residence, court reception halls, mosques, *hammams*, state mint, pharmacy, barracks, court textile factory, plus a large urban quarter on the lowest terrace. This magnificent city was to last for only 50 years. It was sacked and looted during the Civil War (1010–13) that led to the end of the Caliphate of Córdoba and marked the beginning of the *taifa* period.

Above With its series of hillside palaces, Madinat al-Zahra commands an impressive prospect over the surrounding landscape.

Below These horseshoe arches in The Audience Hall in the Great Mosque are richly decorated with panels of carved stone applied to the walls.

Early Islamic Rule in North Africa

THE AGHLABIDS (800–909) RULED THE PROVINCE OF IFRIQIYA IN NORTH AFRICA AND LED INVASIONS OF SICILY, SARDINIA, MALTA AND PARTS OF MAINLAND ITALY.

In 800, the Abbasid Caliph, Harun al-Rashid (reigned 786–809), appointed his army general, Ibrahim ibn al-Aghlab from Khurasan, to pacify and rule the unstable province of Ifriqiya (the area of Tunisia and Eastern Algeria), making him semi-autonomous. The Aghlabids ruled from Kairouan until 909.

THE GREAT MOSQUE

The heart of Aghlabid culture is found in the holy city of Kairouan and, in architectural terms, the jewel in its crown is its magnificent Great Mosque. This was the first building of outstanding quality in the region, and today it is classified as a Unesco World Heritage Site. The mosque was originally founded in 670 by Umayyad general Sidi Uqba b. Nafi, but was entirely renovated in 836 by the Aghlabid ruler Ziyadat Allah (reigned 817–38). It has a large, rectangular courtyard with ablution pool, and a deep hypostyle hall of arcaded columns, with semicircular, horseshoe arches. Many of the 414 marble and porphyry columns are classical spolia, recycled from earlier Roman buildings on the site. The square, three-storey minaret is said to be one of the oldest in the Islamic world.

The most remarkable feature of the interior is the impressive array of early lustre tiles set around the *mihrab* (niche). These were imported from Baghdad in the mid-9th century, and are considered to be the oldest known example of Abbasid tiles still in situ. The surviving 139 examples display a wide variety of designs, including winged palmettes, crowns and peacock-eye motifs. The mosque's *minbar* (pulpit) dates from the 9th century and was made from 300 pieces of imported teak.

OTHER MOSQUES

The design of the Great Mosque at Kairouan was extremely influential, shaping the development of other Aghlabid mosques in Sfax (849), Sousse (850) and Tunis (864). It also had an impact on the Mosque of the Three Doors in Kairouan. Built

Above Kairouan's Great Mosque, rebuilt in 836, was the most influential Aghlabid building – a prototype for early North African architecture.

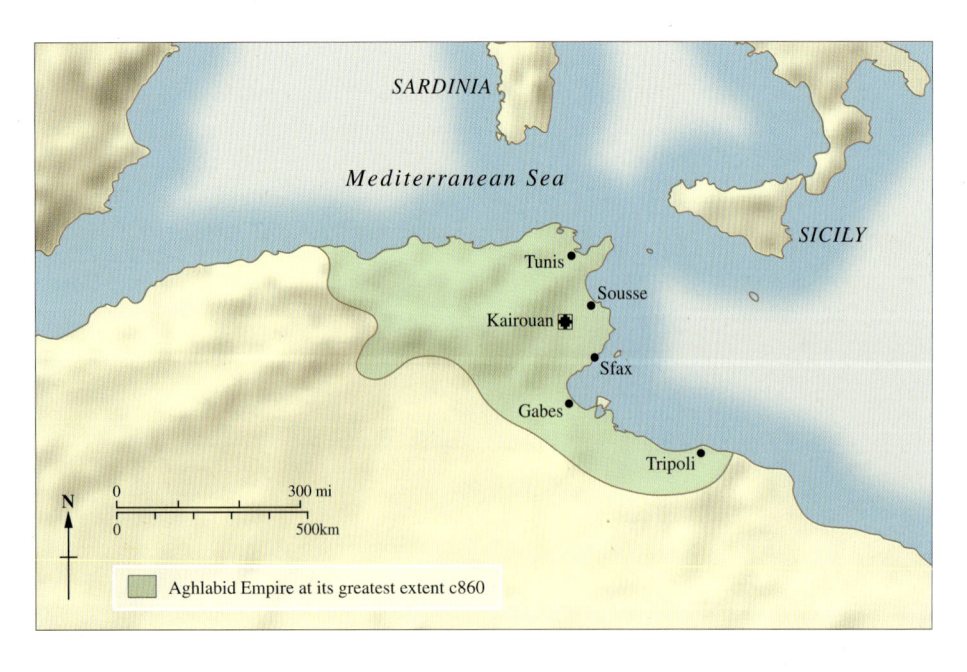

Below The Aghlabid Empire was centred on present-day Tunisia – but extended into Algeria and Libya.

Above These 9th-century lustre tiles from the Great Mosque of Kairouan, Tunisia, feature a variety of vegetal and geometric designs.

in 866 by Muhammad ibn Khayrun, it takes its name from the triple horseshoe arch on the façade, which is surmounted by three bands of decoration, featuring *kufic* inscriptions and floral patterns.

THE BASINS

In a different vein, the Aghlabids created an important civic amenity in Kairouan, a hydraulic system known as the Basins. These two interlinked pools acted as reservoirs, settlement tanks and filters, and provided the city with clean water. They were commissioned by Abu Ibrahim Ahmad ibn al-Aghlab and took four years to complete (859–63).

ISLAMIC *RIBATS*

In the year that Kairouan was granted World Heritage status (1988), Unesco bestowed the same honour on another Aghlabid city: Sousse. This was a major port that held a key strategic and commercial significance, because it was only separated from Sicily by a narrow stretch of water. For this reason, Sousse was well fortified, with powerful ramparts and a *ribat*.

Ribats, which have been described as monastic fortresses, were a distinctive form of Islamic architecture, combining military and spiritual needs. Essentially, they were designed to house the Murabitun (holy warriors), but they also had facilities for prayer and study in times of peace. The minaret at Sousse, for instance, served as a watchtower and a landmark for shipping, as well as its traditional military and religious purpose.

The borders of the Aghlabid territories were protected by a line of *ribats*, with major outposts at Tripoli, Sfax, Monastir, Bizerte and Sousse. The latter is by far the most impressive, but the one at Monastir is also a fine, early example (796). Built by Ziyadat Allah in 821, the Sousse Ribat is notable for its lofty battlements, pierced with arrow slits, its galleries of arcades enclosing the inner courtyard, its rib-vaulting, and the first-floor cells, which were accommodation for the troops.

Above A stairway leads from the courtyard of the Great Mosque of Sousse (850) to the vaulted sanctuary. A long kufic inscription extends above this arcade.

Below Enlarged in the 10th century, the ribat at Monastir has large fortified walls and a tower which served as watchtower and minaret.

ISLAMIC ARCHITECTURE THROUGH THE CENTURIES

THE ALMORAVIDS AND ALMOHADS

THE BERBER DYNASTIES OF THE ALMORAVIDS (1060–1147) AND THE ALMOHADS (1133–1269) RULED THE MAGHREB AND AL-ANDALUS. THEY BUILT MOSQUES AND PALACES AND OVERSAW A SILK-WEAVING INDUSTRY.

The Almoravids were from the western Sahara and established themselves in the Maghreb under religious leader Abdallah ibn Yasin in c.1030–59. Their name derives from al-Murabitun (meaning 'men of the *ribat*'), as the ascetic and highly disciplined followers of ibn Yasin were known; the word *ribat* refers perhaps to a religious institution, a fortified monastery in which the men trained, or simply to a bond of religious brotherhood, a shared commitment to *jihad* (holy war). At the end of the 11th century, the Almoravids extended their power north into al-Andalus and also south of the Sahara in West Africa, eventually creating an empire that covered 3,000km (1,865 miles) from north to south. Their capital was Marrakech.

Almoravid leader Yusuf ibn Tashfin (reigned 1060–1106) first arrived in al-Andalus in 1085, at the invitation of the small Islamic *taifa* kingdoms, requesting support against the Christians. He defeated King Alfonso VI of León and Castile (reigned 1065/72–1109) at the Battle of Zallaka in 1086 and, in 1090, took control of Andalus and defeated the *taifa* kings as well.

ALMORAVID MOSQUES

The Great Mosque of Tlemcen (in Algeria, near the Moroccan border) is a key surviving Almoravid construction, built in 1082 after Yusuf ibn Tashfin led the conquest of the central Maghreb and captured Tlemcen. The mosque is celebrated for its highly decorated minaret and for the splendid horseshoe *mihrab* (niche) and great dome in the prayer hall, both closely based on the Great Mosque of Córdoba. Built by Yusuf ibn Tashfin, the Great Mosque underwent many alterations under the rule of his son Ali ibn Yusuf (reigned 1106–43). The Qarawiyyin Mosque in Fez was expanded and improved with beautiful domed vaults under Ali ibn Yusuf. The mosque had been founded in c.850 by immigrants from Kairouan in Tunisia, and named after them; Ali ibn Yusuf expanded the already large 18-aisle prayer hall to contain 21 aisles – measuring 83m by 44m (272ft by 144ft). It was one of the largest mosques in the Maghreb. Ibn Yusuf's craftsmen also increased the height of the central aisle that leads to the *mihrab* and added five domed vaults decorated with *muqarnas* (tiers of small niches). Under the Almoravids, this mosque was also developed into a major university.

Left The beautifully tiled courtyard at the Qarawiyyin Mosque in Fez.

Above Nine aisles run across the prayer hall in Tinmal's Great Mosque, an example of the Almohad T-plan design.

Other contemporary Almoravid religious foundations include the Great Mosque of Nédroma (near Tlemcen in Algeria), built in 1086, and the Great Mosque of Algiers, built in 1096.

RISE OF ALMOHADS

Known as *al-Muwahiddun* ('those who believe in the oneness of God'), the Almohads swept the Almoravids from power in 1145–47. They were followers of the preacher Imam Muhammad al-Madhi ibn Tumart, a Berber from southern Morocco who declared himself the infallible imam Mahdi. After ibn Tumart's death in 1130, Abd al-Mumin became

80

leader of the movement, defeated the Almoravids at Orhan in north-western Algeria in 1145 and captured Marrakech in 1147.

The Almohads also took control of al-Andalus and made their capital in the city of Seville. However, after 1212, when their leader Muhammad III al-Nasir was defeated at the Battle of Las Navas de Tolosa by a Christian coalition of Aragon and Castile, Almohad power in al-Andalus swiftly failed, and they lost Córdoba (1236), Murcia (1243) and Seville (1248) to Ferdinand III of Castile. Back in the Maghreb, the Almohads survived in Marrakech until 1269, when the city was taken by the rival Berber power of the Merinids.

ALMOHAD T-PLAN MOSQUES

In the Maghreb, the Almohads built a series of mosques to a standard plan, with a many-aisled prayer hall and forecourt in the shape of a rectangle. These are known as T-plan mosques because the prayer hall's central aisle aligned on the *mihrab* met the transept to form a T-shape. Perhaps the principal prototype was the Mosque of Taza in Algeria, founded in 1142 by Abd al-Mumin; another was the Great Mosque of Tinmal (1153), built in the Atlas Mountains around 100km (62 miles) south-east of Marrakech, in memory of Almohad founder Muhammad ibn Tumart.

THE ALMOHADS IN SPAIN

The remains of Almohad buildings can still be found in Seville. The Almohad Great Mosque, constructed in 1172–98, was later the site of the city's Christian cathedral. The minaret and the mosque's main courtyard survive. Today, the minaret serves as the cathedral's bell-tower. It features significant later additions, including a 17th-century Baroque belfry at its top, together with a rotating weathervane, and is called 'La Giralda'. The courtyard is planted with orange trees.

Among the more significant Almohad remains in Seville are parts of the city walls and a 12-sided tower on the banks of the Guadalquivir river near the city gates. The tower was once covered with glazed golden tiles and is known as the Torre del Oro ('Golden Tower'). Originally, it was matched by a similar tower on the opposite riverbank, which was covered with glazed silver tiles and called the Torre de la Plata ('Silver Tower'); the two towers were connected by a chain, which was lifted to allow ships access to the city harbour. Two Almohad palace buildings, the Patio de Yeso and the Patio de Contratacion, survive within the city.

Above Seville's 12-sided Torre del Oro ('Golden Tower') was originally part of the 12th-century city walls.

Above This Almoravid silk cloth (c.1100) survived in a tomb in the Burgo de Osma Cathedral, Spain.

SILK PRODUCTION IN AL-ANDALUS

The history of silk weaving in Spain goes back to the Muslim conquest in the 8th century. Under Almoravid rule the city of Almería became the centre for textile production. According to the geographer Muhammad al-Idrisi (1100–66), in the mid-12th century Almería alone had 800 weaving mills, while the geographer Yaqut notes: 'In the land of Andalus there is not to be found a people who make more excellent brocade than those of Almería.' Generally, under the Almohad rulers figurative decoration on silks disappeared, to be replaced by abstract patterns of geometry and calligraphy.

As with many other Islamic art media, luxurious woven silk textiles were often adopted for use in sacred Christian contexts, such as royal burial, because of their remarkable quality. This (illustrated) silk and gold thread Almoravid fragment was re-used as a shroud for Christian relics of San Pedro de Osma: the design features lions, harpies, griffins, hares and people.

Rabat and Marrakech

THE ROYAL CITIES OF MARRAKECH AND RABAT IN MOROCCO WERE FOUNDED IN THE ALMORAVID AND ALMOHAD ERAS, AND ARE RICH IN ARCHITECTURAL REMAINS OF THE PERIOD.

Marrakech gives its name to the country of Morocco: from Arabic *Marakush*, it came to English by way of Spanish *Marruecos*. The city was founded by Almoravid leader Yusuf ibn Tashfin (reigned 1060–1106) in 1062. He erected a grand palace named Dar al-Hajar ('House of Stone').

ALMORAVID BUILDINGS

A great mosque was built by the Almoravids in Marrakech, but it was destroyed when the city was captured by the Almohads in 1147. However, a small cube-shaped and domed building built over a well survives from the reign of Ali ibn Yusuf (1106–43). Named after its founder, the Qubbat al-Barudiyin is just 8m (26ft) tall. The walls are decorated with polylobed arches derived from those in the Great Mosque of Córdoba and with composite arches (alternately convex and concave curved outlines) based on the arches in the Palace of Aljaferia in Saragossa (1050–83), a product of the *taifa* (small kingdoms) of al-Andalus. The domed interior has magnificent stucco decoration. Historians believe that the building was a place for ritual washing used by those visiting the mosque.

The Almoravid rulers typically installed large, fine wooden *minbars* (pulpits) in their mosques. The beautifully carved *minbar* that once stood in the Great Mosque of Marrakech was ordered by Ali ibn Yusuf in *c.*1120 from renowned craftsmen in Córdoba. It stands 4m (13ft) high and has 1,000 carved panels featuring a complex design of geometric shapes. When the Almohads sacked Marrakech and destroyed the mosque in 1147, they saved the *minbar* and transferred it to the Kutubiyya Mosque that they built in the city.

ALMOHAD MOSQUES

In fact, the Almohads built two Kutubiyya mosques in Marrakech. The first, constructed in 1147, had 17 aisles and was built to a T-plan design with the principal aisle aligned on the *mihrab* (niche) and a pronounced transept cutting across it at right angles to form a T.

However, this building was demolished almost as soon it was finished, perhaps due to a slight mistake made in its alignment with Makkah. The second mosque, built to the south of the first, beginning in 1158 was on a different alignment.

The second Kutubiyya Mosque has five cupolas above the *qibla* aisle (facing the direction of prayer) and six above the transept; there is also a splendid 67.6m (222ft) high minaret with a square tower surmounted by a lantern-shaped section. It contains six floors and a ramp to give the *muezzin* (who makes the call to prayer) access to the platform at the top. Four copper globes adorn the tower: according to local legend, there were originally three gold globes, until a wife of the Almohad ruler Yaqub al-Mansur (reigned 1184–99) donated the fourth globe after giving up all her gold jewellery to compensate for her failure to fast for a single day during Ramadhan. The minaret was the model for the minaret of the Mosque of Hasan in Rabat.

Above Built of red clay, the Bab er Reha gate is part of the 11th-century city wall of Marrakech.

Left Measuring 67.6m (222ft) in height, the elegant minaret of the second Almohad Kutubiyya Mosque in Marrakech was built from 1158.

At Marrakech, the Almohads also laid out fortified city walls that incorporated monumental gates, such as the Bab Agnaou. Yaqub al-Mansur also built a *kasbah*, or fortified palace (citadel), in the city, as well as an associated mosque, the El Mansouria, completed in 1190.

RABAT

The city of Rabat, the modern capital of Morocco, grew from a *ribat*, a fortified camp or monastery, established by the first Almohad ruler Abd al-Mumin (reigned 1130–63) in 1146 as a base from which to launch the military attacks he was planning against al-Andalus.

Above The 12th-century Bab Agnaou gate at Marrakech bears an inscription from the Quran in Maghribi script. It leads into the royal citadel.

Below The unfinished Mosque of Hasan (1195–99) in Rabat contains 200 columns and a half-built, but beautifully decorated, red limestone minaret.

Yaqub al-Mansur gave it the name Ribat al-Fath ('Victory Camp'), from which its modern name derives, and built the fortifications that still survive.

At Rabat, this proud ruler, who took the name al-Mansur Billah ('Granted Victory by God') after he defeated King Alfonso VIII of Castile at the Battle of Alarcos on 18 July 1195, began building the Mosque of Hasan. This mosque was left unfinished, but survives today as a splendid square minaret and long lines of pillars, originally intended to support the roof of the prayer hall. The mosque was a vastly ambitious project: the surviving minaret is on a base 16m (52ft) square and may have been intended to rise to 80m (262ft), while the planned mosque was to cover 178m by 138m (584ft by 453ft) – bigger even than the Great Mosque of Córdoba, which measured 173m by 127m (568ft by 417ft), after it had been extended many times. The Mosque of Hasan may have been left unfinished because Yaqub al-Mansur overreached himself and could not complete such a vast building. After his death in 1199, building work ground to a halt.

THE NASRIDS

THE LAST MUSLIM SULTANS ON THE IBERIAN PENINSULA, THE NASRIDS (1232–1492) WERE RULERS OF THE SMALL KINGDOM OF GRANADA IN SPAIN, WHERE THEY BUILT THE MAGNIFICENT ALHAMBRA CITADEL.

Almohad power in Spain never recovered from the defeat of Sultan al-Nasir by an army led by King Alfonso VIII of Castile in 1212. The Christians captured Córdoba in 1236, the cities of Murcia and Jaén in 1243 and 1245, and Seville in 1248. During this period, several small Muslim kingdoms were established, and one of these was created in Jaén by Muhammad ibn Yusaf ibn Nasr (reigned 1232–73), self-styled Sultan Muhammad I of Arjona, who made his capital in Granada in 1237. Ibn Nasr was a client-ruler under King Ferdinand III, but he managed to pass on his kingdom to his son Muhammad II (reigned 1273–1302), who consolidated Nasrid power in Granada.

The Nasrid kingdom was at its height under Sultan Yusuf I (reigned 1333–54) and Sultan Muhammad V (reigned 1354–9 and 1362–91), both of whom devoted themselves to rebuilding the fortified palace-city of the Alhambra that was the Nasrids' most enduring legacy.

After the reign of Muhammad VII (1392–1408), the power of the Nasrids entered a slow decline as rival family members fought over the sultanate. The final sultan, Muhammad XII, also known as Boabdil, seized the throne from his father Abu'l Hasan Ali in 1482, but the following year he was captured by Christians. Boabdil's uncle took the throne as Muhammad XIII, then King Ferdinand released Boabdil as a vassal-ruler, and the two rivals fought while Ferdinand's army advanced toward Granada. There, Boabdil was forced to hand the city to the Christians in 1492. The 'Reconquista' (reconquest) was complete.

GLORIES OF GRANADA

The Alhambra's name derives from the Arabic words for 'the red one': it is so-called from the reddish colour

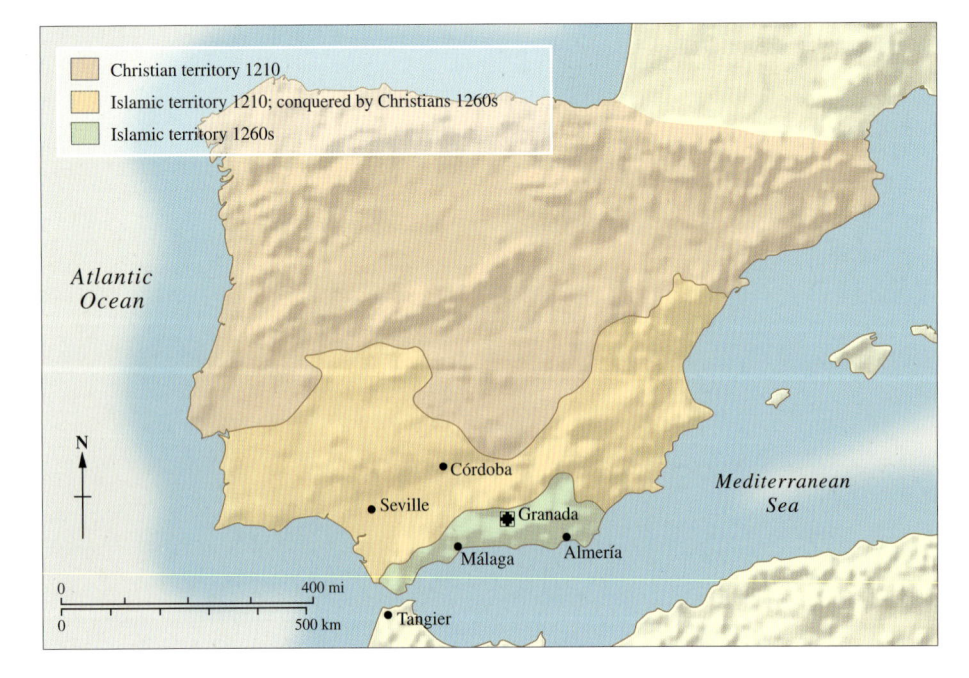

Above A steam bath was part of the harem area of the Comares Palace at the Alhambra. The tiles are original.

of the sun-dried, clay-and-gravel bricks of which its outer walls are constructed. A fort is known from contemporary accounts to have stood on the site as early as 860, but there are no remains dating to earlier than the 11th century, when builders of the Zirid dynasty erected an earlier version of the Alcazaba. The complex began to be established in its current form under the early Nasrid sultans, and the most celebrated features, including the Comares Palace and the Palace of the Lions, date to the reigns of Yusuf I and Muhammad V in the 14th century.

In its final form, the fortified palace-city of the Alhambra stands behind walls 1,730m (5,675ft) long with 30 towers and 4 main gates, on a plateau overlooking the city of Granada. The Alhambra has three main areas: the Alcazaba, or citadel, a barracks area for the guard; the palaces used by the sultan and family; and the madinah, a residential area for officials and artisans.

Left By 1260, Muslim rule in Spain was limited to a small, mountainous area in the south-east of the country.

Above The fortified palace-city of the Alhambra sits on a plateau in front of the Sierra Nevada mountains.

TWO PALACES

Within the palace complex the two outstanding Nasrid buildings are the Comares Palace and the Palace of the Lions. The former was built by Yusuf I around a series of courtyards that led on to reception rooms. Beyond a highly decorated façade, added by Muhammad V in 1370, the main rooms are arranged around the Court of the Myrtles. The main residential areas are off the long sides of the court, while at one end is an administrative complex and at the other a public room with the large Throne Room (or 'Hall of the Ambassadors') occupying the Comares Tower. With its exquisite ceiling of inlaid wood rising to a *muqarnas* dome, it is one of the most beautiful parts of the entire complex.

The Palace of the Lions was added to the Comares Palace by Muhammad V. At the centre of its main courtyard is a marble fountain, its dodecagonal bowl supported by 12 lions. Verses inscribed into the fountain's edge praise the hydraulic system that supplies its water. A colonnade with horseshoe arches runs around the patio and gives access to royal apartments and reception rooms, including the Sala de los Reyes ('Hall of the Kings'), with a dome featuring paintings of people thought to be the principal Nasrid kings. The Sala de los Mocarabes ('Muqarnas Chamber') once had a *muqarnas* dome.

When the city passed into Christian hands, King Charles V of Spain built a large Renaissance-style palace within the walls of the Alhambra in 1526. The Comares Palace and Palace of the Lions were thereafter together called the Casa Real Vieja ('Old Royal Palace'), while the Renaissance building was called the Casa Real Nueva ('New Royal Palace').

MADINAH

In Alhambra, the madinah held stores, a mosque, public baths and the sultans' mausoleum. Many of these were built by Muhammad III (reigned 1302–9). There was also a *madrasa* (college). Outside the Alhambra walls were the Generalife Gardens, incorporating vegetable gardens, ornamental plantings, pavilions, fountains and the summer palace of the Generalife.

Right In the Alhambra's Hall of Justice, a ceiling painting on leather depicts a Christian knight slain by a Muslim warrior.

The Garden in Islamic Architecture

The importance of enclosed and irrigated gardens has a long history in the Middle East. Gardens are often described as an earthly version of the paradise promised in the Quran.

The descriptions of the eternal garden of paradise in the Quran refer to springs, brooks and four rivers containing water, milk, honey and a non-intoxicating type of wine. In a landscape 'as large as heaven and earth', thornless trees provide restful shade and fruits.

Chapter 55, the Surah al-Rahman ('The Merciful'), describes four gardens in paradise, all with flowing waters, trees and fruits. There are references to gates, so the gardens are enclosed by walls. Throughout these gardens are shelters and buildings, including tents, castles, houses and rooms that have running water. The buildings are isolated among green spaces and stretches of water rather than gathered in a settlement, because in contrast to Judaism and Christianity – which both look forward to a 'heavenly Jerusalem' – Islam has no city in visions of the afterlife.

THE GENERALIFE

The Generalife gardens are separated from the Alhambra palace by a gorge, and overlook the palace-city. The name may be derived from the Arabic *jinan al-arif*, meaning 'gardens of the overseer'.

The gardens were laid out during the reign of Muhammad III (reigned 1302–9) and used as a summer retreat; the Nasrid rulers and their courtiers would have strolled through the terraces filled with lush, green planting and cooling fountains.

The lowest terrace – the Patio de la Acequía – was formed as a rectangle and divided into four separate quadrants by two intersecting water channels, with a water basin at the centre.

Below The beautiful Shalimar Gardens in Srinagar, India, were laid out by Mughal Emperor Jahangir in 1619.

Above Fountains and flowing water are central to the design of the Patio de la Acequia in the Generalife Gardens.

USES OF WATER

In its description of paradise, the Quran tells of 'gardens beneath which rivers flow'. With many Islamic cultures rooted in dry regions, irrigation plans were central to the design of gardens. One scheme, developed in pre-Islamic Iran and exported throughout the Islamic world, was to dig canals underground that carried water around the garden down gentle gradients from a raised water source.

As in the Quranic example, the waterway was beneath the garden; it was covered so the water did not evaporate in sunlight. In other places, where the heat was less intense, open canals were used.

In Islamic culture, water is a symbol of life. Control and provision of water were also the gift of the ruler – symbolic of his gracious generosity and responsibility as a fellow Muslim. Fountains, pools and waterways were given prominence so that visitors could enjoy the air-cooling qualities, movement and music of running water. In princely gardens integrated within palace complexes, water flowed in covered canals into the interior of the palace, where it emerged from fountains, ran down tiled walls and fell in waterfalls down stairs.

FOUR-PART GARDEN

The description of the four gardens and four rivers of paradise in the Quran gave resonance to the four-part Persian *chahar bagh* garden design. The *chahar bagh* was named from the Persian words *chahar* (four) and *bagh* (garden). The design was derived from a pre-Islamic source: the gardens in Pasargadae laid out by Cyrus the Great (reigned 576–530BCE), ruler of the Persian Achaemenid Empire.

The *chahar bagh* layout was used for palace gardens and, particularly in Mughal India, for formal gardens surrounding mausolea. In Delhi, Mughal Emperor Akbar (reigned 1566–1605) placed a mausoleum in honour of his father Humayan (reigned 1530–40 and 1555–56) at the centre of a *chahar bagh* garden. Near Agra, the design was used again for the Taj Mahal, the memorial shrine built in 1632–54 by Mughal Emperor Shah Jahan (reigned 1628–58) to honour the memory of his wife Mumtaz Mahal. Here, the tradition was slightly altered: in a normal *chahar bagh* layout, the tomb stands at the centre of the quadrilateral garden, but at the Taj Mahal it is at the northern end overlooking the river Yamuna.

A GREEN SHADE

Many of the early Muslims hailed from arid lands, such as the deserts of Arabia and north Africa, and historians draw on this heritage to explain the love in Islamic culture for well-watered shady places. As well as the Quranic imagery of paradise as a garden, there was a well-established literary tradition in which gardens were revered as blissful places of refuge. Poets conjured the image of shady retreats from the heat of day, where moving water made soothing music. In the Abbasid Empire from the 8th century and in al-Andalus, particularly in the 11th century, the *rawdiya* ('garden poem') was a popular genre. Many Islamic gardens survive attached to palaces and mausolea, but many more have been described in contemporary literary sources. According to these sources, for example, there were 110,000 gardens of fruit trees in Damascus, magnificent parks outside the city walls in Samarra, and miles of canals and gardens in Basra. In al-Andalus, Valencia, Seville and Córdoba were famous for their beautiful gardens.

Above The quadrilateral layout of the chahar bagh *gardens at the Taj Mahal is clear in this 18th-century lithograph.*

Left In Islamic gardens, water in pools, streams and fountains is symbolic both of earthly life and the abundance promised in paradise.

ISLAMIC ARCHITECTURE IN AFRICA

MUSLIMS TRAVELLED FROM NORTH AFRICA ACROSS THE SAHARA AND DOWN THE EAST AFRICAN COAST. THEIR FINE ARCHITECTURAL REMAINS HAVE SURVIVED IN WEST AND EAST AFRICA.

The earliest known mosques in West Africa were established in Tegadoust and Koumbi Saleh, trading centres for the Ghana Empire (750–1076) in the 10th–11th centuries. The empire was based in the land between the upper Senegal and Niger rivers (now eastern Senegal, western Mali and south-western Mauritania), where it grew rich from trade in gold, slaves, salt and ivory. Excavations show that these first West African mosques consisted of a courtyard, prayer hall and square *sawma'a*, or minaret. The empire had many trading contacts; the mosques were for the use of Muslim traders and other travellers, as the natives of the Ghana Empire were pagans.

In the 11th century, the Berber Almoravids of the Maghreb and al-Andalus conquered parts of West Africa. The Almoravids launched a *jihad*, or holy war, in 1062 against the empire under General Abu Baker ibu-Umar, who captured Koumbi Saleh in 1076. The empire fell apart into diverse tribal groups.

MOSQUE OF DJÉNNÉ

In *c.*1240, Prince Sundiata Keita of the small kingdom of Manden (today's northern Guinea and southern Mali) conquered several neighbouring territories creating the Kingdom of Mali. In 1240, a great mud-brick mosque was built in Djénné in Mali. The current structure is one of the most distinctive Islamic buildings in Africa.

Sundiata Keita's nephew Mansu Musa (reigned 1312–37) took the cities of Gao and Timbuktu, and formed an empire. The Mali rulers were staunch Muslims, and traced their lineage to Bilal ibn Ramah (578–642), whom the Prophet Muhammad chose as the first *muezzin* (caller to prayer) of the faith: the Mali princes are said to be descended from Lawalo – one of the seven sons of Bilal, who reputedly settled in Mali in the 7th century.

Above The Djinguereber Mosque in Timbuktu in Mali was built from dried earth in 1327.

BUILDINGS IN TIMBUKTU

When Mansu Musa made the *Hajj* pilgrimage to Makkah in 1324–26 he persuaded the poet and architect Abu Es Haq Es Saheli to return to

Below Built in 1907, the Great Mosque at Djénné is the largest dried earth building in the world.

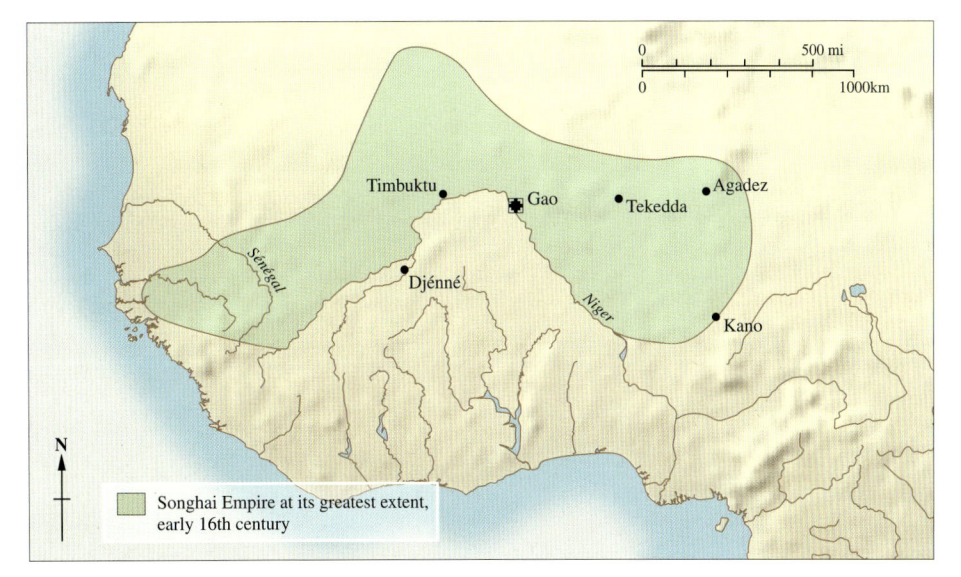

Left The Songhai Empire lasted from the early 15th century to the late 16th century. It followed the course of the river Niger and had its capital at Gao.

West Africa. Es Saheli built mosques and palaces in Gao and Timbuktu, including the Djinguereber Mosque in 1327. This building is made of dried mud bricks and stone rubble, and the walls are rendered in clay. It has a minaret 16m (52ft) in height and a prayer hall with a flat roof supported by mud piers arranged in 25 arcades, three of which have stone horseshoe arches. Above the *mihrab* (niche) there is a conical tower. The mosque, although 14th-century in origin, has been rebuilt several times over the centuries.

Two mosque-*madrasa* (religious college) complexes were built in Timbuktu in this period. The Sankoré Mosque was constructed in the early 14th century, but its oldest surviving buildings date to 1581; the Sidhi Yahya Mosque was built in 1400–40 and named after its first professor, Sidi Yahya Tadelsi. The Sidhi Yahya Mosque was rebuilt in the 16th and 20th centuries, but it retains its original 15th-century minaret. Together the Djinguereber, Sidhi Yahya and Sankoré buildings formed the University of Sankoré, a major teaching institution and force for the dissemination of the faith.

The Mali Empire was eclipsed in the region by the Songhai Empire in the mid-15th century. Major Songhai rulers, such as Ali the Great (reigned 1465–92) and Askia Muhammad I (reigned 1492–1528), supported the Timbuktu mosques. At Agadez, now in northern Niger, Askia Muhammad I is believed to have built the original Great Mosque in 1515. This striking foundation has a rectangular prayer hall with single *mihrab* and a tapering tower minaret with projecting beams. The mosque was rebuilt in 1844.

CHINGUETTI MOSQUE

On the caravan route through the western Sahara at the oasis city of Chinguetti (now in Mauritania), Berber or Arab traders built a great dry-stone Friday Mosque in the 13th or 14th century. The mosque has a square minaret, a courtyard and a flat-roofed prayer hall with walls of split stone and clay, four aisles, a twin *mihrab* and *minbar* (pulpit) and a sand-covered floor.

Crenellations at each corner of the top of the minaret are topped with clay sculptures of ostrich eggs, with a fifth egg sculpture in the centre. When looked at from the west, it identifies the direction of Makkah. By tradition, the area was once home to many ostriches.

EAST AFRICAN BUILDINGS

The oldest surviving religious foundations along the East African coast are the Mosque of Fakhr al-Din in Mogadishu (now capital of Somalia) and the Great Mosque of Kilwa Kisiswani (an island port off the coast of what is now Tanzania). The first of these religious foundations was built in 1269 by the first sultan of Mogadishu. It has a marble-panelled main façade and three doorways leading through into a lobby that is used for ablutions. The lobby opens into a courtyard, beyond which stands an arcaded, five-bay portico with a central dome, and beyond that a prayer hall. The hall has nine bays, with a high dome above the central one; the marble *mihrab* is inscribed with the image of a lamp hanging from a chain.

The Great Mosque at Kilwa Kisiswani has a smaller 11th–12th-century northern prayer hall and a larger 14th-century southern prayer hall. Both parts are covered with vaulted roofs and domes: the mosque is notable as one of the earliest built without a courtyard.

Above The Great Mosque on Kilwa Kisiswani island, East Africa, was built from the 11th century onward.

THE ILKHANIDS AND THEIR ARCHITECTURE

AS THEY SET OUT TO DEMONSTRATE THEIR GREATNESS BY BUILDING ON A GRAND SCALE, THE ILKHANID SULTANS FOLLOWED IRANIAN ARCHITECTURAL TRADITIONS ESTABLISHED IN THE SELJUK ERA.

Former nomads, the Ilkhanid rulers spent winters in the region of Baghdad and summers in grassy pasturelands of north-western Iran. There, the second Ilkhanid Sultan, Abaqa Khan (reigned 1265–82), built the vast, lavishly decorated summer palace of Takht-i Sulayman and the fourth sultan, Arghun Khan (reigned 1284–91), established Tabriz as the capital of the Ilkhanate.

When he came to power, Ghazan Khan (reigned 1295–1304) converted to Sunni Islam, and with his Iranian vizier Rashid al-Din he embarked upon an enormous building programme, constructing *caravanserais* (travellers' inns) along major trade routes and building a congregational mosque and bathhouse in each city. Ghazan Khan also rebuilt the walls of Tabriz, which he developed into a major city of international standing. He then built a grand funerary complex to house his own remains in western Tabriz, with two *madrasas* (religious colleges), an astronomical observatory, library, hospice and other buildings around his tomb. Rashid al-Din constructed a complex in his own name in the eastern part of the city.

ILKHANID MOSQUES

One of the best-preserved mosques of the Ilkhanid period is the Friday, or congregational, Mosque built in 1322–26 under Abu Said, the ninth ruler of the Ilkhanate at Varamin, 42km (26 miles) south of Tehran. The Varamin Mosque was built following the traditional Iranian pattern established under the Seljuks: four *iwans* (halls) built around a central courtyard, with a domed prayer hall with the *mihrab* (niche) behind the *qibla iwan* (the hall in the direction of Makkah).

Above The magnificent dome, spanning an impressive 25m (82 ft), at Uljaytu's tomb at Sultaniyya, in Iran is one of the masterpieces of world architecture.

In Tabriz, however, the mosque of the vizier Ali Shah built in 1315 under the rule of Uljaytu (reigned 1304–16) had a different layout: there was a single *iwan* leading on to the courtyard, which contained a pool and was enclosed by walls 30m (98ft) in length, 10m (33ft) thick and 25m (82ft) high; the *mihrab* was set in a vast semicircular bastion extending behind the *qibla* wall. Originally, there was a grand entrance portal at the far end of the courtyard, and a *madrasa* and hospice for Sufis stood on either side of the *iwan*.

ULJAYTU'S MAUSOLEUM

The eighth Ilkhanid ruler Uljaytu constructed a new capital called Sultaniyya ('Royal Ground') about 120km (75 miles) north-west of Qazvin in north-western Iran, where Arghun Khan had built a

Left Under Hulagu, Genghis Khan's grandson, the Mongol invasions of the 1250s gave the Ilkhanids control over a huge empire.

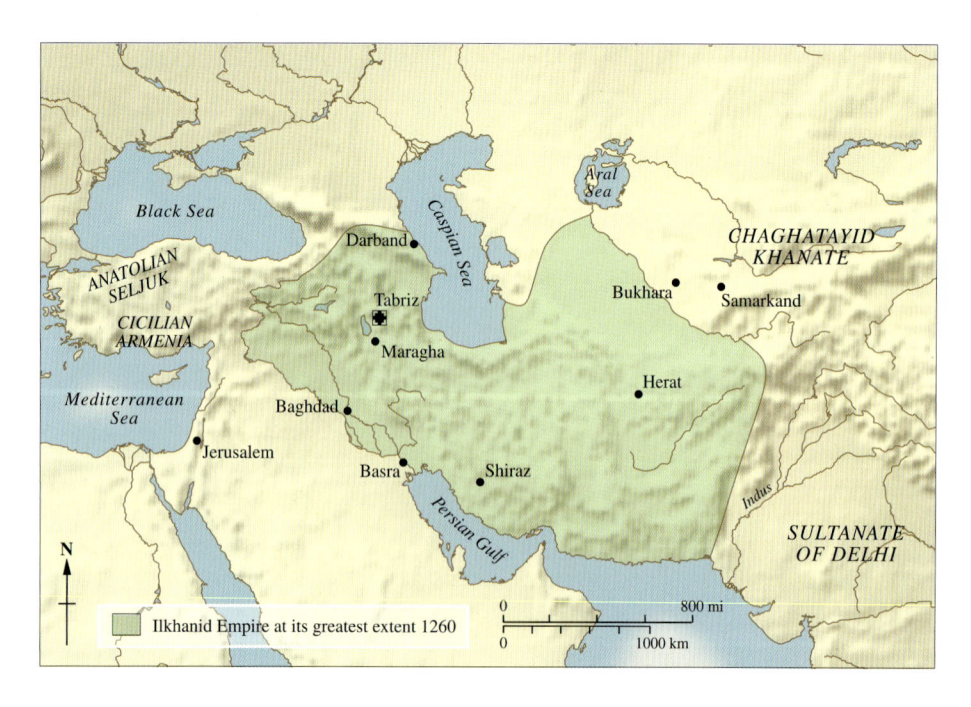

THE ILKHANIDS AND THEIR ARCHITECTURE

Above The octagonal tomb of Sufi saint Abd al-Samad is part of a fine early 14th-century complex at Natanz in Iran that includes a four-iwan Friday Mosque.

summer residence. All that remains today of the city is the Uljaytu's vast octagonal mausoleum, 38m (125ft) in diameter, with eight minarets. It has a beautiful, pointed dome, standing 50m (164ft) high, that was once covered in turquoise tiles. Beneath the dome is an arcaded gallery with a ceiling decorated in coloured stucco and terracotta carving. There are views for miles across the plain from a circuit of vaulted galleries, in which the ceilings are decorated with carved plaster designs painted in patterns markedly similar to those found in the contemporary illuminated manuscripts.

This mausoleum's extraordinary dome is recognized by architects as one of the greatest architectural achievements in the world. According to tradition, it was built on such a grand scale because

Right Calligrapher Haydar picked out floral decoration and sacred phrases on this stucco mihrab of 1310 in the winter iwan at the Friday Mosque, Isfahan.

Uljaytu, who was a Shiah Muslim, was originally planning to move the body of Imam Ali from his tomb at Najaf in Iraq and re-inter it beneath the dome at Sultaniyya. Uljaytu was later dissuaded from this plan and instead made the building his own tomb.

CARVED DECORATION

During Uljaytu's reign, in 1310, a magnificent stucco *mihrab* was added to the winter *iwan* of the Friday Mosque in Isfahan. It was designed and carved by Haydar, the pre-eminent calligrapher of the day, and featured arabesque decoration, floral designs and calligraphic inscriptions. The building of the *mihrab* was ordered to mark the conversion of Uljaytu to Shiah Islam in 1309, an event that had provoked opposition among the mostly Sunni inhabitants of Isfahan.

Haidar's work can also be seen in an inscription band on the north *iwan* at the Friday Mosque in Natanz, central Iran. The mosque was part of a complex built in 1300–10 by vizier Zayn al-Din Mastari around the grave of revered Sufi saint Abd al-Samad, who had died in 1299. The complex included a hospice for Sufis, as well as the tomb and mosque.

91

Takht-i Sulayman

THE SUMMER PALACE OF TAKHT-I SULAYMAN IN NORTH-WESTERN IRAN (C.1275) IS A RARE EXAMPLE OF SURVIVING ILKHANID SECULAR ARCHITECTURE. A NOTED OBSERVATORY WAS BUILT NEARBY.

When Abaqa Khan, the second ruler of the Ilkhanid Empire, built Takht-i Sulayman, he set out to demonstrate his legitimacy as head of an Iranian empire. The complex stands in a breathtaking natural setting. He chose the site on which it was built because it held a ruined sanctuary used for the coronations of the pre-Islamic Sasanian emperors of Iran (226–651). Dragons and phoenixes featured in the lavish tiled decoration of the palace, because these mythical creatures were established Chinese motifs that symbolized imperial authority. Quotations from the *Shahnama* (Book of Kings), the national epic poem of Iran written by Firdawsi in the 11th century, were also incorporated into the decoration.

Below The lake was central to the design of the once-magnificent royal summer palace of Takht-i Sulayman, built by Ilkhanid ruler Abaqa Khan.

The site was located south-east of Lake Urmia in the Azerbaijan province of north-western Iran. It had been called Shiz by the Sasanians and was the location of an important Zoroastrian fire temple at which Sasanian kings performed rituals before they ascended the throne; in the Ilkhanid era it was called Saturiq. The later name Takht-i Sulayman means 'the Throne of Solomon'. The palace stands on an extinct volcano, where a spring flowing into the central crater had created a lake. According to local folk legend, King Solomon bound monsters in the nearby volcano and created the lake that dominates the site.

COURTYARD AND LAKE

The remains at Takht-i Sulayman were excavated from 1959–78. The palace was built around a vast courtyard running north to south, measuring 150m by 125m (492ft by 410ft) and incorporating the lake. The courtyard was surrounded – as was traditional in an Iranian palace (or mosque) – by four *iwans* (halls) situated behind great porticoes.

The south *iwan* was 17m (56ft) wide and featured a grand staircase at the centre rising to a domed hall.

Above Astronomers at work in Hulagu Khan's observatory at Maragha, from a 16th-century edition of the Nusratnama.

At the other end of the complex, the north *iwan* stood before a domed chamber, probably used as an audience room. The courtyard had to be large because the lake's dimensions could not be altered: as a result it is one of the largest four-*iwan* layouts in the Persian tradition.

TWIN PAVILIONS

Beyond the west *iwan* was a flat-roofed hall between two domed octagonal pavilions; this was the sovereign's living quarters. The remains of what must have been a beautiful set of *muqarnas* (vaulting) were found in the southerly pavilion. The northern pavilion – built on the site that the Ilkhanids believed was once the coronation area of the Sasanians – was lavishly decorated. The lower walls of the pavilion were covered in tiles in star and cross shapes; above was a frieze of tiles depicting scenes and quotations from the *Shahnama* (Book of Kings) and Chinese symbols of kingship.

Archaeologists also discovered a square stucco plaque with sides measuring 50cm (20in), covered in drawings of part of a *muqarnas* vault at Takht-i Sulayman. Historians believe the drawings were used as a guide by workmen to help them put cast units together to form the dome. From contemporary accounts we learn that designs for buildings of this kind were often drawn up in the capital before being sent to the site in question; this plaque is one of the few pieces of evidence that this occurred.

MARAGHA OBSERVATORY

At the Ilkhanids' summer capital Maragha, 30km (19 miles) west of Takht-i Sulayman, Hulagu Khan (*c*.1216–65) built an astronomical observatory atop a hill around 500m (1,640ft) north of the town, beginning in 1259. The director was Nasir al-Din al-Tusi (1201–74), the notable scientist and astronomer, working with a large team of eminent scientists. There was a central tower of four storeys with a quadrant measuring no less than 45m (148ft) in diameter, a foundry used for making astronomical instruments and a library that reputedly held 400,000 volumes. Observations made at the observatory in 1260–72 were recorded in Persian in the *Zij-i Ilkhani* (Ilkhanid Tables), which included data tables for working out the positions of the planets. By tradition, Hulagu Khan attributed his military successes to the advice he received from astrologers, so to ensure future success he built the observatory and funded the collection of information for the *Zij-i Ilkhani*. The Maragha scientists sought to resolve inconsistencies with the geocentric model of the universe and their work influenced the Polish astronomer Nicolaus Copernicus.

Above This celestial brass globe (1275), at Maragha, was signed by 'Muhammad ibn Hilal, astronomer from Mosul'.

BAHRAM GUR

The palace of Takht-i Sulayman was decorated with a number of pictorial tiles illustrating episodes from the *Shahnama* (Book of Kings). One example shows the popular story of Bahram Gur: the king was out hunting antelopes on a camel, with his female slave Azada riding behind him. She asked Bahram Gur to transform a male antelope into a female, and a female into a male, so he fired two arrows that knocked the horns from the head of a male antelope, before firing two more to create 'horns' on the head of a female antelope. Unimpressed, Azada laughed at him and declared that practice had simply made him perfect. Bahram Gur was maddened and threw her from her perch, and she was trampled underfoot.

Above Hunting scenes were a favourite subject for palace decoration. This tile shows riders bringing down an antelope.

ISLAMIC ARCHITECTURE THROUGH THE CENTURIES

THE TIMURID DYNASTY

TURKIC CONQUEROR TIMUR IS KNOWN CHIEFLY FOR HIS RUTHLESSNESS. YET, HE AND THE SUCCESSORS OF HIS DYNASTY CREATED AN IMPRESSIVE ARCHITECTURAL AND CULTURAL LEGACY.

Probably the greatest conqueror in Islamic history, Timur (reigned 1370–1405) rose from being a minor chief near Samarkand, to rule an empire stretching from Anatolia to the borders of China. He achieved this despite a birth handicap that won him the nickname of Timur Lenk ('the Lame') – his upper thigh, right knee and right shoulder were malformed and he could get about only by using crutches or on horseback. The variations of his name, such as Tamerlane or Tamburlaine, are European corruptions of Timur the Lame. In 1941, Soviet scientists examined his skeleton and found evidence of these disabilities.

A MONGOL DESCENDANT

Timur was descended from the Barlas tribe, a Mongol tribal group that settled in Transoxiana (roughly in modern Uzbekistan). With his brother-in-law Amir Husayn, he won control of Transoxiana by 1366; then he turned against Husayn and in the ancient city of Samarkand declared himself sole ruler in 1370. His culture was Turkic: he used the Turkic title *amir* rather than the Mongol *khan*. But he set out to restore the Mongol Empire created by his ancestors, and kept marriage ties with Genghis Khan's bloodline.

Despite having defeated many Muslim rulers, Timur presented himself as a religious warrior, or *ghazi*. His conquests were brutal. According to estimates, 17 million people were killed in the course of his campaigns; he sacked and burnt many ancient cities, creating gruesome pyramids of his victims' heads, and laid waste to vast areas. He died at the age of 69 in 1405 while leading an invasion of China. Yet, the Timurid dynasty he founded survived until 1526, despite dynastic in-fighting, and in India more than 300 years longer still, as the Mughal Empire that ended only in 1857, which was founded by an Asian Timurid prince, Babur (1483–1530), a direct descendant of Timur.

Above The battered remains of the vast 50-m (164-ft) tall entrance portal is all that survives of Timur's Aq Saray Palace in Shahr-i Sabz (or Kesh).

TIMURID PATRONAGE

On campaign, Timur spared artisans and craftsmen when he could, and dispatched hordes of conscripted masons, stucco workers, painters, tilers, potters, weavers and glassmakers to Samarkand. There, they reputedly worked on splendid palaces, fitted with carpets and decorated with mosaics and murals depicting his conquests, but these structures are now lost.

In Timur's lifetime, and in the Timurid era that followed, when princes of the dynasty competed

TIMUR'S REPUTATION

Timur was celebrated in Renaissance Europe as the embodiment of ruthless conquest, particularly for his defeat and capture of Ottoman Sultan Bayezid I at the Battle of Ankara in July 1402, followed by his humiliation of Bayezid in captivity. According to traditional (but probably invented) tales of these events, Timur kept Bayezid in a cage and used his kneeling body as a footstool when mounting his horse. Timur was the subject of the play *Tamburlaine the Great* (1590) by English dramatist Christopher Marlowe, and of the opera *Tamerlano* (1724) by Handel. Today, he is celebrated as a national hero in the former Soviet republic of Uzbekistan, independent since 1991; an equestrian statue of the conqueror stands in the capital, Tashkent.

Left An equestrian statue of Timur has been erected in Tashkent, where the conqueror is celebrated as a hero of Uzbekistan.

as patrons of architecture and the arts, magnificent mosques, *madrasas* (religious colleges) and palatial tomb complexes were built in the major cities of the empire, such as Samarkand and Herat. These buildings were characterized by their vast size and beautiful facing of multicoloured tile mosaic.

In his hometown of Shahr-i Sabz (or Kesh), 80km (50 miles) south of Samarkand, Timur built the grand Aq Saray Palace ('White Palace'), with a decorated entrance portal 50m (164ft) high bearing the inscription: 'If you have doubts as to our power, just look at the buildings we raise.' He also built a grand memorial complex named Dar al-Sadat ('House of Power'), which appears to have contained a domed chamber and mausoleum. The Dar al-Sadat was seemingly intended to house Timur's own remains. Both these grand buildings survive only in fragments.

BIBI KHANUM MOSQUE

In Samarkand in 1399–1404, Timur oversaw the construction of the Bibi Khanum Friday (congregational) Mosque, which contained a prayer hall with a dome 44m (144ft) tall that measured 140m by 99m (460ft by 325ft), making it one of the largest mosques in the world. The entrance portal stood between polygonal towers covered in mosaic decoration, and behind it the courtyard was surrounded by galleries beneath domes that were supported by marble columns. There were two smaller domed rooms at the courtyard's cross-axis and a tall, thin minaret at each corner. Soon after construction parts of this enormous building began to fall apart under the weight of its own bricks, which was not helped by the region's frequent small earthquakes. In the 1970s it was rebuilt by the Soviet Union at third of its original size.

Above Small domed side chambers at the Bibi Khanum Friday Mosque in Samarkand are exquisitely tiled in geometric patterns and bands of Quranic inscriptions.

In Bukhara in 1400–50, the Kalan Friday Mosque was built on the same model, but with a polygonal niche at the entrance portal; the galleries around the courtyard have 288 domes held on pillars, and the prayer hall has a grand *maqsura* (private prayer area) with a beautifully tiled *mihrab*.

MADRASAS OF ULUGH BEG

Timur's grandson Ulugh Beg is remembered as a man of learning, a mathematician and astronomer, and the builder of three great *madrasas*: at Bukhara in 1418, at Samarkand in 1420 and at Gishduwan in 1437. The *madrasa* at Bukhara has a tall entrance portal with pointed arch and two-storey arcade sections on each side leading to corner towers; behind the entrance a square hall gives access to two domed side chambers (one a mosque for winter use, and one a classroom) and the courtyard, which has two *iwans* (halls).

The *madrasa* in Samarkand had a *pishtaq* (projecting portal) 45m (148ft) tall in the entrance façade, which faces the city's main square. The *madrasa* covers 81m by 56m (266ft by 184ft): its interior courtyard, measuring 30sq m (98sq ft), has a minaret at each corner and four *iwans*, as well as 50 student rooms arranged around the yard over two storeys. In the rear wall there is a rectangular mosque set between domed chambers. This was a highly prestigious *madrasa* and it hosted many great religious and secular scholars of the Timurid period. The *madrasa* at Gishduwan has a grand entrance portal, but is more modest, with just four sets of student rooms on each side of the courtyard. Ulugh Beg also built an important astronomical observatory in Samarkand in 1428–29.

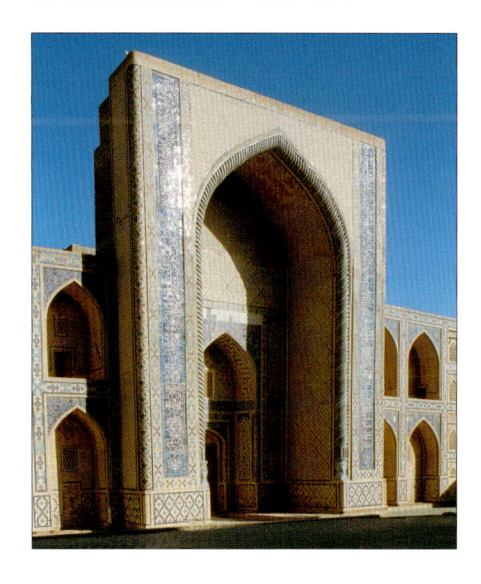

Above The magnificent entrance portal to Ulugh Beg's madrasa at Bukhara was built in 1418.

SAMARKAND TOMBS

TIMUR'S CAPITAL SAMARKAND, NOW IN UZBEKISTAN, IS CELEBRATED FOR DOMED MAUSOLEA DECORATED WITH EXQUISITE TILE WORK AND MOSAICS, BUILT IN THE LATE 14TH TO 15TH CENTURIES.

One of the grandest of the Samarkand tombs is the Gur-e Amir (Lord's Tomb) mausoleum, initially built in 1403 to house the remains of Timur's favourite grandson, Muhammad Sultan. The Gur-e Amir was built as part of a complex containing a *madrasa* (religious college) and a *khanqa* (hospice), around a walled courtyard with a minaret at each corner. Today, only the entrance portal, part of one minaret and the foundations of the *madrasa* and *khanqa* remain in addition to the mausoleum, which has been substantially restored.

A DYNASTIC MAUSOLEUM

Timur had built a mausoleum for himself in his hometown of Shahr-i Sabz. However, on his death in 1405, his body could not be carried to Shahr-i Sabz because the route was blocked by snow, so instead he was buried in the Gur-e Amir Mausoleum. Ulugh Beg oversaw the completion of the mausoleum, and added a grand entrance portal to the complex in 1434: the beautifully tiled portal bears the name of its builder Muhammad ibn Mahmud al-Banna al-Isfahani. During Ulugh Beg's reign, the Gur-e Amir tomb became established as the dynastic mausoleum. Along with Timur and Muhammad Sultan, it was the burial place of Timur's sons Shah Rukh and Miran Shah, and of Ulugh Beg himself.

The mausoleum is octagonal on the outside but has a square chamber within, 10m (33ft) long on each side, and supporting a high drum with decorative facing beneath a ribbed, pointed, azure blue dome 34m (112ft) high. The outside of the drum bears a *kufic* inscription, set in tiles, declaring that 'Allah is eternal', and there are geometric patterns of glazed and plain bricks. This particular use of glazed bricks arranged in geometric patterns within groups of unglazed bricks has become known as the *banna'i* technique.

Above The interiors of the mausolea in the Shah-i Zinda complex in Samarkand are tiled in intricate patterns. No two decorative schemes are the same.

The inside of the building is lavishly fitted and decorated. The internal dome rises to a height of 26m (85ft), its inner surface once coloured with relief work of gilded papier-mâché; hexagons of onyx and painted decoration cover the lower walls rising to a cornice of *muqarnas* (stalactite-like decorative vaulting), and above, an inscription band. Each wall has a rectangular bay beneath *muqarnas* domes. In the south-east corner of the square chamber, steps lead down to the cross-shaped, domed burial crypt beneath. Some historians identify this breathtaking domed building as the model for the mausolea built by the Mughal descendants of the Timurids in India, notably the Tomb of Humayan in Delhi and the Taj Mahal in Agra.

SHAH-I ZINDA COMPLEX

Another beautiful collection of tombs in Samarkand is the Shah-i Zinda ('Living King') complex. This was built up over the years

Left The tomb chamber beneath the Gur-e Amir mausoleum in Samarkand contains the bodies of Timur and several of his descendants.

Right Remains of the Gur-e Amir complex include the grand entrance portal and the distinctive mausoleum, with its ribbed dome set upon a cylindrical drum.

1360–1434 in the vicinity of the reputed Tomb of Qutham ibn Abbas, the cousin of the Prophet, which had been restored in 1334–60. According to tradition, after Qutham ibn Abbas came to the region in the 7th century to preach the new faith founded by Muhammad, he was beheaded but escaped down a well or crevice, where he is said to be living still.

Arranged along a stepped pathway that runs 70m (230ft) to the north from the old city walls, the tombs in this complex were mostly single-room structures. A monumental entrance marks the start of the complex and was added by Ulugh Beg after 1434.

Many of the entrance portals are beautifully decorated with tile mosaics, some with gold leaf added; there are also glazed bricks, glazed terracotta, wall paintings, wood carvings, *muqarnas*, stucco, coloured glass and painted ceramic pieces; and there are beautiful calligraphic inscriptions in both Arabic and Persian that quote from the Quran and from poetic elegies.

There are fine examples of work produced with the minai or *cuerda seca* techniques that were also used by Safavid craftsmen in the holy buildings of Isfahan. *Cuerda seca* means 'dry cord' and refers to lines of a black substance used to mark out areas of glaze: the artists applied the glaze within these lines, which burnt away in the kiln.

OTHER COMPLEXES

Elsewhere in Samarkand, the Ishrat Khane ('Place of Joy') mausoleum complex was built by Ishrat Khane,

Below The necropolis of Shah-i Zinda stands in an elevated position, just beyond the ancient city limits of Samarkand.

wife of Timurid ruler Abu Said in 1464. The structure has survived mostly in its original state without renovation. It has a large, beautifully decorated entrance portal and sizeable central chamber beneath a dome raised on overlapping arches, beneath which is the octagonal domed burial chamber.

The palatial mausoleum Aq Saray (c.1450) stands close to the Gur-e Amir complex, but all that remains is the central chamber, with corner rooms, and a hall attached on the north side. The surviving interior decoration is beautiful, with the finest tile mosaics and relief work painted in blue and gold below elegant vaults.

ISLAMIC ARCHITECTURE THROUGH THE CENTURIES

TIMURID HERAT

THE TIMURID DYNASTY MOVED ITS CAPITAL TO HERAT IN THE EARLY 15TH CENTURY. THIS ANCIENT CITY ENJOYED A RENAISSANCE, DURING WHICH SEVERAL IMPRESSIVE MONUMENTS WERE BUILT.

The conquests of Timur had established a powerful empire in the East, but this threatened to disintegrate after his death in 1405, as bitter rivalries surfaced. Shah Rukh – Timur's only surviving son – decided against moving to his father's base in Samarkand. Instead, he chose Herat as the new capital and appointed his son, Ulugh Beg, as governor of Samarkand.

AN ESTABLISHED CITY

Herat, in present-day Afghanistan, was an old city with an illustrious past. Pre-Islamic Persian rulers as well as early Muslim dynasties had recognized the city for its military and commercial importance. It also had an impressive cultural reputation and was known in the Islamic world for its high-quality metalwork. Yet, before Shah Rukh's time, the Mongols had demolished the city and, in 1381, Timur had sacked it again.

The accession of Shah Rukh opened a new chapter for Herat. He set about rebuilding the city, transforming his court into a major artistic centre. He is probably best remembered as the patron of a number of outstanding illuminated manuscripts, while the surviving architectural monuments are more closely associated with his wife, Gawhar Shad.

MOSQUE OF GAWHAR SHAD

In nearby Mashhad, Gawhar Shad commissioned a new mosque (1416–18) as part of the renovations around the shrine of Imam Reza, a popular destination for pilgrims. The building is especially famous for its outstanding tile work. Though Islamic architects had for a long time adorned the domes and façades of their buildings with colourful glazed tiles, this art form reached its peak during the Timurid period. The mosque at Mashhad is a fine example, featuring extensive sections of cut-tile mosaic.

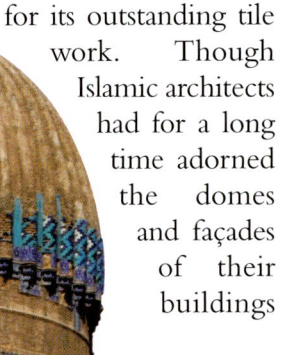

Above The shrine of Abdullah Ansari at Gazargah lies within a hazira – *an enclosed burial ground* – *located within a four-*iwan *courtyard.*

MUSALLAH COMPLEX

The mosque was designed by Qavam al-Din Shirazi (d.1438), one of the most successful of the Timurid architects. When finished, the queen commissioned him to undertake an even more ambitious project – a complex of buildings in Herat. These included Gawhar Shad's mausoleum, a *madrasa* (religious college) and a congregational mosque.

The complex must have been spectacular, but only two minarets and the tomb have survived. Much of it was destroyed during military campaigns in the 19th century, and by an earthquake in 1932. The best-preserved section is the domed

Left Gawhar Shad's mausoleum in Herat has a distinctive ribbed cupola.

mausoleum, which rests on a 16-sided drum base. Eight Timurid princes were buried here, along with Gawhar Shad herself. Only two minarets remain from the *madrasa* and the mosque, but their glazed tiles embellished with floral motifs and *kufic* inscriptions are a hint of their former splendour.

OTHER MAJOR PROJECTS

Progress on the complex of Gawhar Shad was slow, taking almost 20 years to complete. This was because, in 1425, Shah Rukh diverted the architect to build the Abdullah Ansari funerary shrine at Gazargah, just outside Herat.

Ansari was a 12th-century Sufi mystic, revered as the *pir* (wise man and guardian) of Herat. His tomb had long been a place of pilgrimage for Sunnis, and Qavam al-Din's new shrine added to its prestige. The most impressive feature there is a massive *pishtaq* (monumental portal), 30m (98ft) high, which soars over the tomb. The decorations include *banna'i* designs, another form of tile work favoured by the Timurids. Here, the technique was to lay the glazed bricks on their ends, to form zigzag patterns or angular inscriptions.

Qavam al-Din's last commission was a *madrasa* at Khargird, which was completed after his death. The structure is now in ruins, but there are enough remains to clearly demonstrate its similarity to the Ansari shrine. This is evident from the panels of glazed-brick decoration and the arrangement of the entrance bays.

Another important Timurid monument in the region is the Funerary Mosque of Abu Nasr Parsa at Balkh, a spiritual leader in Herat who died in 1460. The mosque was begun shortly after his death, but its completion date is unclear. The entrance has a huge *pishtaq*, and the mosaic decoration displays Chinese influences.

Above The intricate carvings in Ansari's tomb complex at Gazargah are centred on a 16-point star, flanked by two stylized trees.

Below At Abu Nasr Parsa's shrine at Balkh, the cut-tile mosaics combine floral and geometric designs.

SAFAVID ISFAHAN

BUILDING STATELY MOSQUES, PALACES AND A BAZAAR AROUND A NEW CENTRAL *MAIDAN*, OR SQUARE, SAFAVID SHAH ABBAS I TRANSFORMED ISFAHAN INTO A FITTING CAPITAL FOR HIS DYNASTY'S PERSIAN EMPIRE.

The sublime architecture built by Shah Abbas I (reigned 1587–1629), fifth and greatest ruler of the Safavid dynasty, is regarded as the supreme achievement of the Safavid era. Situated on the river Zayandeh Rud in central Iran about 340km (211 miles) south of Tehran, Isfahan had been a town of note as far back as the Parthian Empire (238BCE–226CE), and a capital under the Seljuk Turks (11th–14th centuries). It reached a golden age when Shah Abbas made Isfahan the new Safavid capital and began a grand building programme in 1598.

A NEW CITY CENTRE

Abbas I made a new centre by laying out a vast rectangular *maidan*, or square, known as Maidan-e Shah (King's Square), and now renamed Maidan-e Imam, or Imam Square. Covering 8ha (20 acres), the *maidan* was built in 1590–95, initially as a public space for state ceremonial, military and sporting events. In a second building stage, completed by 1602, a double-storey arcade of shops was laid out around the perimeter.

On the north side of the *maidan* the shah oversaw the building of a covered two-storey bazaar entered by a grand portal decorated with a tile mosaic of Sagittarius the archer, because the city was founded under this astrological sign, and frescoes showing Abbas I's military victories over the Uzbek Shaybanid dynasty. The bazaar contained a 140-room royal *caravanserai*, baths, a hospital and the royal mint.

TWO MAJOR MOSQUES

On the east side of the square, the Lutfallah Mosque, named after the scholar Shaykh Lutfallah Maisi al-Amili, was erected in 1603–19. A grand entrance portal on the square gives access to the mosque's prayer hall, a single square-domed room measuring 19m (62ft) on each side, and set at a 45-degree angle to the portal, so that the *mihrab* (niche) and *qibla* wall (indicating the direction of prayer) could be aligned to Makkah. The inner dome is finely decorated with glazed tiles in a sunburst design at the apex and medallions filled with floral designs running down the dome's sides. This was the shah's private oratory.

On the south side of the *maidan* another great entrance portal, finely decorated with tiers of *muqarnas* (stalactite-like decoration) domes and tile mosaic, gives access to the Masjid-e Imam, or Imam's Mosque. Originally known as the Masjid-e Shah (King's Mosque), this large congregational mosque was built in 1611–30 to replace the older Friday Mosque in the Seljuk part of Isfahan.

Its traditional layout consists of a courtyard measuring 70m (230ft) on each side, surrounded by arcades and with an *iwan* (hall) in the centre of each side, with a domed prayer hall behind the *qibla iwan*. As with the Lutfallah Mosque, the entrance *iwan* fronts the square, but the main part of the complex behind is shifted 45 degrees so that the *qibla* wall is aligned to Makkah. The side *iwans* on the courtyard lead into

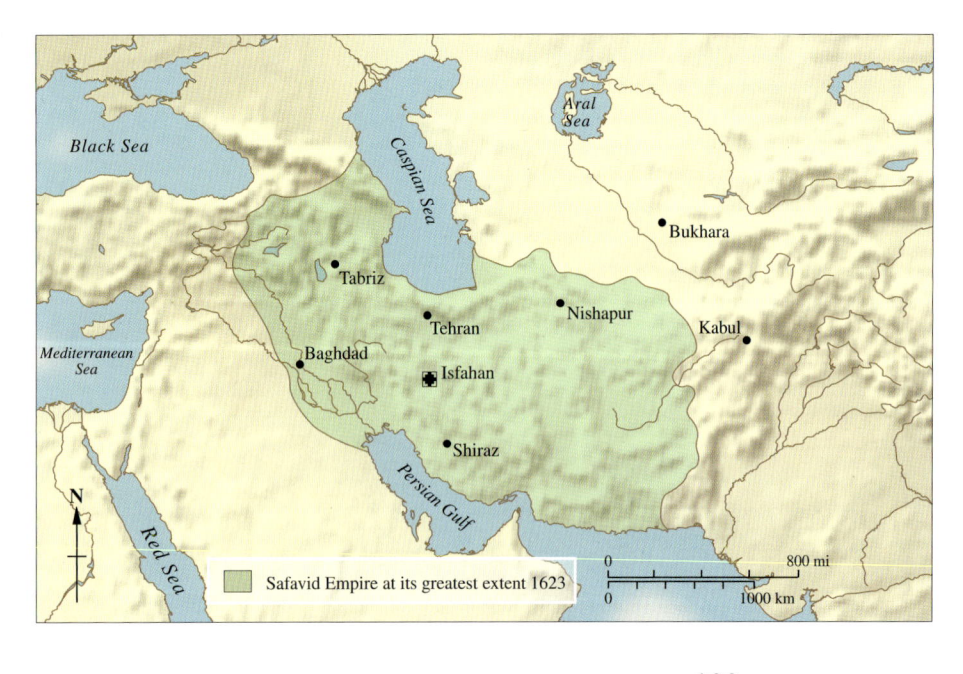

Above The ceiling in the music room at the Ali Qapu Palace on Maidan-e Imam. The Ali Qapu was originally just a gateway into the royal gardens.

Left The Safavid Empire reached its peak under Shah Abbas I (reigned 1587–1629). He made Isfahan the capital city.

Right *The interior of the Lutfallah Mosque in Isfahan is decorated with ceramic tiles on every surface.*

domed chambers, while behind the arcading on each side of the main courtyard is another arcaded yard that was used as a *madrasa* (religious college). There are four minarets, but the call to prayer was given from a small building, called *guldasta* in Persian, situated above the west *iwan*. The grand dome above the prayer hall is 52m (170ft) tall; like the Gur-e Amir in Samarkand, it has a double shell, with a bulbous outer dome rising above its inner dome.

GARDENS AND PALACES

On the west side of the *maidan*, Abbas I built the Ali Qapu ('Highest Gate'). Originally an entrance to the royal gardens, this was reworked as a palace with a raised veranda, or *talar*, that was used as a royal viewing platform when displays, parades or sporting events, such as polo matches, were held on the *maidan*.

The Ali Qapu was the entrance to 7ha (17 acres) of royal parkland containing pavilions, garden palaces and walled gardens. In the park, the Chihil Sutun ('Forty Columns') Palace built by Shah Abbas II (reigned 1642–66) stands beside a rectangular pool. The palace has a flat-roofed *talar* supported by tall pillars of the kind built in pre-Islamic Persia. Despite its name, the palace has only 20 pillars: it appears to have 40 because they are reflected in the pool. The palace contains a large hall and many murals of court life. Also in the gardens is the Hasht Behesht ('Eight Heavens') Palace, built by Shah Sulaiman I (reigned 1666–94).

Below *The view across the square looks south to the Masjid e-Imam which is angled toward Makkah.*

RIVERSIDE IMPROVEMENTS

Shah Abbas I's redevelopment of Isfahan also included the laying out of the Chahar Bagh esplanade from the *maidan* to the river Zayandeh. This splendid avenue was lined with the palaces of leading nobles. Great bridges were built across the river. The Si-o Se Pol ('Thirty-three Arch Bridge'), constructed in 1602 by Allahvardi Khan, general to Shah Abbas I, is 300m (984ft) long and has pavilions from which pedestrians can take in the view. New Julfa, a quarter for Armenian merchants, was built on the opposite bank.

ISLAMIC ARCHITECTURE THROUGH THE CENTURIES

MUGHAL TOMBS

ARCHITECTURE UNDER THE MUGHALS ACHIEVED A WONDERFUL BLEND OF HINDU AND PERSIAN STYLES. THE MOST SPECTACULAR EXAMPLES ARE MONUMENTAL TOMBS, OFTEN IN A GARDEN SETTING.

Though the glorification of the dead is alien to the spirit of Islam, there are many outstanding tombs built in Islamic lands. 'The most beautiful tomb,' according to the Prophet Muhammad, 'is one that vanishes from the face of the earth.' Yet magnificent tombs were built by rulers to perpetuate and glorify their names or at the desire of a community of believers to honour their saints. The tombs of rulers were often built by the rulers themselves, whereas those of saints were the gift of their disciples.

Sher Shah (reigned 1540–45), the Afghan ruler who seized the throne and forced Humayun into exile, built his own monumental mausoleum at Sasaram. At the time it was completed, in 1545, it was the largest tomb ever built in India. Its setting in the middle of an artificial lake and its octagonal shape are both allusions to the Islamic notion of paradise. The tomb rises in three tiers of diminishing size and is crowned by a Hindu-style dome.

Below The red sandstone exterior of Humayun's imposing tomb in Delhi is picked out in relief with white marble.

Above The shadowed interior of the Tomb of Salim Chishti at Fatehpur Sikri is lit by intricately carved marble latticework windows, or jalis.

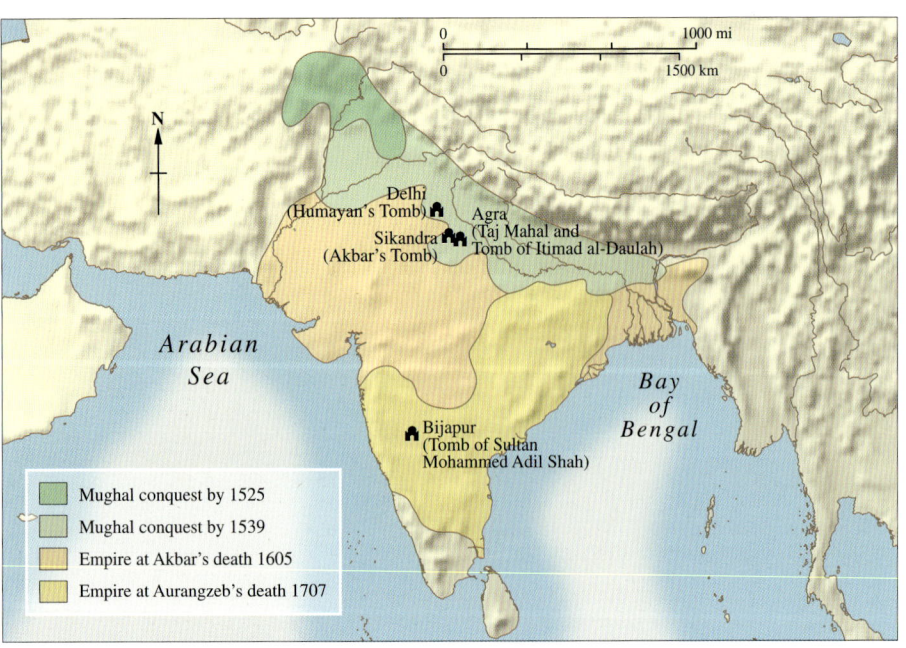

TOMB OF HUMAYUN

Humayun's mausoleum in Delhi was, and remains, a fine example of Indo-Islamic architecture and was one of the first of many garden tombs built during the Mughal period. It was probably built my Humayun's son Akbar. Construction began in 1562 and continued for nine years. Set on a wide, high platform, the mausoleum has four double-storey pavilions set in a square, creating a central space between them. The space is crowned by a white marble dome mounted on a high drum. The red sandstone exterior is picked out in relief with white Makrana marble. Inside the tomb, a system of corridors allows for the circumambulation of the central cenotaph (a monument for a person whose remains are elsewhere). High walls surrounding the garden are intersected by four gates.

Humayun's son, Akbar (reigned 1556–1605), ordered the construction of a tomb at Fatehpur Sikri to honour Shaykh Salim Chishti, the saint who had

Left The growth of the Mughal Empire across the subcontinent and the sites of the major Mughal tombs.

MUGHAL TOMBS

Above With three tiers of diminishing size, the Tomb of Sher Shah at Sasaram is crowned by a Hindu-style dome.

predicted the birth of his son, Jahangir. Built of luminous white marble, the tiny tomb lies at the feet of the red sandstone walls of the city's great mosque. The tomb's canopy is inlaid with ebony and mother-of-pearl. Jahangir (reigned 1605–27) added exquisite marble screens, mosaic flooring and a walkway paved in marble.

GARDEN TOMBS IN AGRA

The garden setting of Akbar's own tomb at Sikandra, near Agra, follows the same basic design as Humayun's tomb. Set in a *chahar bagh*, or four-part garden of Persian origin, the tomb consists of five storeys, surmounted by red domed kiosks supported on pillars. The tomb's upper storey is open to the sky, and in the centre is Akbar's white marble cenotaph. His actual grave lies in a domed hall at ground level, reached through a portico. The tomb complex is entered by an imposing gateway. At its four corners rise white marble minarets.

OTHER IMPORTANT TOMBS

The tomb of Itimad al-Daulah in Agra was built in 1622–28 by Nur Jahan, the wife of Jahangir, for her parents. The mausoleum, set in a garden, is entirely clad in white marble with subtle inlays in yellow and green stone, differing from earlier use of red sandstone. A small pavilion on the roof is surmounted by a square dome. Here lie the two cenotaphs, surrounded by marble screens. Every inch of the whole mausoleum, inside and out, is decorated with geometrical patterns, floral designs in marble mosaic and *pietra dura* inlay, using semi-precious stones, such as topaz, onyx and lapis lazuli.

Right This corner of the Tomb of Itimad al-Daulah at Agra shows the pietra dura *inlay on the exterior of the building.*

At Bijapur in the Deccan lies another noteworthy mausoleum, the Tomb of Muhammad Adil Shah (reigned 1627–57). Known as Gol Gumbaz, this mausoleum boasts one of the largest domed spaces in the world – 4.9m (16ft) larger than the dome of St Paul's in London. At each corner of the building is an impressive domed octagonal tower.

103

THE TAJ MAHAL

ONE OF THE MOST FAMOUS MAUSOLEA IN THE WORLD, THE TAJ MAHAL AT AGRA MARKS THE MOMENT WHEN INDO-ISLAMIC ARCHITECTURE REACHED A PEAK OF PERFECTION.

The future Shah Jahan (reigned 1628–58), Prince Khurram, was the favourite of his grandfather Akbar and of his own father, Jahangir. A fine soldier, it was Prince Khurram who was responsible for the military successes of Jahangir's reign. To honour his son's victories, his father bestowed on him the title Shah Jahan, or 'King of the World'. While still a prince, he had already demonstrated a passion for architecture and gardens and had carried out a number of building projects, including the Shahi Bagh (Princely Garden) at Ahmadabad and the wonderful Shalimar Gardens in Lahore.

On Shah Jahan's accession to the throne, the prodigious wealth at his command enabled him to carry out not only an extravagant building programme but to maintain a court whose magnificence was the envy of all. The sums he expended on his tombs, hunting pavilions, palaces and gardens, even entire planned cities, such as Shahjahanabad in Delhi, would seem astonishing even today. The emperor took a close personal interest in all these undertakings. His pride in his magnificent buildings is reflected in the famous couplet inscribed on the Diwan-i-Khas in the Red Fort at Delhi: 'If there be a paradise on earth, it is this, it is this, it is this!'

THE EMPEROR'S WIFE

The peak of the ruler's architectural achievements is the Taj Mahal, built as a tomb for his favourite wife, Mumtaz Mahal, who was a niece of Jahangir's formidable queen Nur Jahan. Mumtaz Mahal played a discreet but important role in Shah Jahan's government. She was, wrote a Mughal chronicler, the emperor's 'intimate companion, colleague, close confidante in distress and comfort, joy and grief'. He was utterly devoted to her and although he had other wives, he had children only by her. When she died in 1631 while giving birth to his 14th child, he was devastated. It is said that he shut himself up in his private

Below Often considered the finest example of Mughal architecture, the Taj Mahal sits at the end of a 300m (980ft) square chahar bagh *garden.*

Above The decoration on the Taj Mahal includes Hindu-influenced design elements, such as this lotus flower, beautifully carved in white marble.

quarters and refused to eat. When he emerged eight days later, his hair and beard had turned white.

OUTSIDE THE TOMB

The grief-stricken emperor chose a site for his wife's tomb on a bend in the river Jumna at Agra. Instead of following the usual practice of positioning the tomb at the centre of a garden, he placed it at the end overlooking the river, so it is visible at the horizon. The tomb, built by some 20,000 workers over 20 years, is set on a marble terrace, which in turn stands on a wide platform, flanked by two red sandstone buildings. At each corner, at a distance from the tomb, are four marble minarets, 42m (138ft) high.

All four sides of the tomb are identical, but it can only be entered from the garden side. The garden is bisected by a broad, straight canal that stretches from the tomb to the main gateway, an elegant two-storey building of red sandstone. In the centre of the canal lies a square pool in which the inverted reflection of the Taj seems to hang suspended. The huge dome, shaped like a lotus bud – a typically Hindu motif – culminates in a gilded bronze finial. The entire building is faced with pure white Makrana marble decorated with *parchin kari*, a type of inlay stonework that characterizes many of Shah Jahan's buildings.

INSIDE THE TAJ MAHAL

The interior of the tomb consists of a central octagonal chamber, which contains the cenotaphs of Shah Jahan and his wife. Linked to each other, and to the central chamber, are four side chambers. A white marble trelliswork screen surrounds the cenotaph, filtering the light entering the tomb chamber. For the Mughals, light served as a metaphor for divine light, symbolizing the true presence of God.

Shah Jahan's severe illness in 1657 led to a rivalry between his four sons, in which the third son, Aurangzeb, killed his brothers, declared his father unfit to rule and seized the throne. Shah Jahan lived for another seven years, imprisoned inside the Agra fort in one of his own palaces, overlooking his most sublime creation.

Above The cenotaphs of Shah Jahan and his wife Mumtaz Mahal lie at the heart of the Taj Mahal. An exquisite octagonal marble screen, or *jali*, surrounds the cenotaphs.

Below Extensive stone inlay decoration on the exterior of the Taj Mahal includes calligraphy, abstract forms and designs based on plant forms.

ISLAMIC ARCHITECTURE THROUGH THE CENTURIES

RED FORT

AT THE HEART OF SHAH JAHAN'S NEW CITY STOOD THE RED FORT, A VAST WALLED COMPLEX OF PALACES AND ASSEMBLY HALLS FROM WHICH HE RULED WITH UNRIVALLED POMP AND CEREMONY.

In 1639, Shah Jahan founded a new city at Delhi. He named it Shahjahanabad, meaning 'the abode of Shah Jahan'. The city of 2,590ha (6,400 acres) supported a population of 400,000. The Friday Mosque, the largest mosque in India at that time, was built on a hillock. Shahjahanabad became the new capital of the Mughal Empire.

According to the emperor's librarian: 'It first occurred to the omniscient mind that he should select on the banks of the [Jumna] river some pleasant site, distinguished by its genial climate, where he might found a splendid fort and delightful edifices…through which streams of water should be made to flow, and the terraces of which should overlook the river.'

A NEW PALACE-FORTRESS

As the emperor had desired, a structure was sited on the banks of the Jumna. Known today as the Red Fort, the complex was situated on Shahjahanabad's eastern edge, dominating the new imperial city but separated from it by walls of red sandstone over 1.8km (1 mile) in circumference. With its palaces, audience halls, bazaars, gardens, mansions for the nobility and an estimated population of 57,000, the Red Fort was a city within a city.

In 1648, nine years after work on the complex began, the Red Fort was dedicated in a magnificent ceremony. The buildings were decorated with impressive textiles embroidered with gold, silver and pearls, and costly gifts, such as jewelled swords and elephants, were distributed to members of the imperial family and nobility.

Above Red sandstone, pillars with intricate low-relief carving and marble flooring are used to decorate this building in the Red Fort.

Below One of the two imposing entrances to the Red Fort. The fort was a city within a city, housing a bazaar, many workshops and 50,000 people.

CANAL OF PARADISE

The great palace-fortress could be entered by two gates, the massive red sandstone Lahore Gate and the Delhi Gate. The Lahore Gate led to a long covered bazaar street, the Chatta Chowk, whose walls were lined with shops. The principal buildings and the emperor's private quarters were sited along the river side of the fort on a terrace some 600m (2,000ft) long.

A shallow marble watercourse, known as the Canal of Paradise, ran through the centre of all these exquisite marble pavilions. Water for the Mughals was just as vital an element in their architecture as it was in their gardens. 'There is almost no chamber,' reported a 17th-century visitor, 'but it hath at its door a storehouse of running water; that 'tis full of parterres, pleasant walks, shady places, rivulets, fountains, jets of water, grottoes, great caves against the heat of the day, and great terraces raised high, and very airy, to sleep upon in the cool: in a word, you know not there what 'tis to be hot.' This Mughal love of water is particularly evident in the Shah Burj ('King's Tower') pavilion, where the water ripples down a marble *chador*, or water chute, into a lotus-shaped pool, and from there flows into the Canal of Paradise.

COURTLY QUARTERS

In a commanding position at the centre of the fortress-palace was the Diwan-i-Am ('Hall of Public Audience'), which contained the marble throne from which Shah Jahan presented himself to his court. The Diwan-i-Khas ('Hall of Private Audience'), the most richly decorated of all the fort's buildings, was where Shah Jahan, seated on a gem-encrusted peacock throne, held the equivalent of cabinet meetings. Built of white marble, the pavilion's interior was richly embellished with floral *parchin kari* stone inlays, precious stones and a ceiling made of silver and gold.

Next to the Diwan-i-Khas lay the Khwabagh, or emperor's private quarters (now called the Khass Mahal). Every day at dawn the emperor presented himself to his people from the balcony of an octagonal tower, which overlooked the river bank. Here too were staged fabulous spectacles, such as elephant fights and military reviews. Also along the riverside were the *zenanas*, or women's quarters, and the *hammam*, or bathhouse. Cool in summer and heated in winter, the *hammam* was ideal for discussing affairs of state in private.

Above Beautiful cusped arches enliven the Sawan Pavilion, named after a month in the rainy season. It is one of two pavilions in the Red Fort's garden.

There were two major gardens, the Moonlight Garden and the Lifegiving Garden, where the hyacinths 'made the earth the envy of the sky' and 281 fountains played. The fort's other areas held numerous specialist workshops that supplied the vast court with everything it needed.

Below The Diwan-i-Khas was used to hold meetings. It held Shah Jahan's peacock throne, before it was plundered by Iranian invader Nadir Shah in 1739.

LAHORE

THE CITY OF LAHORE IN NORTHERN INDIA REACHED A PEAK OF ARCHITECTURAL GLORY DURING THE RULE OF THE MUGHALS. FROM 1584 TO 1598, IT SERVED AS THE IMPERIAL CITY.

During most of the Mughal dynasty, the imperial capital was moved to different cities. When the emperor and his army set off on campaign, his entire establishment went with him, from the ladies of the harem to the treasury and from the court artists to the menagerie. However, several cities did become – and remained for a while – the official Mughal capital.

Akbar (reigned 1556–1605) used Agra as his capital until 1571, when he moved it to his newly built city, Fatehpur Sikri. Within 15 years, he had transferred his capital to Lahore in the Punjab. Lahore remained the capital until 1598, when Akbar moved it back to Agra. However, Lahore, which was strategically situated along the routes to Afghanistan, Multan and Kashmir, continued to be one of the most important Mughal cities after Agra until 1648, when Shah Jahan built his new capital at Delhi.

MUGHAL FORT

During his residence at Lahore, Akbar constructed a fortified palace on the edge of the city overlooking the river Ravi, on the site of an earlier fort. The walls of Akbar's fort were brick, a traditional building material of the region. Under Jahangir (reigned 1605–27), Lahore gained increasing prominence – the city was described by Europeans as one of the greatest in the East. The fort was substantially remodelled, and several audience halls and residential pavilions, with private courtyards and gardens, were added.

The fort's exterior walls were decorated with hundreds of brilliantly coloured tiles, a material common in Lahore, arranged in complex geometric patterns. Other tiled mosaics depicted elephant fights, camels, the Virgin Mary and Jesus, while the emperor's bed chamber had friezes of angels around the ceilings.

Above In the Shish Mahal, tiny pieces of mirror on the walls and ceilings create shimmering, reflective surfaces.

AFTER JAHANGIR

In 1627, Jahangir died on the way to Kashmir. His queen, Nur Jahan, constructed his mausoleum at Shadera near Lahore. Set in a large square garden, the tomb's exterior is decorated with marble inlay and the cenotaph inlaid with semi-precious stones representing tulips and cyclamen. Nur Jahan's own tomb in Lahore bears a moving epitaph: 'On the grave of this poor stranger, let there be neither lamp nor rose. Let neither butterfly's wing burn nor nightingale sing.'

Jahangir's succeeding son, Shah Jahan (reigned 1628–58), was born in Lahore. Like his father, he extended the fort and built several other structures in the city. Here, as elsewhere, he was closely involved in the design of his buildings. His love for white marble is evident in the Shah Burj, built inside the fort for his exclusive use. Within the Shah Burj he built the Shish Mahal

Left The exterior walls of Lahore's fort are made of brick; they are profusely decorated with panels of pictorial tiles and cut-tile mosaic.

('Glass Palace'), so-called because its walls and ceilings were inlaid with a mosaic of mirrors, which created a shimmering effect, that was especially noticeable at night when the interior was lit by lamps.

One of the most beautiful tiled buildings in Lahore is the Wazir Khan Mosque, built in 1634 by Wazir Khan, Shah Jahan's governor of the Punjab. Four towering minarets dominate the building, which is set on a plinth and entered through a high portal. Every inch of the walls is faced with coloured tile mosaics depicting floral sprays, arabesques and calligraphy.

SHALIMAR GARDENS

Shah Jahan's most spectacular addition to Lahore was the Shalimar Gardens, the greatest of the Mughal water gardens. Constructed in 1641–42, the garden is rectangular in shape and has numerous marble pavilions of intricate design and exquisite workmanship. The garden has three terraces, with two changes of level. At the centre of the middle terrace lies a square pool, said to have contained 152 fountains. Looking out across the pool is the emperor's marble throne.

BADSHAHI MOSQUE

Set in a vast courtyard, the Badshahi Mosque was built in 1674 by Aurangzeb (reigned 1658–1707). With its trio of white domes, octagonal minarets and imposing arched portal, the mosque is the largest place of prayer constructed during the Mughal era. Some walls are covered with intricate geometric patterns, others with a mass of tiny flowers and floral sprays springing from vases. Moulded plaster lattices adorn the vaults and domes, taking on an almost textile quality. Although responsible for the construction of this great mosque, Aurangzeb seldom visited Lahore. Probably because the city lacked an imperial presence, by the second half of the 17th century it was in a state of rapid decay.

Above Lahore's Shalimar Gardens, the greatest of all Mughal water designs, were laid out by Shah Jahan.

Below The courtyard of Aurangzeb's Badshahi Mosque in Lahore can hold tens of thousands of believers for prayers.

Early Ottoman Architecture

IN THE 14TH AND EARLY 15TH CENTURIES, THE OTTOMANS BECAME POWERFUL IN THE EASTERN MEDITERRANEAN. THEIR ARCHITECTURAL STYLE WAS INFLUENCED BY BYZANTINE MODELS.

A succession of victories against the weakened Byzantine Empire allowed the Ottomans to expand their dominion at a fast rate. In 1326, Orhan Gazi (reigned 1324–62) conquered Bursa, a town near the southern coast of the Sea of Marmara that became his capital. The crossing into Europe in 1349 shifted the weight of conquest west, and Edirne was declared the new capital after its capture by Murad I (reigned 1362–89) in 1365.

MERGING TRADITIONS

Both early Ottoman capitals alongside Iznik, a town near Bursa conquered in 1331, preserve a large number of early Ottoman buildings. These modest in scale but ambitious structures can be viewed as Ottoman variations on traditional themes. However, their experimental plans and novel ideas cannot be explained without taking into account the main outside influence on the Ottomans, which was Byzantium.

While adopting the fiscal and administrative structures of the fading empire for practical reasons, the Turkish sultans also tried to emulate the splendour and continue the legacy of an ancient Mediterranean imperial tradition. They aspired to the conquest of Constantinople, the ultimate imperial Roman city of the East. Ottoman builders made use of the Byzantine repertoire of architectural forms and techniques that were drawn from buildings within their conquered lands.

DOMED SPACES

The predominance of domes found within Ottoman architecture has been attributed to both an Islamic tradition developed by the Seljuks and a Byzantine influence. However, it is in the treatment of space under the dome and in the techniques adopted in order to support it that Ottoman originality and Byzantine inheritance are better demonstrated. The earliest surviving Ottoman mosques were cubic buildings crowned with relatively large domes resting on pendentives or squinches that bridged the triangular spaces between the corners of the walls and the perimeter of the domes. However, it was their builders' constant concern to expand the space under the dome without breaking up its unity with bulky supports or blind walls. An easy solution was to increase the number of domes and place them on arches resting on columns or pillars.

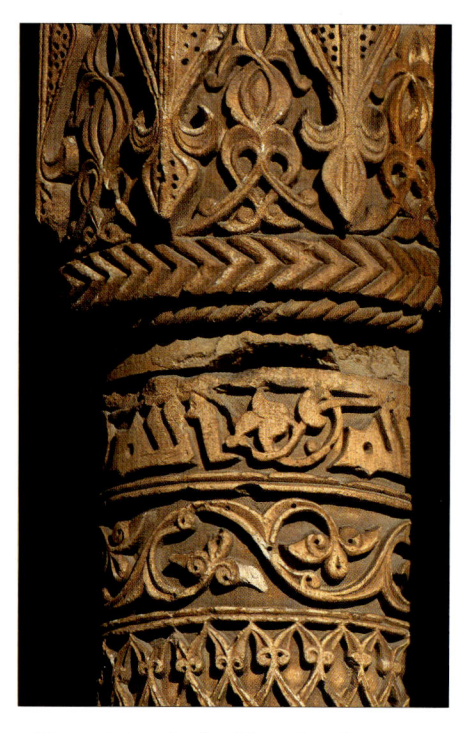

Above A band of calligraphy forms part of the ornate decoration on this 1396 column from the western portal of the Ulu Çami in Bursa.

Left The Ottoman Empire was formed by Turkish tribes from Anatolia. The expanding state included Bursa to the east and Edirne to the west.

EARLY OTTOMAN ARCHITECTURE

Above Huge square pillars inside the early 15th-century Eski Çami in Edirne support the arches and domes above.

EARLY EXPERIMENTATION

The Ulu Cami (Great Mosque) in Bursa, built in 1396–1400 for Sultan Bayezid I (reigned 1389–1402), is the most representative example of this multidomed type. Despite its significant ground area, the forest of 12 columns necessary to support 20 domes marred the desired feeling of expansiveness. The same problem had been faced a thousand years earlier by the builders of the Early Christian period, and several solutions had been proposed, most popular being the domed cross-in-square plan, in which a central domed square space is surrounded by eight square spaces of equal or similar proportions. The Eski Cami Mosque in Edirne (1403–14) can be viewed either as a concentrated version of the Ulu Cami, with only nine domes supported by four pillars, or as a version of the nine-bay solution, a plan not unknown to Islamic architecture but better developed within the Byzantine world.

Further proof of the Byzantine origin of this idea is the late 14th-century Didymoteicho Mosque, in which the central bay is wider and crowned with a dome, whereas the surrounding eight bays are smaller and covered with barrel or cross vaults. This arrangement appears frequently in Byzantine buildings that were scattered within the newly conquered Balkans, for example at the 1028 church of Panagia 'ton Chalkeon', in the administrative and trade centre of Thessaloniki, conquered in 1430.

Given the conscious adoption of a Byzantine prototype for most Ottoman mosques after the conquest of Constantinople in 1453, it would be reasonable to assume that a similar desire to include Byzantine, and ultimately Roman, imperial elements within the designs of early Ottoman architecture had encouraged these experimental plans, although they proved to be short-lived.

Nevertheless, the century that predated the 1453 conquest has offered innovative buildings. An elegant example is the Uç Serefeli Mosque (1438–47) in Edirne, built for Murad II (reigned 1421–44, 1445–51) and featuring a 24-m (79-ft) wide dome resting unusually on a hexagon instead of a square or octagon. The side pillars prevent unimpeded views of the four side bays, but the effect is novel and challenging, and is unique within early Ottoman architecture.

Right The impressive 15th-century Uç Serefeli Mosque (1438–47) was the first in Edirne to have a large courtyard adjoining the prayer hall.

CONSTANTINOPLE (ISTANBUL)

THE OTTOMANS GAINED A NEW PRESTIGIOUS CAPITAL WHEN THEY TOOK CONSTANTINOPLE IN 1453. THE CITY ALSO PROVIDED THEIR BUILDERS WITH THE PROTOTYPE FOR THEIR GREAT MOSQUES.

Istanbul, the Turkish version of the Greek words *eis ten polin*, or 'to the City', became the official name of the city on the Bosphorus only as late as 1930. Until that date, it was still called Constantinople, 'the city of Constantine', a name reflecting its Roman and Byzantine imperial past. The grandeur of this capital of three successive empires inspired several sieges by Muslim rulers, but the prize of conquest was reserved for Sultan Mehmet II (reigned 1444–46, 1451–81), who consequently assumed the epithet of Fatih, 'the Conqueror.'

THE FATIH MOSQUE

The first mosque to be built in the soon-to-be-regenerated capital still bears the same name, Fatih Mosque (1462–70), and despite collapsing and being reconstructed in 1771, it retains its original plan. Like the pre-1453 mosques of Bursa, Edirne and Didymoteicho, it has a large central domed roof and some lateral bays, but it also presents the first occurrence of a feature that later would develop into the main characteristic of classical Ottoman mosques: a large semidome that supports the main dome on the *qibla* side (toward the direction of prayer) over a long and narrow bay, unlike the square side bays to the left and right. Significantly, this bay is separated from the domed central bay by an arch supported by pillars that recede to the sides, creating the illusion of a unified roof consisting of the central dome and the semidome.

THE HAGIA SOPHIA PLAN

This effect was undoubtedly inspired by the patriarchal church of Byzantine Constantinople and eventually mosque of the Ottomans, Hagia Sophia (Ayasofya),

Above The interior decoration of the reconstructed Fatih Mosque follows the Baroque style of 18th-century Ottoman architecture.

a building laden with imperial connotations. Built between 532 and 537, it was an inventive and short-lived answer to the problem of a large floor area sheltered by a domed roof. The 'Hagia Sophia plan' was popular with Ottoman builders and characterized 16th-century mosque architecture.

The original 'Hagia Sophia plan,' as in the 6th-century cathedral, was finished with a second semidome opposite, creating an elongated oval shell. The complete version first appeared in the Sultan Bayezid Mosque in Istanbul, built for Bayezid II (reigned 1481–1512) around the turn of the century, in which the central core (semidome-dome-semidome) was flanked to the right and left by eight domes arranged over eight bays.

The most faithful Ottoman version of the plan was erected between 1550 and 1557 by Sinan

Left This aerial view of the Sultan Bayezid Mosque (1501–6) gives some idea of its of its innovative roofing system.

(1489–1588), the principal architect of the Ottoman Empire, for Sultan Suleyman 'the Magnificent' (reigned 1520–66). The Süleymaniye Mosque, the high point of classical Ottoman architecture, bears a striking resemblance to the Byzantine cathedral in both proportions and ground plan, although the lofty arches opening to the right and left toward the side bays represent a step forward by alleviating the restricting effect of the church's side walls.

BEYOND THE PROTOTYPE

While little innovation can be seen in the floor plans of sultanic mosques because they adhere to a venerated prototype, the architectural designs of smaller buildings are often more original. The graceful Şehzade Mosque, built by Sinan in 1543 to commemorate the son of Suleyman I, was a symmetrical departure from the Hagia Sophia plan. Two lateral semidomes balancing the ones on and opposite the *qibla* side create a strong central focus complementing the single large dome. The pillars carrying the main arches are pushed toward the outside walls to allow the play of curved surfaces on the top half of the building's interior to counterbalance the strong vertical lines of the supports. By this stage, walls are simple screens bridging the gaps between load-bearing elements and they are profusely pierced with stained-glass windows in symmetrical arrangements.

Buildings other than mosques, erected around the Ottoman Empire in great numbers, were built within the traditions of earlier Islamic architecture. Surrounding mosques and supporting them financially were complexes of shops and *hammams* (bathhouses), creating income to cover the running costs of mosques and charitable institutions complementing their social role, such as *imarets* (public kitchens) and *madrasas* (religious colleges).

Above A drawing of the Süleymaniye Mosque shows the system of domes and semi-domes based on the Hagia Sophia plan.

Below The Hagia Sophia's domed structure interior decoration and fenestration inspired Ottoman architects.

Topkapi Palace

THE WORLD-FAMOUS TOPKAPI PALACE PRESERVES MOST OF ITS ORIGINAL ARCHITECTURAL LAYOUT, ALONG WITH AN REMARKABLE MUSEUM COLLECTION FROM THE IMPERIAL TREASURY.

Founded by Mehmet II in the 1450s, the Topkapi is one of the best-known palace complexes in the Islamic world. Built on the acropolis of ancient Constantinople, it overlooks the Golden Horn, the Sea of Marmara and the Bosphorus, and was an ideal location for the new centre of Ottoman power. The Topkapi (or Cannon Gate) Palace was built shortly after the Ottoman conquest of Constantinople in 1453. Initially known as the New Palace, this was the seat of administration only – the royal family was housed in another palace, known later as the Eski Saray or Old Palace. They moved to the Topkapi after the harem was built in the late 16th century.

AN ORDERED UNIVERSE

The palace is organized around a sequence of courtyards, with increasingly restricted privilege of access and high security. This sequential layout articulated the state hierarchies with great clarity.

Much more than the sultan's residence, the Topkapi Palace was the seat of government for the entire Ottoman Empire. It was home to hundreds of courtiers, soldiers and slaves. The imperial complex included the Divan, where government ministers met, as well as military barracks, workshops, the royal mint, state treasury and enormous kitchens situated around beautifully planted and well-maintained garden courtyards. The harem was restricted to the royal family and their servants, and within these quarters were facilities to serve the residents' needs.

Being an imperial residence for some four consecutive centuries, the interiors of the palace were regularly updated and rearranged, to follow new changes in interior fashions, or to renovate after occasional house fires. The splendid palace rooms therefore show the tastes of different periods – from 16th-century Iznik tiled pavilions to 18th-century Baroque *trompe l'oeil*.

There was an exacting order that permeated everyday life within the enclosure. Specific groups were admitted at particular areas during determined times to perform prescribed duties. Some quarters were altogether out-of-bounds, except to a few. Famously, the only non-eunuch adult male allowed in the harem was the sultan himself.

HIERARCHICAL LAYOUT

The Gate of Majesty leads into the first court, where the Imperial Mint and the 8th-century church of Hagia Irene, used in Ottoman times as a warehouse and armoury, still stand. Upon arriving at the Gate of Salutation or Middle Gate, everyone but the sultan had to dismount in order to proceed into the second court. The second court was the main gathering place for courtiers, the location of the grandest audiences with the sultan and the point of access to various areas of the palace – the chimneyed kitchens, rebuilt by Sinan after a fire in 1574; the Outer Treasury; the Divan, seat of the government council; the Tower of Justice and the inner harem.

From here, through the Gate of Felicity, or Gate of White Eunuchs,

Above This reception room is in the sultan's private quarters of the palace.

Left A dense array of buildings form the Topkapi Palace, originally called the Yeni Saray, or 'New Palace'. The Tower of Justice can be seen here (right).

the few that were granted access by the sultan could enter the third court, surrounded by the Chamber of Petitions, or Throne Room, the Library of Ahmet III (reigned 1703–30), the Mosque of the Aghas, the Kiosk of the Conqueror (housing the Inner Treasury), the Dormitory of the 39 Senior Pages (the sultan himself being the 40th 'page') and the sultan's apartments.

ROUTE TO THE HAREM
The sultan accessed the harem from the third court – a complex of palatial proportions. The individual apartments featured mosques, ancillary service rooms, *hammams* (bathhouses) and warehouses.

Finally, in the innermost fourth court, visitors can nowadays enjoy the views and lofty quarters once reserved for the sultan, among them the superbly decorated Baghdad Kiosk and Circumcision Chamber, standing between decorative pools. The slopes leading to the sea are still planted with gardens, and give a flavour of the tranquil atmosphere surrounding the palace. In 1853, the imperial household moved out of the Topkapi Palace, to the more modern Dolmabahçe Palace on the shores of the Bosphorus.

Above The Circumcision Chamber was clad with the finest tiles manufactured during the peak of Iznik production.

Below The love of flowers is apparent in the 18th-century Fruit Room, where painted wooden panels of fruit and flowers decorate the walls and ceiling.

Damascus, Aleppo and Iznik

AS THEY EXTENDED THEIR TERRITORIES, THE OTTOMANS BUILT NOTABLE STRUCTURES IN OTHER CITIES, SUCH AS THE ANCIENT SYRIAN CENTRES OF DAMASCUS AND ALEPPO AND IN IZNIK.

The highly attractive Dervish Pasha Mosque in Damascus was built in 1574 by the Ottoman governor of the city, Dervish Pasha. The use of the traditional Syrian architectural feature of *ablaq* (bands of alternating black-and-white stone) gives the main façade a distinctive look. The entrance consists of an arched doorway with an Arabic inscription naming patron and date and a polygonal minaret with conical roof above. Within, there is a rectangular open-air courtyard with polychrome paving and at its centre a 16-sided fountain; on the yard's south side stands the prayer hall's five-bay portico with five small domes supported by white stone columns. From the courtyard a spiral staircase climbs to the minaret.

The prayer hall is a typically Ottoman square-domed space, with side aisles, each with three smaller domes. The main dome has 16 arched windows. To the south, the *qibla* wall (facing the direction of prayer) is covered with geometric patterns in multicoloured marble; its *mihrab* (niche) arch has a rectangular frame with diamond-and-star decoration made of coloured stones, and is flanked by marble columns. The niche has vertical stripes of white and black marble, and the semidome above it contains white, red and black marble laid in a zigzag decoration. The *minbar* (pulpit) is also marble.

The other walls of the prayer hall are covered with panels of Persian-style tiles and also contain coloured-glass windows. The mosque also has a *madrasa* (religious college) and the shrine of the governor, who died in 1579.

Another fine 16th-century Ottoman mosque in Damascus is the al-Sinanieh Mosque, built on the Bab al-Jabieh Square just outside the city wall by Governor Sinan Pasha in 1590–91. Like the Dervish Pasha Mosque, the al-Sinanieh also has a striking *ablaq* façade, a rectangular open-air court and a seven-dome prayer hall. It is particularly celebrated for its beautiful cylindrical minaret covered with green and blue tiles.

AZEM PALACE

Near the citadel and south of the Umayyad Mosque in the Old City of Damascus, the splendid Azem Palace was built in 1749 as the residence of Asad Pasha al-Azem, Ottoman governor of Damascus. It comprises several buildings arranged in three wings. The first, the *haremlik*, is a private residential area for the governor and his family, containing baths and kitchens as well as lavish accommodation. An interesting touch is that the baths are an exact replica, scaled down in

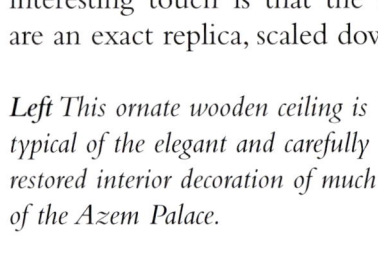

Above The Azem Palace baths, built in imitation of the main city baths, are now dilapidated, but visitors can see that they were once beautifully decorated.

Left This ornate wooden ceiling is typical of the elegant and carefully restored interior decoration of much of the Azem Palace.

Above The minaret of the Ottoman-era al-Sinanieh Mosque in Damascus rises above the façade decorated in black-and-white *ablaq* stonework.

the architects used the *ablaq* technique, creating a pleasing decorative effect in their combination of marble, basalt, limestone and sandstone in the walls; within, the bedroom ceilings were fitted wooden panels bearing paintings of natural scenes, and there were marble mosaics and *muqarnas* (stalactite-like decoration) corners. The palace was damaged in 1925 during the Syrian revolt against French control in the region, but has since been carefully restored and today is a Museum of Arts and Popular Traditions.

ASAD PASHA KHAN

In 1751–52, Governor Asad Pasha al-Azem also built a magnificent *khan* (lodging place) on Suq al-Buzuriyyah in Damascus' Old City. Covering 2,500sq m (27,000sq ft), the *khan* is laid out in traditional style over two floors around a central courtyard: the ground floor contains shops, while on the upper level 80 rooms are arranged as accommodation for merchants.

The courtyard is divided into 9 equal areas, each covered with a dome standing on a drum containing 20 windows; an octagonal fountain stands beneath its own dome in the centre of the courtyard. It has a magnificent monumental entrance portal with carved stone decoration as well as a beautiful *muqarnas* semidome.

IN ALEPPO AND IZNIK

The Ottomans left a proud architectural legacy in other cities of the empire, notably Aleppo in Syria and Iznik (now in Turkey). Of particular note in Aleppo is the Khan al-Wazir, probably the city's most beautiful *khan*, constructed in 1678–82 on the traditional pattern with buildings arranged around a courtyard, with shops and storage on the ground floor and merchants' accommodation on the upper floor. It has splendid ornamented window frames and a black-and-white marble *ablaq* façade with an arched entrance door.

Among the many Ottoman buildings in Iznik is the Nilufer Hatun Imareti, a charitable hospital built by Sultan Murad I (reigned 1362–89) in 1388 and named after his mother Nilufer Hatun. A five-bay entrance portico leads into a domed central court, and beyond it a raised vaulted building that contains a *mihrab* indicates that it may have been used as a prayer hall.

size, of the main baths in Damascus. The second, the *khadamlik*, or servants' quarters, is attached to the family quarters. The third, the *salamlik*, is a guest wing, and contains grand reception areas, including a hall with a beautiful internal fountain, and superb courtyards with water features; the grounds were kept lush by waters diverted from the river Barada. The palace combines opulent interiors with serene exteriors: once again,

Right In Iznik, the Nilufer Hatun Imareti of 1388, once a charitable hospital, was restored in 1955 and is now the city's principal museum.

ISLAMIC ARCHITECTURE THROUGH THE CENTURIES

REVIVALIST TRENDS

MANY ARTISTS OF THE MODERN AGE – BOTH EUROPEANS VISUALIZING MUSLIM CULTURE AND THOSE FROM WITHIN THE MUSLIM WORLD – HAVE BEEN INSPIRED BY THE HERITAGE OF THE ISLAMIC MIDDLE EAST.

In the 19th century, a number of important Western European artists admired the achievements of the Islamic artistic past and revived these traditional methods in their own work.

Prominent among these artists was English tile designer and potter William de Morgan (1839–1917), a friend and collaborator of the artist, writer and designer William Morris (1834–96). Both men were notable figures in the Arts and Crafts aesthetic movement, which turned away from mass production in the wake of the Industrial Revolution, instead celebrating individual craftsmanship.

William de Morgan began to work in ceramics in 1863. He was a great experimenter, and in c.1873 rediscovered the techniques of tin-glazing and lustre that had been invented in 9th-century Iraq. He also began to use a colour palette (including turquoise, dark blue and green) and imagery (including fabulous creatures and repeating geometric motifs) derived from wares made by Iznik craftsmen in the Ottoman Empire during the 16th century.

LEIGHTON'S 'ARAB HALL'

In the 1870s, English artist and sculptor Frederic Lord Leighton (1830–96) built a magnificent 'Arab Hall' as part of an extension to his house in Holland Park in London. The hall was intended to house and display Lord Leighton's large collection of Damascus and Middle-Eastern tiles, and the interior was based on the banqueting hall of the summer palace of La Zisa, which was built in Palermo, Sicily, by Fatimid craftsmen working in Norman Sicily in 1166.

The hall's grand decoration includes an epigraphic frieze of tiles with an inscription quoting from Surah 54, verses 1–6, beginning 'In the name of the long-suffering Allah, ever merciful, who has taught

Left Leighton House's Arab Hall contains an indoor fountain as well as beautiful tiling, slender columns and muqarnas vaulting.

Above English craftsman William de Morgan's Persian-style dish draws inspiration from the designs of 16th-century Iznik ceramics.

me the Quran…'. Richard Burton may have acquired this for Lord Leighton in Sind, Pakistan: he certainly sourced tiles for Leighton in Jerusalem.

Upstairs is a 17th-century wooden *zenana*, a box-like construction designed for segregating women from men during worship, which Lord Leighton transported to London from a mosque in Cairo, along with a 17th-century stained-glass window from a Damascus mosque.

IRANIAN PAINTERS

The revival of miniature painting in early 20th-century Iran is an example of how artists tried to resurrect historic traditions and techniques. A key figure in the renewal was Mirza Hadi-Khan Tajvidi, who in 1929 established the Madraseh-i Sanaye'-i Qadimeh ('School of Traditional Arts') in Tehran. He taught many artists there who formed the School of Tehran.

Other notable painters in this revival included Mohammad Ali Zavieh, Shayesteh Shirazi and Hossein Behzad. Born in Tehran, Behzad produced paintings in an archaizing style imitating traditional Timurid and Safavid manuscript paintings. He won international renown as a miniaturist, beginning with his illustrations to works by the Persian poet Nizami (1141–1209), completed in 1915, and continuing with illustrations to the *Rubáiyát of Omar Khayyám* (1048–1123), finished in 1936. He received several international awards, and many of his works were collected and housed in the Behzad Museum in the Saad Abad Palace in Tehran.

In the wake of these artists came a generation of Iranian painters who were both inspired by the great Persian miniature tradition and introduced modern techniques from other areas of the arts. Among these is Mahmoud Farshchian. Born in Isfahan and educated in the fine arts both in Iran and in Europe, Farshchian won wide acclaim with works inspired by the Iranian epic the *Shahnama* (Book of Kings) and the works of the Sufi mystical poet Rumi (1207–73).

Other artists in this generation include Mohammad Bagher Aghamiri, Majid Mehregan and Ardshir Mojarrad-Takestani.

TRADITIONAL BUILDINGS

Particularly in Africa, some modern architects have maintained traditional forms when constructing mosques. For example, the Great Mosque of Niono in Mali, completed by master mason Lassina Minta with local workmen in 1973, was built in line with centuries-old local Islamic building traditions with wooden beams and walls of clay bricks and roofs made from matting and earth. A number of the historic mosques of the region, such as the Great Mosque of Djénné, were rebuilt in the 20th century using similar materials and craftsmanship. The Great Mosque of Niono has a vast prayer hall covering approximately 726sq m (7,815sq ft). The Niono Mosque won an Aga Khan Award for Architecture in 1981–83.

Above The Grand Mosque of Djénné, Mali (1906), is one of several 20th-century West African mosques built from clay and wood in the traditional style.

Above John Frederick Lewis drew on memories of life in Cairo for his Orientalist work, An Intercepted Correspondence *(1869).*

IMAGINING THE EAST: 'ORIENTALIST PAINTERS'

From the late 18th century and throughout the 19th century in Britain, many Western artists were drawn to scenes of life in the Orient – which often meant the Mediterranean coastline of Egypt, Syria, Turkey and Palestine. These artists represented harem, bazaar or city scenes, especially in the cities of Istanbul, Damascus, Cairo and Jerusalem, at this time all part of the declining Ottoman Empire. One of the leading Orientalist painters was John Frederick Lewis, who had lived for ten years in Cairo, and later made his name in England with images such as *Harem Life, Constantinople* (1857), *Edfu, Upper Egypt* (1860) and *The Seraff: A Doubtful Coin* (1869). The exotic appeal of Orientalist art lay in authentic reportage of foreign landscape and architecture, as well as in the sexual mores of the harem. Artists made close study of Islamic domestic architecture, and painstakingly reproduced latticework screens, as in *An Arab Interior* (1881) by Arthur Melville, but their actual knowledge of local genre situations was extremely restricted.

THE MODERN AGE

AFTER THE 18TH CENTURY, ART AND ARCHITECTURE WERE INFLUENCED BY EUROPEAN STYLES, AND IN CAIRO AND ELSEWHERE URBAN DESIGNERS ADOPTED STRAIGHT-BOULEVARD CITY PLANNING.

By the 1800s, the Ottoman Empire was in decline, and the balance of political and financial power swung westward. Former Ottoman territories, such as Greece and Serbia, won independence; North Africa came under varying degrees of Western colonial control.

In many Islamic countries, political and social reforms brought government and administration closer to Western models: in the Tanzimet Period (from the Arabic word for 'Reordering') in 1839–76, Ottoman sultans Abdulmecid I (reigned 1839–61) and Abdulaziz (reigned 1861–76) introduced reforms of the army, administration, judiciary and education systems; in 1861, Tunisia was the first Islamic country to adopt a constitution and established itself as a Western-style constitutional monarchy. In line with this, architecture and the arts turned to Western models.

THE BALYAN ARCHITECTS

In Istanbul from the 1820s onward, the architects of the Armenian Balyan family produced mosques in a style influenced by Western Baroque and Empire styles. Krikor Balyan designed the Nusretiye Mosque, built in 1823–36 for Sultan Mahmud II (reigned 1808–39). The mosque was called the Victory Mosque to celebrate the abolition by Mahmud II of the janissary troops who had been behind many revolts, and their replacement with a Western-style military.

Garabet Amira Balyan and Nigogayos Balyan, Krikor's son and grandson, were responsible for several mosques: the Dolmabahçe Mosque (1853–55), the Ortakoy Mosque (1854–56) and the Buyuk Mecidiye Mosque, finished in 1855. These have a Western European look, using marble and grand paintings in place of tiles as decoration.

Above Three Western styles of architecture – Baroque, Rococo and Neoclassical – combine in the Dolmabahçe Palace. Its ceilings are covered with 14 tonnes of gold.

These two men also designed the Dolmabahçe Palace, built in 1844–55, for Sultan Abdulmecid I. The palace stands in what was once a harbour on the Bosphorus, indeed where Mehmet II had once anchored 70 ships. The harbour was later reclaimed for use as royal gardens and the name of the palace means 'filled garden'. Its white marble façade, 284m (932ft) long, faces on to a quay 600m (1,968ft) in length. The Dolmabahçe was the first European-style palace in Istanbul: its interior was beautifully designed by the French decorator Charles Séchan (designer of the Paris Opera) and was lavishly appointed, with the world's largest chandelier, weighing 4.5 tonnes and containing 750 lights, in the Exhibition Hall and a celebrated staircase with banisters made from Baccarat crystal.

Left The Dolmabahçe Mosque stands on a site measuring 25sq m (269sq ft) close to the Dolmabahçe Palace beside the waters of the Bosphorus.

MUHAMMAD ALI MOSQUE

In this period, Egypt was ruled by the Khedives, descendants of Muhammad Ali Pasha (1769–1849). He was an Albanian officer, sent to the country as part of an Ottoman force following the invasion of Egypt by French general Napoleon Bonaparte. Muhammad Ali had taken power and established himself as Wali (Ottoman governor) in 1805, and founded a dynasty that ruled until 1952. In the Cairo Citadel, he built a Grand Mosque in the Ottoman style in 1824–48.

The Muhammad Ali Mosque was at first planned in the local Mamluk style by a French architect named Pascal Coste, but the designs of Greek architect Yusuf Bushnaq were preferred. The mosque has a large main dome and four half-domes with Ottoman spindle minarets, modelled on the 1599 Yeni Valide Mosque in Istanbul.

The Muhammad Ali Mosque was the largest mosque built in the first half of the 19th century, and superseded the nearby Mamluk Mosque of al-Nasir Muhammad as the state mosque of Egypt. It was built on the grounds once occupied by Mamluk palaces, which were destroyed on Muhammad Ali's order. In choosing the Ottoman instead of the Mamluk mosque style, Muhammad Ali made it clear that Egypt was aligned with the Ottomans. At the same time, the decorative style used displayed a strong European influence and harmonized with that used in the contemporary Empire and neo-Baroque mosques of Istanbul, designed by the Balyans.

Muhammad Ali's grandson, Ismail Pasha (reigned 1863–79), was pro-Western. He added a new area on Cairo's western edge in the style of Paris, as remodelled by Baron Georges-Eugène Haussmann, and built a rail network in Egypt. He declared in 1879, 'My country is no longer part of Africa; now we are in Europe. It is natural, therefore, for us to set aside our former ways and to take on a new organization suitable to our social conditions.'

Above The main dome of the grand Muhammad Ali Mosque (1824–48) in Cairo is 21m (69ft) in diameter, and is flanked by Ottoman-style minarets.

EFFECTS ON OTHER ARTS

These changes had varied effects in other arts. In metalwork, for example, Western influence was felt from the 18th century onward by the elite craftsmen of Istanbul, who produced Baroque and Rococo decorative designs. The craftsmen made mirrors, trays, ewers and coffee sets with intaglio (stone-carved) decoration. Floral decoration became more expansive, with engravings of bouquets and baskets of flowers, bows and ribbons.

In the 19th century, the severe Ottoman decline had dispiriting effects on metalwork and the arts. Except for those that were donated to mosques or mausolea, many gold and silver pieces held in the imperial palace were melted down. However, Western influence had little effect on calligraphy, the Islamic art form par excellence.

Right This clock from the Dolmabahçe Palace clearly shows how Western styles – particularly Baroque – influenced late Ottoman metalwork.

MODERN ARCHITECTURE

SOME OF THE MOST DYNAMIC ARCHITECTURE OF THE LATE 20TH AND EARLY 21ST CENTURIES WAS CREATED IN THE ISLAMIC WORLD, USING MODERN DESIGNS THAT HONOUR THE ISLAMIC TRADITION.

The vast King Faisal Mosque in Islamabad is a symbol of modern Pakistan. Built in 1976–86 under the supervision of Turkish architect Vedat Delakoy, it combines the modern and the traditional: it is based on the design of a central dome with spindle minarets used over centuries by the Ottomans, but here the main dome is opened out into a great folded roof resembling a tent. It is made of concrete without external decoration. The scale is vast: the mosque is part of a complex covering 5,000sq m (53,820sq ft) that can hold 300,000 members of the faithful.

The prayer hall contains a large chandelier, calligraphy by Pakistani artist Sadeqain Naqqash and tiles by Turkish artist Menga Ertel. On the west wall the *kalimah* (the affirmation of faith) is written in *kufic* script set in mosaic.

The King Faisal Mosque is the state mosque of Pakistan, and one of the world's largest mosques; it was named after King Faisal of Saudi Arabia, who suggested its construction in 1966 and afterward funded the building.

OTHER MOSQUES

There are several other modern mosques of note, including the Freedom Mosque (or Istiqlal Mosque) in Jakarta, Indonesia, built in 1955–84 by architect Frederick Silaban, using concrete and steel. The large prayer hall covers an area of 36,980sq m (398,050sq ft) and the mosque can hold 250,000 people. It is the state mosque of Indonesia.

Abdel-Wahed el-Wakil built the King Saud Mosque in Jeddah, Saudi Arabia, completed in 1989. It covers 9,700sq m (104,410sq ft) and has a minaret 60m (197ft) tall. It pays tribute to both Iranian and Mamluk architecture, celebrating the four-*iwan* (hall) design of Iranian tradition in that it contains a rectangular courtyard and four *iwan*-like openings in the surrounding wall, and honouring Mamluk architecture in Cairo in the pointed dome shape and the minaret style. The main dome is 42m (138ft) tall and 20m (66ft) across.

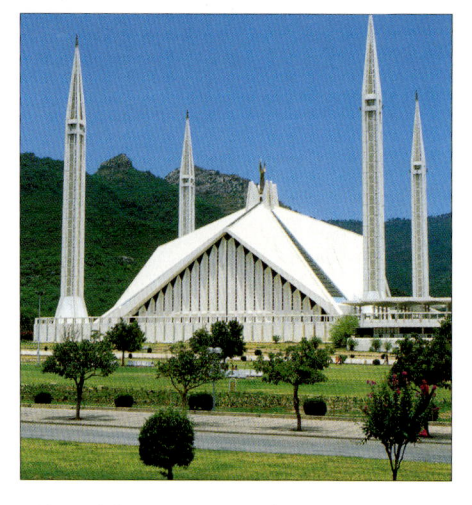

Above The King Faisal Mosque (1966–86) stands at the northern edge of Islamabad, where the city gives way to the foothills of the Himalayas.

COMMERCIAL BUILDINGS

In this same period, the vast scale of secular architecture built in Islamic countries is a good representation of their wealth and status. Hotels, apartment blocks and offices have been built in a dynamic, glamorous style.

In Tehran, Iran, the distinctive Azadi Tower was designed in 1971 by architect Hossein Amanat. Initially called the Shayad Tower ('Memorial of Kings'), it was renamed the Azadi (Freedom) Tower after the 1979 Iranian Revolution. The tower contains 8,000 blocks of white marble stone from the region of Isfahan, and was built by the pre-eminent Iranian stonemason Ghaffar Davarpanah Varnosfaderani. It stands at the centre of a great square that was the setting for many of the demonstrations

Left In the rectangular prayer hall of the Freedom Mosque in Jakarta, Indonesia, 12 great columns support a spherical dome 45m (148ft) in diameter.

MODERN ARCHITECTURE

Above A luxury restaurant within the golden sphere atop the Al Faisaliyah building revolves so that diners have a changing view of Riyadh, Saudi Arabia.

and rallies of the Iranian Revolution, and it continues to be a focal point for protest.

Many modern buildings that set new standards for size have been built in Saudi Arabia and the countries of the United Arab Emirates. In Riyadh, the twin towers of the Al Faisaliyah Centre and the Kingdom Centre are the two tallest buildings in Saudi Arabia. The Kingdom Tower, 311m (1,020ft) tall with 43 floors, was completed in 1999. It contains offices, a hotel, private apartments, restaurants, fitness clubs and shopping floors; there are also three mosques, including the world's highest, the King Abdullah Mosque, on the 77th floor and a public viewing platform at the top at a height of 270m (886ft). The Kingdom Centre was designed by Ellerbe Becket/Omrania. The Al Faisaliyah Centre, completed in 2000 and 267m (876ft) tall with 30 floors, contains offices and shopping areas. The four main corner beams of the centre bend in to join at the tip and beneath them is a great golden ball containing a restaurant. It was designed by UK architects Foster and Partners.

Dramatic skyscraper hotels were built in Dubai, United Arab Emirates, in the late 20th and early 21st centuries. The highly distinctive Burj al-Arab ('Tower of the Arabs') was built in 1994–99 to designs by architect Tom Wright in the shape of a boat's sail on a man-made island 280m (919ft) offshore from Jumeirah Beach. It has 60 floors and stands 321m (1,053ft) tall, making it the second tallest hotel in the world, outdone only by the Rose Tower, 333m (1,093ft) tall, on Shaykh Zayed Road, also in Dubai. The Rose Tower has 72 floors and was built in 2004–7.

INSPIRATIONAL AIRPORT

A notable building complex in Saudi Arabia is the Dhahran International Airport, built in 1961 and designed by American architect Minoru Yamasaki (1912–86). The airport's blend of traditional Islamic architectural forms with modern elements was highly influential. Its flight control tower has the appearance of a minaret, and the distinctive terminal featured for some time on Saudi banknotes. In 1999, after the building of the King Fahd International Aiport, the Dhahran International Airport was made into a air base of the Royal Saudi Air Force.

Right The iconic Burj al-Arab hotel in Dubai, United Arab Emirates, mimics the shape of the sail used in the traditional Arab sailing vessel, the dhow.

Glossary

ABLAQ Typically Syrian use of alternating dark and light masonry, often marble.
ARABESQUE Decorative geometric ornament based on stylized vegetal forms, such as tendrils and creepers.
ARCH A curved area in a building used to spread the weight of the structure above it to the walls, pillars or columns below; important in Islamic architecture, especially for supporting large domes.
ASHLAR Dressed stone blocks.
AZULEJO Tin-glazed ceramic tiles produced in Islamic Spain.

BAB Gate.
BAZAAR Turkish term for covered marketplace and business centre in Islamic towns and cities, also known as *souk* in Arabic.

CALLIGRAPHY The art of beautiful writing; in Islam stylized written Arabic is revered as the highest art because it gives visible form to the words of the holy Quran.
ÇAMI Congregational mosque used for Friday prayers (Turkish; called *jami* in Arabic).
CARAVANSERAI Secure and often fortified lodging for merchants and travellers, their animals and goods, usually on a trade route. Known as *han* in Turkish, and *khan* in Arabic.
CASBAH See citadel.
CHAHAR BAGH Persian-style, four-part garden layout.
CITADEL Enclosed, fortified section of a city or town, known as *casbah* (from Arabic *qasaba*) in North Africa.
CLOUD BAND Decorative motif of curling clouds in Chinese art, used throughout Islamic art from the 14th century onward.
CUERDA SECA (in English, 'dry cord') Use of lines of a greasy black substance to mark out and contain areas of glaze applied to tiles, enabling artists to contain the colours.

DRESSED STONE Building stone that has been shaped or 'finished' prior to use.

GUNBAD Tomb tower.

HAMMAM Bathhouse.
HAN See *caravanserai*.
HYPOSTYLE Hall with flat roof supported by columns; type of mosque in which the flat roof of the prayer hall is supported by rows of columns.

INLAYING The technique of inserting one material into another to create a decorative effect, often used in metalwork to add a precious metal, such as gold or silver, to decorate a less expensive metal body, such as bronze or brass.
IWAN Vaulted hall with one side left open, giving on to the courtyard of a mosque or *madrasa*.

JAMI Or *masjid-i-jami*; congregational mosque used for Friday prayers (Arabic; *çami* in Turkish).

KAABAH Islam's most sacred shrine, a cube-shaped building in the Masjid al-Haram (Holy Mosque) at Makkah; Muslims must face toward the *Kaabah* when praying.
KHAMSA Five in Arabic; in Persian a *khamsa* is a group of five books; in Islamic Africa a *hamsa* (sometimes *khamsa*) is a hand-shaped, good-luck symbol used in jewellery.
KHAN See *caravanserai*.
KHANQA A monastery for Sufis.
KITAB Book; al-Kitab or kitab Allah (Book of God) are sometimes used as terms for the Quran.
KUFIC Early Arabic script, named after city of Kufa in Iraq.
KULLIYE Complex of religious buildings centred on a mosque with other establishments, such as *madrasa*, *caravanserai*, *hammam*, kitchens and sometimes hospitals, typically built by wealthy subjects of the Ottoman sultans.

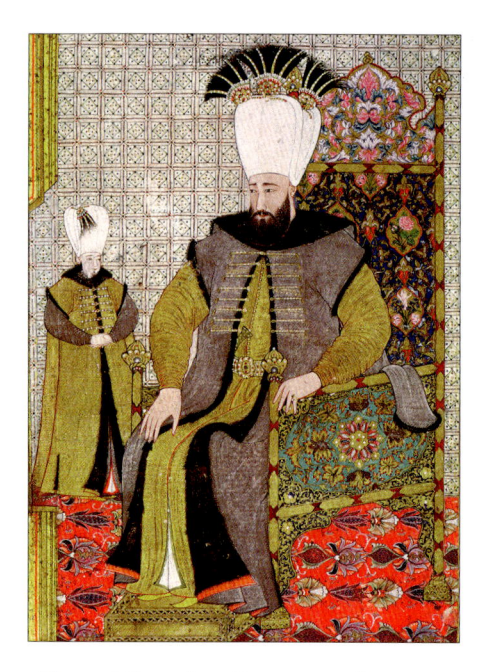

Above Like other Ottoman sultans, Ahmet III (reigned 1703–10) was a great patron of the arts.

LUSTREWARE Ceramics finished with metallic glazes that produce a shining effect. Developed in Abbasid Iraq in the 9th century.

MADRASA Islamic educational establishment, often associated with a mosque, where students studied the Quran, law and sciences.
MAGHRIBI Cursive form of Arabic script; developed in western Islamic lands.
MAIDAN Open square, usually in the centre of a town or city.
MAQSURA Private area in a congregational mosque used by a ruler or governor, often lavishly decorated.
MASHHAD Shrine; tomb of martyr or Sufi saint.
MASHRABIYA Turned-wood openwork screen.
MASJID See mosque.
MIHRAB Wall niche in form of arch indicating the correct direction of prayer (toward Makkah).

GLOSSARY

MINAI An overglaze technique for decorating pottery used in Kashan Iran in the 12th–13th centuries.

MINARET Tower attached to a mosque, once used as a watchtower but now the place from which the Muslim faithful are called to prayer.

MINBAR Pulpit in mosque from which the *khutbah* prayer or sermon is pronounced.

MOSQUE Muslim place of gathering and prayer. In Arabic, *masjid* ('place of prostration').

MUEZZIN Anglicized form of the Arabic *muadhdhin*, the individual who calls faithful to prayer, traditionally from the minaret of a mosque.

MUHAQQAQ Cursive script used in calligraphy; one of the 'six hands' of calligraphy identified in the 10th century by Ibn Muqla (d.940).

MUQARNAS Small, concave stalactite vaults, often painted or tiled, used widely in Islamic architecture.

MUSALLA Enclosed area with *qibla* wall, where large numbers can gather to worship; known as *Namazgah* in Persian.

NASKH Style of Arabic script.

NASTALIQ Calligraphic script, used mainly for Persian rather than Arabic.

PISHTAQ Arched portal leading to an *iwan* at the entrance of a mosque, *madrasa* or *caravanserai* in Iran.

QASR Palace or castle.

QIBLA The direction of prayer, toward the *Kaabah* at Makkah, in which Muslims face when praying.

QUBBAH Dome or domed tomb.

QURAN The word of Allah (God), as revealed to the Prophet Muhammad in 610–32; the main source of guidance and authority for Muslims.

Right Blue tiles decorate an arched panel in the Friday Mosque in Isfahan, Iran.

RIBAT Fortified monastery, a base for *jihad*, or religious war.

RIWAQ Arcades running around the four sides of the courtyard in an Arabic-style courtyard mosque.

SAHN Courtyard of a mosque.

SHADIRWAN Fountain inside a palace room or the courtyard of a mosque.

SHAHNAMA Book of Kings. Epic Persian history written by Firdawsi between 977–1010. The text has been illustrated in various media.

SHEREFE Balcony on minaret used when issuing a call to prayer.

SURAH A chapter in the Quran (plural *suwar*).

TALAR Columned hall (Persian).

THULUTH Large and elegant cursive calligraphic script.

TIRAZ Robes given as mark of honour, embroidered with Quranic verses and the name of the donor.

TUGHRA Stylized monogram-signature incorporating the name of an Ottoman sultan.

TURBE Mausoleum.

ULAMA Islamic legal and religious scholars (Arabic, singular *alim*).

VIZIER Administrator; chief minister (Anglicized form of the Arabic *wazir*).

WAQF Pious endowment supporting a *masjid*, *madrasa* or secular institution, such as a *bimaristan* (hospital).

WIKALA Hostel for merchants and travellers within a city.

YURT Round tent used by Central Asian nomads.

ZIYADA The enclosure or courtyard between mosque precincts and outer walls.

INDEX

Abbasids 9, 28, 37, 44–7, 74, 78
Afghanistan 24, 52–3, 54–6, 60, 98
Aghlabids 78–9
Agra 103, 108; cenotaphs 105; Taj Mahal 26, 87, 96, **104–5**; Tomb of Itimad al-Daulah 103; Tomb of Mumtaz Mahal 26, 104–5
Aksaray 31, 61, 63
Aleppo 64–5, **68–9**, 116–17; citadel 29, 68–9; Madrasa al-Firdaus 68–9; Mosque of Abraham 68
Algeria 78, 80–1
Alhambra 29, 84–5; Comares Palace 84–5; Generalife Gardens 86; Hall of the Kings 85
Almohads **80–1**, 82–3
Almoravids **80**, 82, 88
Amasya 62–3
Anatolia 8, 60–1, **62–3**, 67, 94, 110
al-Andalus 74, 80–1, 83, 87, 88
Ankara 63
architects: the Balyans 120, 121; Es Saheli 89; modern 121–3; Sinan, Mimar 19, 25, 31; Yamasaki, Minoru 123
architecture: African **88–9**; the garden in **86–7**; Ilkhanid **90–1**, 92; modern 117–21, **122–3**; Mughal 104–5; Ottoman **110–11**;

Below Entrance portal and mausoleum at the Gur-e Amir complex, Samarkand, Uzbekistan.

Persian 100–1; Samanid 52
astrolabes 21
astronomy 92–3, 95; observatories 92–3, 95
Aswan: cemeteries 26, 49; Tombs of the Martyrs 27
Ayyubids 64, **66–7**, 68–9

Baghdad 8, 18, 24, 28, 31–3, **44–5**, 46, 52, 56, 59, 66, 74–5, 90; Mustansiriya *madrasa* 24, 67; Tomb of Zumurrud Khatun 44
Balkh: Funerary Mosque of Abu Nasr Parsa 99; Nuh-Gunbadh Mosque 52
Basra 44, 64
Bukhara 52–3, 60, 95; Mausoleum of Ismail Samani 52–3; Ulugh Beg's *madrasa* 95
Bursa 17, 110, 112; Ulu Çami 110–11
Byzantines 8, 19, 21, 36–9, 50, 74, 110

Cairo (al-Qahira) 11, 24, 27, 28, 32, 48–9, 66–7, 70–3, 118–21; Bab al-Futuh 49; Ibn Tulun Mosque 23; Khan al-Khalili bazaar 31; Madrasa of al-Salih Najm al-Din Ayyub 67; Mosque of al-Maridani 70; Mosque of al-Mu'ayyad 70; Muhammad Ali Mosque 121; al-Nasir Muhammad complex 72, 121; Qalawun complex 72; Salah al-Din Citadel 66–7, 70; Salar al-Jawli complex 72–3; Sanjar al-Jawli complex 72–3; Sultan Barquq Mosque 22; Sultan Hasan complex 22, 25, 71
caravanserais 30–1, 57, 58, **60–1**, 62–3, 73, 90, 100
cemeteries 26, 49
Chinese influence 92–3, 99
cities and citadels **28–9**, 66–70
Constantinople *see* Istanbul
Córdoba **76–7**, 80–1, 84, 87; Great Mosque (Mezquita) 18, 21, 74, 76, 80, 82; Madinat al-Zahra 28, 77

Damascus 8–9, 32–3, 37, 44, 64, 66, **68–9**, 69, 70, 74–5, 87, **116–17**, 118; Al Sinovich Mosque 116–17; Azem Palace 116–17; Great Mosque 18, 37, **40–1**, 56, 69
Delhi 55, 87, 106; Diwan-i-Khas 107; Red Fort **106–7**; Sawan Pavilion 107; Tomb of Humayan 26, 96, 102–3
desert palaces **42–3**; Qasr al-Hayr al-Sharqi 37; Qasr al-Hayr al-Gharbi 42–3; Qasr al-Mshatta 43; Qasr Amra 42; Ukhaydir 44–5
Djénné 88; Great Mosque 88, 119
Dubai: Burj al-Arab 123

East Africa 89
Edirne 112; Eski Çami Mosque 111; Selimiye Mosque 19; Uç Serefeli Mosque 111
Egypt 11, 22, 24–5, 27, 28, 32, 36–7, 45, 48, 66–7, 70, 121
ewers 43, 73

Fatehpur Sikri 28, 108; Tomb of Salim Chisti 28, 102
Fatimids 26–8, **48–9**, 50–1, 74
Fez: Qarawiyyin Mosque 24, 80
Fustat 66–7

gardens **86–7**, 101
Gazargah: shrine of Abdullah Ansari 98–9
Ghaznavids 53, **54–5**, 63
Ghurids **54–5**
gold 7, 71, 120

126

Granada 29, 84, 86; *see also* Alhambra
gunbads 27, 58–9
Gurgan: Gunbad-i-Qabus 27, 54

Hajj 6, 7, **32–3**, 88
Hama: Nur al-Din Mosque 65
hans 30–1, 60–1
heraldry 73
Herat 95, **98–9**; Musallah complex 98–9

Ibn Battuta (traveller) 32–3
Ilkhanids 27, **90–1**, 92–3
India 11, 26, 28, 54–5, 86, 94, 96, 102–9
Iran 8, 18–20, 24–5, 27–9, 31, 37, 45, 52–3, 54–60, 90–2, 122
Iraq 8–9, 27, 28, 31–3, 37, 44–7, 64, 66
Isfahan 29, **100–1**; Ali Qapu Palace 100–1; Chahar Bagh complex 25; Friday Mosque 19, 20, 56–7, 91; Imam Mosque 57, 100–1; Imam Square 100–1; Shaykh Lutfallah Mosque 28, 100
Islam: Five Pillars of Islam 7; Shiah Islam 8–9, 37, 49, 52, 56, 59, 65, 67, 91; Shiite Islam 8; Sufi Islam 53, 58; Sunni Islam 24, 52–3, 56, 59, 64–5, 66–7, 90, 99
Islamabad: King Faisal Mosque 122
Istanbul (Constantinople) 19, 27, 29, 110, **112–13**, 113, 119–21; Dolmabahçe Mosque 120; Dolmabahçe Palace 120; Fatih Mosque 29, 112; Hagia Sophia 19, 112–13; Süleymaniye Mosque 19, 25, 27, 112–13; Sultan Ahmet Mosque 19; Sultan Bayezid Mosque 112; Topkapi Palace 29, 63, **114–15**
Italy 78
Iznik 62, 110, 116–17; Nilufer Hatun Imareti 117

Jakarta: Freedom Mosque 122
Jerusalem (al-Quds) 20, 49, 64, 66, 118, 119; Al-Aqsa Mosque 20, 64; Dome of the Rock 16, 20, **38–9**, 64, 72
Jordan 10, 32–3, 42–3

Kaabah 6–7, 18, 20, 30, 32, 39, 40
Kairouan 78–80; Great Mosque 18, 78
Kayseri 63
khanqas 65, 73
khans 117
Khurasan 18, 44, 52–3, 54
Kilwa Kisiswani: Great Mosque 89
Konya 27, 31, 62–3; Ince Minareli *madrasa* 10, 24, 63; Karatay *madrasa* 63; Sırçali *madrasa* 59
Kufa 37, 44–5; Grand Mosque 8
kulliyes 25, 62

Lahore 26, **108–9**; Akbar's fort 108; Badshani Mosque 109; Shalimar Gardens 109; Shish Mahal 108–9
Leighton's 'Arab Hall' 118
literature 53, 65; *Romance of Varqa and Gulshah* 63; *Shahnama* (Book of Kings) 54, 93, 119

Madinah 6–7, 20, 22, 49, 66; Mosque of the Prophet 6, 18, 20
Madinat as-Salam 44
madrasas 10, **24–5**, 31, 57, **58–9**, 62–3, 65, 67–9, 72–3, 85, 89, 90, 95, 98–9, 101, 113, 116; Seljuk *madrasas* 24
Mahdia 48–9
Makkah 6–7, 18, 20–1, 27, 30, **32–3**, 36, 39, 40, 49, 58, 66, 75, 82, 88, 90, 100
Mali 88–9, 119
Mamluks 10–11, 25, 69, **70–1**, 72–3
maqsuras 22, 40, 56, 71, 95
Maragha 27, 58; Hulagu Khan's observatory 92–3
Marrakech 80–1, **82–3**; Bab Agnaou gate 83; Bab er Reha gate 82; Kutubiyya Mosque 82
Mashhad 9, 60, 98
mashhads 27
mausolea 11, 26–7, 29, 52–3, 58, 62–3, 71, 85–7, 90–1, 96–8, 104–5; Mamluk **72–3**
Merv 57, 60; Mausoleum of Sanjar 58
mihrabs 18–23, 40–1, 46, 49, 56–8, 61, 63, 69, 76, 78, 80–1, 89, 90–1, 95, 100, 116

Above Detail of ornate inlay work at Emperor Akbar tomb at Sikandra, Agra, India.

minarets 41, 55, 57, 65, 79, 81–3, 99, 117, 121
minbars 19, 22, 64, 69, 82, 89, 116
Monastir: *ribat* 79
Mongols 64, 90, 98
monuments **58–9**
Morocco 24, 80, 82–3
mosaics 16, 39, 41, 96, 99, 108
mosques 6, 8, **18–19**, 20–5, 27–31, 37, 40–1, 44, 46–7, 49, 50, 52, 55–7, 61–3, 64–5, 67–72, 74–6, 78–83, 85, 148, 89, 90–1, 95, 98–9, 100–1, 106, 109, 110–14, 116–17, 119–23; Arab-style 18; central-dome 19; four-*iwan* 18–19, 56–7, 59, 71, 91; Ilkhanid 90; interiors of **22–3**; *jami* 19; *masjid* 19; T-plan 80–1; Ulu Çami 62–3
Mosul **64–5**
Mshatta 43
Mughals 26–8, 94, 96, 102–9
muqarnas 50–1, 68–9, 93, 96, 118

Nasrids **84–5**
Natanz: Tomb of Abd al-Samad 91
New Delhi: Qutb-al-din Aybak 11
Nigde: Ala al-Din Çami 62
Niono: Great Mosque 119
Nishapur 52
North Africa 8, 74, **78–9**, 80–3, **88–9**

INDEX

Ottomans 18–19, 25, 27, 29–31, 33, 69, 110–17

palaces 27, 29, 46–7, 48–9, 50–1, 62–3, 67, 69, 70, 77, 80–2, 84–7, 90, 92–3, 94–5, 100–1, 114–15, 120; *see also* desert palaces
Persia 37, 52, 54, 58, 86, 100–1
pilgrimage 7, 9, 30–1, **32–3**, 39, 88, 99

al-Qahira *see* Cairo
Qajars 8
qibla 18–19, **20–1**, 22–3, 40, 49, 58, 63, 71, 82, 90, 100, 113, 116
al-Quds *see* Jerusalem
Quran 7, 11, 16, 23, 30, 39, 83, 86, 87

Rabat **82–3**; Mosque of Hasan 82
Rayy: Tomb of Toghrul Beg 58
Riyadh 123; Al Faisaliyh building 123

Safavids 25, 100
Samanids **52–3**
Samarkand 11, 52, 60, 94–5, **96–7**, 98; Bibi Khanum Friday Mosque 95; Gur-e Amir Mausoleum 35, 96–7; Shah-i Zinda complex 96–7; Shah-i Zinda Mausoleum 11; Ulugh Beg's observatory 95
Samarra 45, **46–7**, 47, 54, 87; Bab al-Amma 28, 46; Great Mosque 28, 34, 46; Qasr al-Ashiq 46–7

Below Domed interior of a tomb in the Shah-i-Zinda necropolis, Samarkand.

Sasanians 8, 39, 43
Sasaram: Tomb of Sher Shah 102–3
Seljuks 10, 24, 27, 30–1, **56–7**, 58–63; Anatolian **62–3**
Seville 81, 84, 87; Great Mosque 81; Torre del Oro 81
Shahr-i Sabz: Aq Saray Palace 94–5
Sicily **50–1**, 78–9; Church of San Cataldo 50; summer palace of La Zisa 50–1; Palatine Chapel 50–1
Sivas: Gök Madrasa 62
Sousse 78–9; Great Mosque 79
Spain 18, 21, 28–9, 45, **74–5**, 76–7, 81, 84–5; *see also* al-Andalus
Srinagar: Shalimar Gardens 86
stonework 77, 117
stucco 37, 38, 43, 45, 47, 91
Sultaniyya 28; Uljaytu's Mausoleum 90–1
Syria 8, 18, 29, 32, 36–7, 42–3, 48, 64–5, 66, 68–70, 117

Tabriz 90
Takht-i Sulayman, palace of 90, **92–3**
Tehran 122
tiles 20, 35, 78, 84, 96, 101, 115, 118; Bahram Gur tile 93; Iznik 39
Timbuktu 89; Djinguereber Mosque 88–9
Timurids **94–5**, 98–9
Tinmal: Great Mosque 80–1
Toledo: Bab al-Mardum Mosque 75
tombs **26–7**, 28, 44, 49, 54, 58–9, 62–3, 81, 90–1, 99; Fatimid 27; Mughal **102–3**; in Samarkand **96–7**; *see also* mausolea
trade **30–1**
Tunisia 18, 48, 78, 80
Turkey 10, 19, 24–5, 28–30, 61, 117
Turkmenistan 57–9, 61

Umayyads 8–9, 28, 32, **36–7**, 38–43, **74–5**, 76, 78
United Arab Emirates 123
Uzbekistan 10–11, 13, 52, 60, 94, 96

Yemen 32, 66

Zangids of Mosul **64–5**

ACKNOWLEDGEMENTS

The publishers have made every effort to trace the photograph copyright owners. Anyone we have failed to reach is invited to contact Toucan Books, 111 Charterhouse Street, London EC1M 6AW, United Kingdom.

akg-images 16, 23b, 36t, 47t, 67t, 78b, 91t, 93bl, 105t, 110tr, 117b.
Alamy 4bml, 4mr, 10tm, 11bm, 12tm, 22b, 27b, 43t, 43b, 49, 50t, 50b, 51t, 52t, 58b, 60b, 65t, 66bl, 68, 69br, 70t, 70b, 71t, 71b, 72t, 72b, 91b, 102t, 107b, 111t, 112t, 116b, 117t, 118b, 120t, 120b, 127.
Ancient Art & Architecture Collection 5bml, 37t, 59t.
The Art Archive 7, 13br, 14tm, 18t, 19r, 21b, 22t, 24t, 25b, 30t, 30b, 32tr, 33br, 39b, 40t, 41b, 44t, 53b, 62t, 65b, 73b, 92t, 113t, 125.
Art Directors/ArkReligion.com 4bl, 4br, 5bl, 18b, 19tl, 24b, 28t, 29t, 45t, 56t, 61t, 94b, 108t.
The Bridgeman Art Library 5bmr, 8b, 20b, 45b, 47b, 51b, 74b, 87t, 93r, 118t, 119b, 124.
Corbis 6t, 6b, 8t, 9t, 9b, 11bl, 11br, 20t, 26t, 27t, 31t, 31b, 38t, 38b, 39t, 40b, 54b, 57t, 61b, 63t, 64t, 67t, 73t, 80t, 85b, 87b, 90t, 99b, 103t, 111b, 112b, 122b, 128.
Getty Images 3, 33tr, 75b.
Heritage-Images 15.
iStockphoto.com 1, 17.
Paul Harris Photography 107tr.
Peter Sanders Photography 75tl, 76tr.
Photolibrary 2, 5br, 12tl, 14tl, 14tr, 21t, 23t, 28b, 29b, 37b, 46t, 53t, 57b, 66t, 69t, 74t, 76b, 77t, 77b, 78t, 79t, 81t, 82t, 83t, 83b, 85t, 86t, 86b, 88t, 94t, 95b, 96t, 96b, 97t, 97b, 100t, 101t, 101b, 102cl, 104t, 104b, 105b, 108b, 109t, 109b, 113b, 114b, 115t, 115bc, 116t, 119t, 121t, 122t, 123t, 123b, 126.
Photoshot 60t.
Rex Features 52b.
Robert Harding 10tr, 12tr, 13bl, 13bm, 25tr, 34, 35, 41t, 42t, 54tr, 55b, 59b, 64b, 82b, 88b, 92b, 95t, 98t, 98bl, 99t, 103b, 106b, 114t, 121b.
Shutterstock 26b.
Sonia Halliday Photographs 42br.
Werner Forman Archive 48t, 58t, 63b, 79b, 80b, 81b, 84t, 89b, 106t.
Maps produced by Cosmographics, UK.